YAMAHA
SERVICE MANUAL

FOR

SERIES DT1

(1968—1971)

INCLUDES

DT1A - DT1B - DT1C

DT1S - DT1E

G.Y.T. - MX

A FLOYD CLYMER PUBLICATION by:
www.VelocePress.com
Copyright 2024 Veloce Enterprises

PREFACE

TRADEMARKS & COPYRIGHT

Yamaha ® is the registered trademark of the Yamaha Motor Co.Ltd. This publication is not sponsored by or endorsed by the trademark owner. We recognize that some words, model names and designations, for example, mentioned herein are the property of the trademark holder. We use them for identification purposes only. This is not an official publication however; it may include works of the trademark holder.

INTRODUCTION

Welcome to the world of digital publishing ~ the book you now hold in your hand was printed using the latest state of the art digital technology. The advent of print-on-demand has forever changed the publishing process, never has information been so accessible and it is our hope that this book serves your informational needs for years to come. If this is your first exposure to digital publishing, we hope that you are pleased with the results. Many more titles of interest to the classic automobile and motorcycle enthusiast, collector and restorer are available via our website at www.VelocePress.com. We hope that you find this title as interesting as we do.

NOTE FROM THE PUBLISHER

The information presented is true and complete to the best of our knowledge. All recommendations are made without any guarantees on the part of the author or the publisher, who also disclaim all liability incurred with the use of this information.

INFORMATION ON THE USE OF THIS PUBLICATION

This manual is an invaluable resource for those interested in performing their own maintenance. However, in today's information age we are constantly subject to changes in common practice, new technology, availability of improved materials and increased awareness of chemical toxicity. As such, it is advised that the user consult with an experienced professional prior to undertaking any procedure described herein. While every care has been taken to ensure correctness of information, it is obviously not possible to guarantee complete freedom from errors or omissions or to accept liability arising from such errors or omissions. Therefore, any individual that uses the information contained within, or elects to perform or participate in do-it-yourself repairs or modifications acknowledges that there is a risk factor involved and that the publisher or its associates cannot be held responsible for personal injury or property damage resulting from the use of the information or the outcome of such procedures.

WARNING!

One final word of advice, this publication is intended to be used as a reference guide, and when in doubt the reader should consult with a qualified technician.

NOTICE

This manual has been written by Yamaha Motor Company for use by Authorized Yamaha Dealers and their qualified mechanics. In light of this purpose it has been assumed that certain basic mechanical precepts and procedures inherent to our product are already known and understood by the reader.

Without such basic knowlege, repairs or service to this model may render the machine unsafe, and for this reason we must advise that all repairs and/or service be performed by an Authorized Yamaha dealer who is in possession of the requisite basic product knowledge. Other information is produced by the U. S. distributor, Yamaha International Corporation, and is necessary to provide total technical coverage regarding the product. The Research, Engineering, and Service Departments of Yamaha are continually striving to further improve all models manufactured by the company. Modifications are therefore inevitable and changes in specifications or procedures will be forwarded to all Authorized Yamaha Dealers and will, where applicable, appear in future editions of this manual.

YAMAHA DT1 SERIES SERVICE MANUAL

1ST REVISED EDITION
APRIL 1971

LIT 1161-214-99

FORWARD

This Service Manual is directed to acquaint both the owner and mechanic with the operation, service and maintenance of the DT1 series motorcycle as manufactured by Yamaha Motor Co., Ltd., Hamakita, Japan, during the model years 1968 through 1971. In essence, it is the original DT1E (1971) Service Manual with appropriate information for earlier models. In the rear of the manual you will also find G.Y.T. Kit and Motocross model information.

The DT1 was Yamaha's first fully street legal motorcycle designed to enable the owner to ride on the street, use for trail or enduro riding or convert (with factory available parts) into a competition-ready scrambler or motocrosser. It "made" the off-the-road market what it is today and we at Yamaha are justifiably proud of the marque.

This manual, and the technical and service information enclosed, should be closely followed to enable you to properly maintain the machine, thereby ensuring continuous good performance and long service life.

YAMAHA SERVICE DIVISION

Contents

Chapter 1 General 1
- 1—1 Features 1
- 1—2 External View 2
- 1—3 Specifications 3
- 1—4 Performance Curves 5
- 1—5 Tools and Instruments for Shop Service 6

Chapter 2 Yamaha Antolube 8
- 2—1 What is Yamaha Autolube? 8
- 2—2 Features of Yamaha Autolube 8
- 2—3 Handling the oil Pump 8

Chapter 3 5-Port Cylinder Induction System 11
- 3—1 Construction and Features Design of the 5-port Induction System 11

Chapter 4 Engine 12
- * Engine Exploded View
- 4—1 Engine Removal 12
- 4—2 Cylinder Head 15
- 4—3 Cylinder 16
- 4—4 Piston Pin 17
- 4—5 Piston Ring 18
- 4—6 Piston 18
- 4—7 Flywheel Magneto 20
- 4—8 Crankcase Cover (R.H.) 21
- 4—9 Clutch 22
- 4—10 Primary Drive Gear 26
- 4—11 Kick Starter Mechanism 27
- 4—12 Shift Mechanism 29
- 4—13 Drive Sprocket 31
- 4—14 Crankcase 32
- 4—15 Transmission Assembly 34
- 4—16 Crankshaft 36
- 4—17 Bearings and Oil Seals 39
- 4—18 Carburetor 41
- 4—19 Air Cleaner 43

Contents

Chapter 5 Chassis 45
    5 – 1 Front Wheel 45
    5 – 2 Rear Wheel 48
    5 – 3 Rear Wheel Sprocket 52
    5 – 4 Tires and Tubes 53
    5 – 5 Front Forks 53
    5 – 6 Rear Shocks 55
    5 – 7 Gas Tank 56
    5 – 8 Rear Swing Arm 57
    5 – 9 Steering Head 58
    5 –10 Oil Tank, Battery Box and Tool Box 59
    5 –11 Frame 59
    5 –12 Handlebars 59
    5 –13 Miscellaneous 59

Chapter 6 Electrical System 60
    6 – 1 Discription 60
    6 – 2 Table of Component Parts 60
    6 – 3 Connection Diagram 60
    6 – 4 Ignition System—Function and Service 61
    6 – 5 Ignition Timing 61
    6 – 6 Ignition Coil 61
    6 – 7 Condenser 62
    6 – 8 Charging System 62
    6 – 9 Battery 64
    6 –10 Checking the Main Switch 65
    6 –11 Spark Plug 65
    6 –12 Lighting and Signal Systems 65

Chapter 7 Conversion for Competition 67
    7 – 1 List of GYT Parts 67
    7 – 2 GYT Competition Parts 68
    7 – 3 Additional Modefication 69
    7 – 4 Specifications (GYT) 69
    7 – 5 Setting the Ignition Timing 69
    7 – 6 Check and Service Prior to Racing 70

Continued

Contents

Chapter 8 Miscellaneous Service Information

8 — 1 Conversion Tables 71
8 — 2 Wiring Diagrams 73
8 — 3 DT1A Model Changes (1968) 77
8 — 4 DT1A to DT1B Model Changes (1968 to 1969) 85
8 — 5 DT1 Series Parts and Service Bulletins 93
8 — 6 DT1B - DTIC - DT1S - DT1E Motocross Series Data 107

CHAPTER 1 GENERAL

1-1 Features of Yamaha Enduro 250

1. Single Cylinder 5-port Engine

The Yamaha DT1 250 c.c. single cylinder engine is the first of its kind ever produced by Yamaha.
The iron sleeved aluminum cylinder is of 5-port design and its improved scavenging efficiency results in optimum engine performance in all gears from 2,500 to 6,000 R.P.M.

2. Convenient and Reliable Yamaha Autolube

Yamaha Autolube—automatic oil injection lubrication system—is well known for its performance and reliability. Like every other Yamaha model, the Yamaha Enduro 250 also employs the world-renowned Autolube.

3. 5-Speed Wide Ratio Transmission

The Yamaha Enduro 250 assures steady engine performance, from low speed off-road riding to high speed road work, because of the wide ratio 5-speed transmission. (DT1A-DT1B employ close ratio)

4. Convenient Primary Kickstarter

The primary kickstarter enables the engine to be started either in gear or in neutral.

5. Easy Riding Position and Superb Maneuverability

The light-weight sturdy frame combined with the component parts are ideal for off-the-road riding. Agile, and with a comfortable riding position, the Yamaha Enduro 250 exhibits superb maneuverability and handling over rough terrain.

6. Competition Designed Front Forks and Rear Shocks

The Yamaha Enduro 250 has telescopec front forks with internal coil springs such as used for competition racers.
The front forks provide excellent handling qualities over the roughest terrain with longer stroke and superb dampening capacity. The rear shocks have 3-way adjustable springs with a longer stroke.
This insures stability under even the roughest condition. (DT1E – 5 Way Adjustable)

7. Separate Tachometer and Speedometer with a Reset Odometer for Mileage Calibration.

A separate tachometer is provided to enable the rider to make best use of the engine power.
The speedometer combined with a trip meter allows the rider to the reset the mileage for enduros.

8. Trials Universal Tires for Off-the-road and On the Road Riding.

Trials universal tires for off-the-road and on the road riding are equipped as standard. They are ideal for off-the-road riding as well as on the road riding.

9. Alternate* GYT Parts for Competition Riding.

The GYT kit parts for competition engine tuning are available. You can convert your DT1 into a motorcrosser by simply installing GYT parts and removing all unnecessary parts (DT1C and E model motocross parts can be used as an alternative to the DT1A GYT Kit.)
* Genuine Yamaha Tuning

GENERAL - Features and External View

1-2 External View

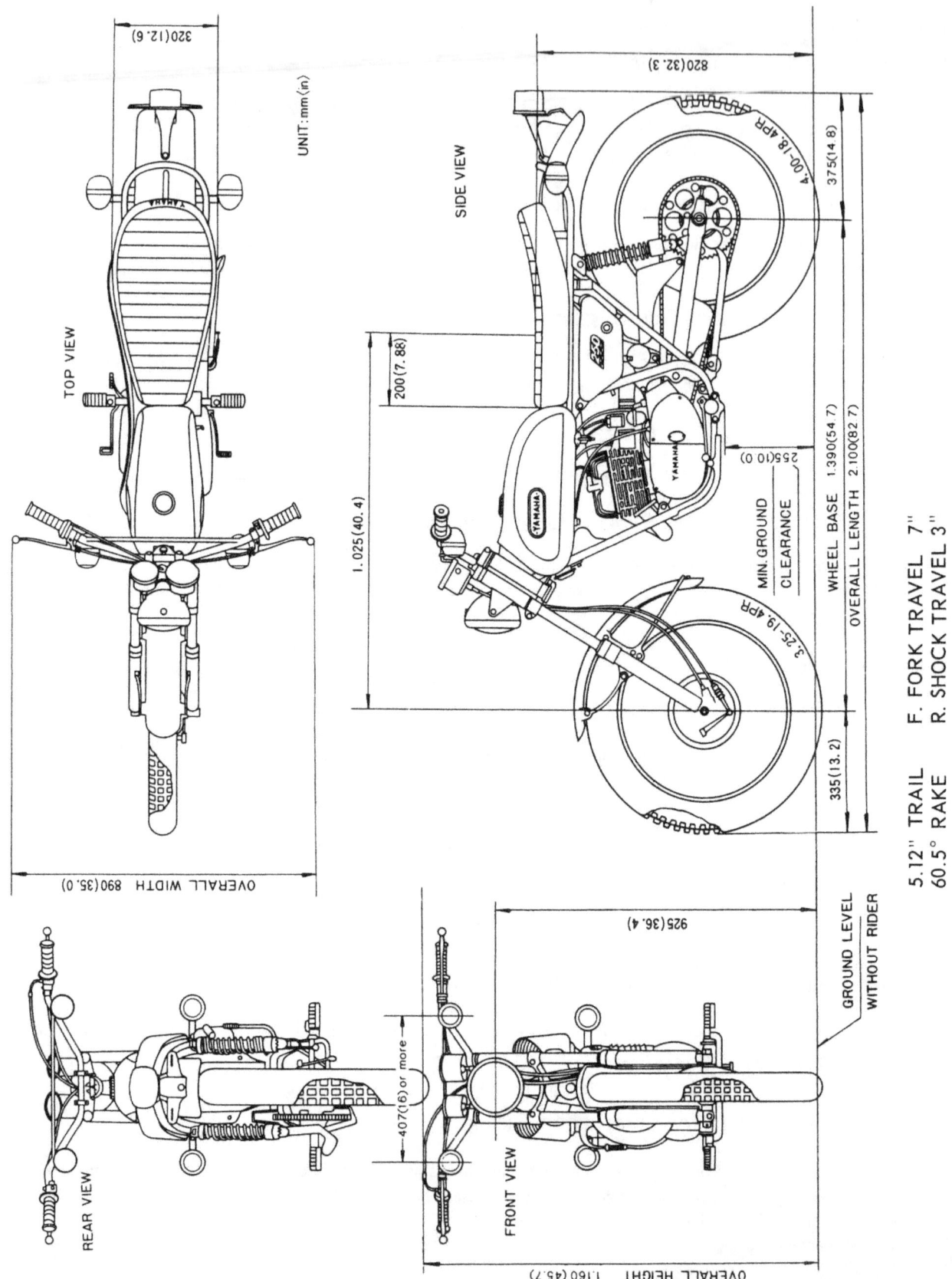

CHAPTER 1 GENERAL

1-1 Features of Yamaha Enduro 250

1. Single Cylinder 5-port Engine

The Yamaha DT1 250 c.c. single cylinder engine is the first of its kind ever produced by Yamaha.
The iron sleeved aluminum cylinder is of 5-port design and its improved scavenging efficiency results in optimum engine performance in all gears from 2,500 to 6,000 R.P.M.

2. Convenient and Reliable Yamaha Autolube

Yamaha Autolube—automatic oil injection lubrication system—is well known for its performance and reliability. Like every other Yamaha model, the Yamaha Enduro 250 also employs the world-renowned Autolube

3. 5-Speed Wide Ratio Transmission

The Yamaha Enduro 250 assures steady engine performance, from low speed off-road riding to high speed road work, because of the wide ratio 5-speed transmission. (DT1A-DT1B employ close ratio)

4. Convenient Primary Kickstarter

The primary kickstarter enables the engine to be started either in gear or in neutral.

5. Easy Riding Position and Superb Maneuverability

The light-weight sturdy frame combined with the component parts are ideal for off-the-road riding. Agile, and with a comfortable riding position, the Yamaha Enduro 250 exhibits superb maneuverability and handling over rough terrain.

6. Competition Designed Front Forks and Rear Shocks

The Yamaha Enduro 250 has telescopec front forks with internal coil springs such as used for competition racers.
The front forks provide excellent handling qualities over the roughest terrain with longer stroke and superb dampening capacity. The rear shocks have 3-way adjustable springs with a longer stroke.
This insures stability under even the roughest condition. (DT1E – 5 Way Adjustable)

7. Separate Tachometer and Speedometer with a Reset Odometer for Mileage Calibration.

A separate tachometer is provided to enable the rider to make best use of the engine power.
The speedometer combined with a trip meter allows the rider to the reset the mileage for enduros.

8. Trials Universal Tires for Off-the-road and On the Road Riding.

Trials universal tires for off-the-road and on the road riding are equipped as standard. They are ideal for off-the-road riding as well as on the road riding.

9. Alternate* GYT Parts for Competition Riding.

The GYT kit parts for competition engine tuning are available. You can convert your DT1 into a motorcrosser by simply installing GYT parts and removing all unnecessary parts (DT1C and E model motocross parts can be used as an alternative to the DT1A GYT Kit.)
* Genuine Yamaha Tuning

1-2 External View

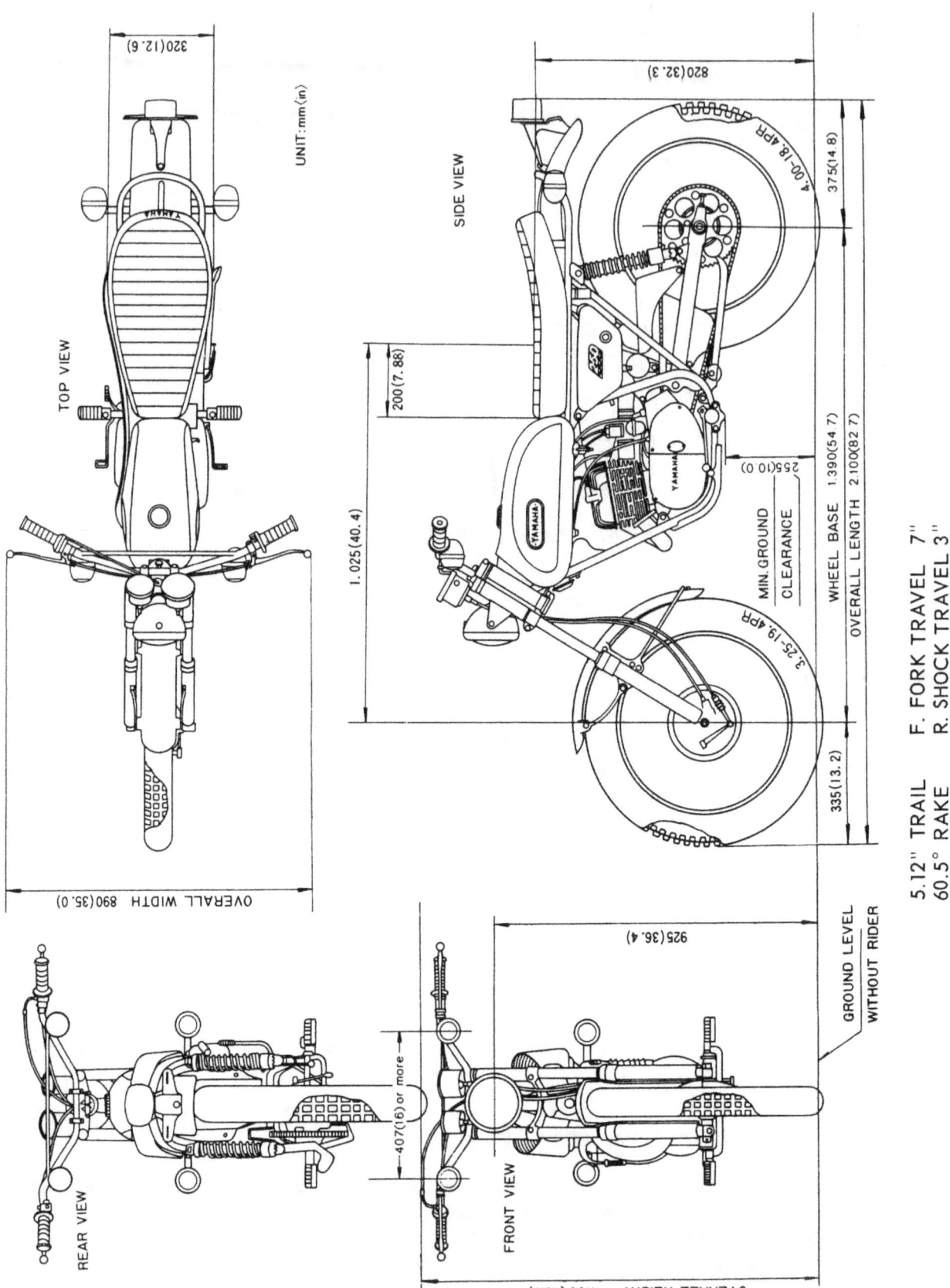

5.12" TRAIL   F. FORK TRAVEL 7"
60.5° RAKE   R. SHOCK TRAVEL 3"

ALL MODELS

Chassis:		
Frame		Tubular-Double loop
Suspension system, front		Telescopic fork
Suspension system, rear		Swinging arm
Cushion system, front		Coil spring oil damper
Cushion system, rear		Coil spring oil damper
Steering system		
Steering angle		49° both right and left
Caster		60.5°
Trail		5.12 in (130 mm)
Braking system:		
Type of brake		Internal expansion
Operation system, front		Right hand operation
Operation system, rear		Right foot operation
Tire size		
Front		3.25-19-4PR
Rear		4.00-18-4PR
Dynamo		
Model		FZA-1BL
Manufacture		Mitsubishi Elec
Battery		
Model		MV1-6D
Manufacture		Nippon Battery
Capacity		6V 2AH
Lighting		
Headlight		6V 35W/35W
Taillight/Stoplight		6V 5.3W/17W
Flasher light (DT1E)		6V 17W
Meter light		6V 3W x 2
Tanks		
Gasoline tank capacity		2.5 gals (9.5 liters)
Oil tank capacity		1.7 qts (1.6 liters)

		DT-1	DT-1 GYT
1.	MODEL		
2.	BORE x STROKE (mm)	70x64	70x64
3.	CAPACITY (cc)	246	246
4.	COMPRESSION RATIO	6.8:1	8.2:1
5.	IGNITION TIMING BEFORE T.D.C. (inch)	0.126	2.091
	IGNITION TIMING BEFORE T.D.C. (mm)	3.2	2.3
6.	CONTACT BREAKER POINT GAP SETTING (inch)	0.011-0.013	0.011-0.013
	CONTACT BREAKER POINT GAP SETTING (mm)	0.30-0.35	0.30-0.35
7.	SPARK PLUG & SPARK GAP (mm) NGK	B-7E 0.5-0.6	B9E-B9EN 0.5-0.6
8.	VOLTAGE REGULATOR ADJUSTMENT (volt/rpm)		
9.	CUTOUT RELAY ADJUSTMENT (volt)		
10.	CONDENSOR CAPACITY (microfarad)	0.0016-0.0018	0.0016-0.0020
11.	PISTON CLEARANCE-SKIRT (inch)	0.040-0.045	0.040-0.050
	PISTON CLEARANCE-SKIRT (mm)		
12.	CARBURETOR TYPE (Mikuni)	VM26SH (214E) ※※	VM30SH (214M) ※※
	MAIN JET (#)	150	210
	AIR JET	0.5	0.5
	NEEDLE JET	0-2	0-4
	JET NEEDLE	5D1-3	8J-5D05-3
	CUT AWAY	2.5	
	PILOT JET (#)	35	80
	AIR SCREW (turns out)	1-1/2	1/2
	STARTER JET (#)	50	60
13.	PRIMARY REDUCTION RATIO	65/21 3.095	65/21 3.095
14.	SECONDARY REDUCTION RATIO	44/15 2.93	44/14 3.143
15.	GEAR BOX GEAR RATIO & 1st	29/13 20.25	29/13 21.70
	OVERALL GEAR RATIO 2nd	26/16 14.75	26/16 15.81
	3rd	23/19 10.99	23/19 11.78
	4th	21/21 9.08	21/21 9.73
	5th	19/23 7.50	19/23 8.04
16.	GEAR BOX OIL CAPACITY (quart)	1.06	1.06
17.	OIL TANK CAPACITY (quart)	1.7	1.7
18.	FUEL TANK CAPACITY (gallon)	2.4	2.4
19.	FRONT FORK OIL CAPACITY (oz) @	7.1 oz each	7.1
	FRONT FORK OIL CAPACITY (cc) @	210 cc each	210
20.	TIRE SIZE FRONT	3.25x19	3.25x19
	TIRE SIZE REAR	4.00x18	4.00x18
21.	TIRE PRESSURE FRONT (lb.)	12-14 10※	10
	TIRE PRESSURE REAR (lb.)	16-18 12※	12
22.	CHAIN TENSION (UP & DOWN) (inch)	0.20-0.25	0.20-0.25※
23.	OIL PUMP ADJUSTMENT STROKE MIN. (mm)	1.85-2.05	1.85-2.05※
	STROKE MAX. (mm)		
	OPERATING CABLE ADJUSTMENT	At Idle	At Idle

※Without Autolube; follow oil manufacturer's recommendation - premix oil to gas ratio.

	MODEL	DT1B	DT1C	DT1C-MX	DT1-E	DT1E-M
1.						
2.	HORSEPOWER @ RPM	21-7000	23 @ 7000	30 @ 7000	23 @ 7,000	30 @ 7,000
3.	TORQUE @ RPM	16.8-5000	17.5 @ 6500	22.4 @ 6500	17.5 @ 6,500	22.4 @ 6,500
4.	BORE & STROKE (mm)	70 x 64	70 x 64	70 x 64	70 x 64	70 x 64
5.	ENGINE DISPLACEMENT	246cc	246cc 15 cu. in.	246cc 15 cu. in.	246cc 15.0 cu. in	246cc 15.0 cu. in
6.	NET WEIGHT (Appx.)	232	232 lbs.	229 lbs.	245 lbs.	232 lbs.
7.	COMPRESSION RATIO	6.8:1	6.4:1	8.2:1	6.8:1	8.2:1
8.	IGNITION TIMING B.T.D.C. (mm) Retarded	.126	-	-	-	-
	Advanced	3.2mm ± 0.1	3.2mm ± .1	2.3mm	3.2mm ± .1	2.3mm ± .1
9.	CONTACT BREAKER POINT GAP SETTING (mm) (inch)	.011 - .013"	.3-.35mm .011-.013"	.3-.35mm .011-.013"	.30-.40mm .012-.015"	.30-.40mm .012-.015"
10.	SPARK PLUG AND GAP (mm)	B7E (N) .5 - .6mm	B-7E .5-.6mm	B-10EN .5-.6mm	B-8ES .5-.6mm	B-10EN .5-.6mm
11.	VOLT. REG. ADJ. (Volts @ rpm - no load)	MAGNETO	MAGNETO	MAGNETO	MAGNETO	MAGNETO
12.	CUTOUT RELAY ADJ. (Cut in voltage)	MAGNETO	MAGNETO	MAGNETO	MAGNETO	MAGNETO
13.	CONDENSER CAPACITY (Microfarad)	0.22uF	0.22uF	.22uF	.22uF	.22uF
14.	PISTON SKIRT CLEARANCE (mm) (inch)	.040 - .045	.040-.045mm .0016-.0018"	.045-.050mm .0018-.0020"	.040-.045mm .0016-.0018"	.045-.050mm .0018-.0020"
15.	CARBURETOR TYPE & MANUFACTURER	VM26SH	VM26SH Mikuni	VM30SH	VM26SH Mikuni	VM30SH Mikuni
	MAIN JET (M.J.)	160	#160	#210-220	#160	#210-220
	AIR JET (A.J.)	.5	0.5	0.5	-	0.5
	NEEDLE JET (N.J.)	0 - 2	0-2	0-4	0-2	0-2 (or 0-4)
	JET NEEDLE - clip position (J.N.)	5D1-3	5D1-3	5D5-4	5D1-3	5D5-4
	CUTAWAY (C.A.)	2.5	2.5	3.5	2.5	3.5
	PILOT JET (P.J.)	35	#35	80	#35	#80
	AIR SCREW (Turns out) (A.S.)	1½	1½	1	1½	1.0
	STARTER JET (S.J.)	60	#60	60	#60	#60
	FLOAT LEVEL (mm) (F.L.)	14.1*	15.1mm	25.5mm	15.1mm	25.5mm
16.	AIR FILTER TYPE	Wet foam	Wet foam rubber	Wet foam rubber	Wet foam rubber	Wet foam rubber
17.	PRIMARY REDUCTION RATIO & METHOD	3.095 (65/21)	65/21 3.095 gear	65/21 3.095 gear	65/21 3.095 gear	65/21 3.095 gear
18.	SECONDARY REDUCTION RATIO & METHOD	2.933 (44/15)	44/14 3.143 chain	44/14 3.143 chain	44/14 3.143 chain	44/14 3.143 chain
19.	TRANS. GEAR RATIOS 1st (Internal) (No. teeth) (Overall)	2.231 (29/13)	2.533 38/15 24.644	2.250 36/16 21.888	2.533 38/15 24.64	2.250 36/16 21.89
	2nd	1.624 (26/16)	1.789 34/19 17.408	1.650 33/20 16.051	1.789 34/19 17.41	1.650 33/20 16.05
	3rd	1.211 (23/19)	1.304 30/23 12.689	1.261 29/23 12.267	1.304 30/23 12.69	1.261 29/23 12.27
	4th	1.000 (21/21)	1.000 26/26 9.728	1.000 26/26 9.728	1.000 26/26 9.73	1.000 26/26 9.73
	5th	.826 (19/23)	0.767 23/30 7.458	0.793 23/29 7.714	0.767 23/30 7.46	0.793 23/29 7.71
20.	TRANS. OIL CAPACITY (Qt.)	1000cc (1.06 qt.)	1.06	1.06	1.06	1.06
21.	OIL TANK OR ENGINE SUMP CAPACITY (Qt.)	1.7	1.7	1.7	1.7	1.7
22.	FUEL TANK CAPACITY (U.S. Gal.)	2.5	2.5	2.5	2.5	2.5
23.	FRONT FORK OIL CAPACITY	7.1 210cc	7.1 oz. 210cc	7.1 oz. 210cc	5.9 oz 175cc	5.9 oz. 175cc
24.	TIRE SIZE (Front)	3.25 x 19	3.25 x 19	2.75 x 21 knobby	3.25-19	2.75-21 knobby
	(Rear)	4.00 x 18	4.00 x 18	4.00 x 18 knobby	4.00-18	4.00-18 knobby
25.	TIRE PRESSURE (Lbs.) (Front) (off road)	14	14	14	13	13
	(Rear) (off road)	17	17	17	16	16
26.	DRIVE CHAIN TENSION (Up & down freeplay) MAX. (mm)	20mm (25/32")	20mm 25/32"	20mm 25/32"	20mm 25/32"	20mm 25/32"
27.	OIL PUMP STROKE ADJUSTMENT MIN. (mm)	.20 - .25	.20-.25mm	.20-.25mm	.20-.25mm	.20-.25mm
	MAX. (mm)	1.85 - 2.05	1.85-2.05mm	1.85-2.05mm	1.85-2.05mm	1.85-2.05mm
		At idle	At idle	At idle	At idle	At idle

GENERAL - Performance Curves

1-4 Performance Curves

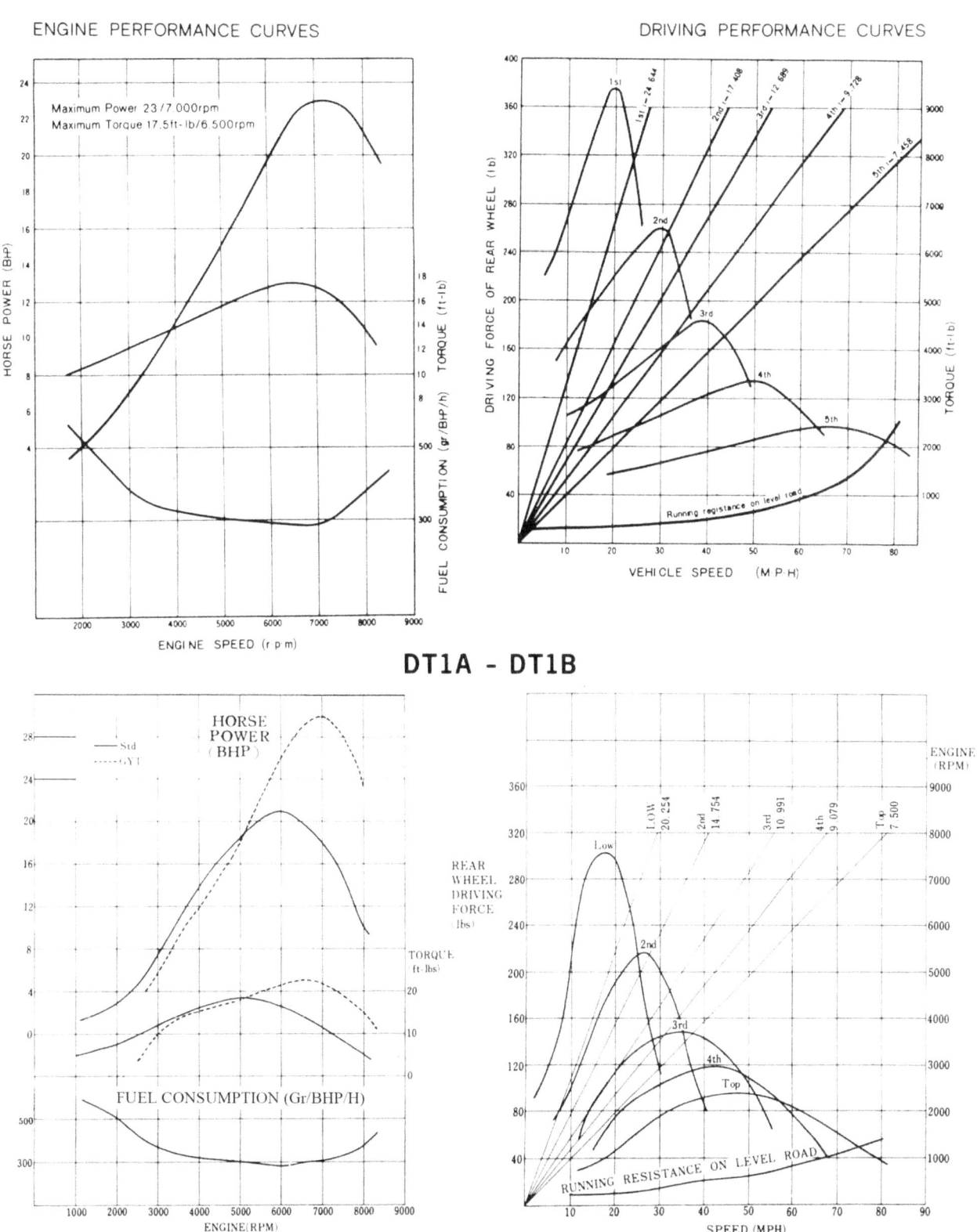

DT1C - DT1E - DT1S

DT1A - DT1B

GENERAL - Service Tools

1-5 Tools and Instruments for Shop Service

The following tools and instruments ar required to service the DT1-E

1. General Tools

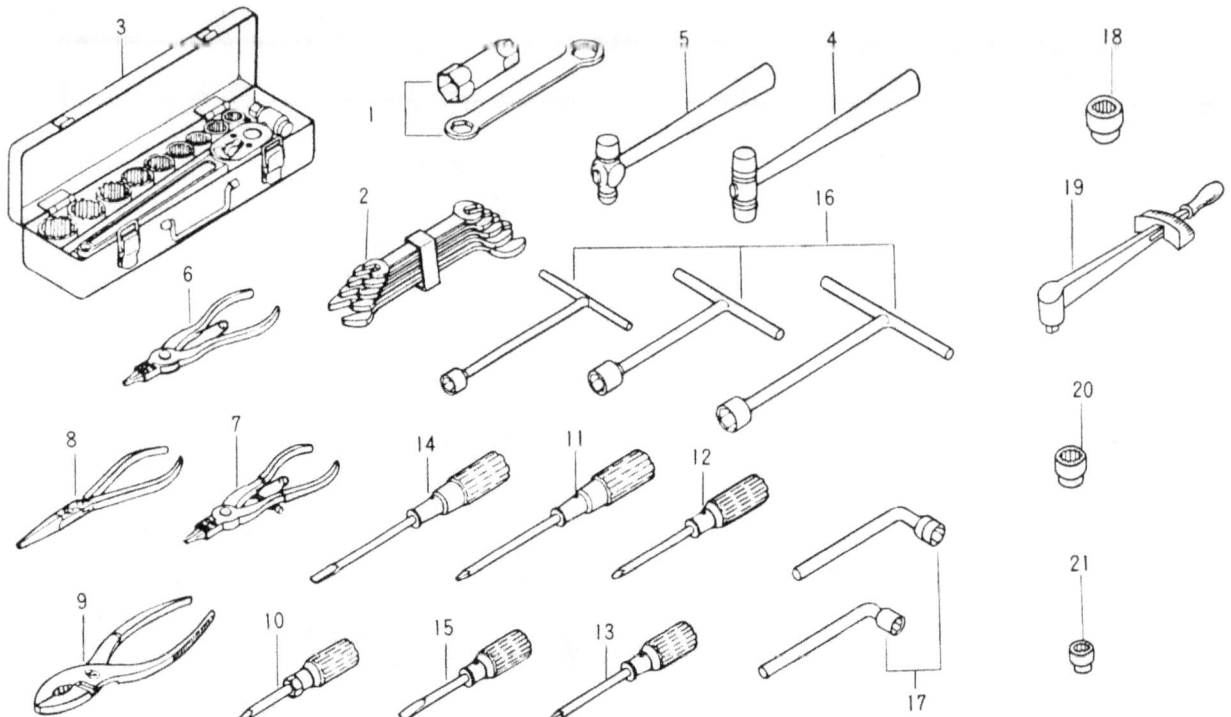

1) Plug wrench 23 x 29mm
2) A set of wrenches
3) A set of socket wrenches
4) Plastic tip hammer
5) Steel hammer
6) Circlip pliers (ST type)
7) Circlip pliers (TR type)
8) Needle nose pliers
9) Pliers
10) Phillips-head screwdriver
11) Phillips-head screwdriver (L)
12) Phillips-head screwdriver (M)
13) Phillips-head screwdriver (S)
14) Slot-head screwdriver (M)
15) Slot-head screwdriver (S)
16) T-handle socket wrench

Fig. 1-4-1

2. Special Tools and instruments

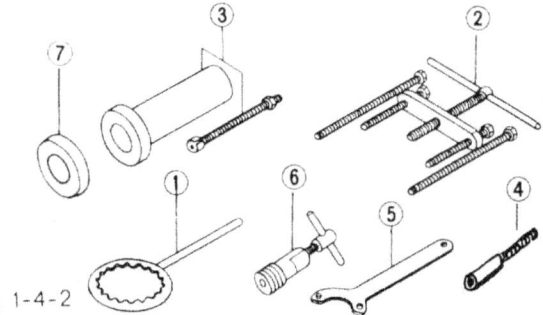

Fig 1-4-2

1) Clutch holding tool (for R5 and YM2)
2) Crankcase disassembling tool
3) Crankshaft assembling tool (for YF1 and YG1)
5) Flywheel magneto holding tool
6) Flywheel magneto puller
4) Stand, dial gauge adaptor
7) Crankshaft puller pot adaptor

In addition, an electro-tester, tachometer (engine r.p.m. meter) hydrometer, etc. are needed.

GENERAL - Service Tools

3. Other Materials

1) Yamaha Bond (No.5)
2) Autolube oil
3) Grease
4) Wiping material
5) Overhauling stand
6) Parts tray
7) Oiler
8) Oil jug

Fig 1-4-3

The use of a wooden box as shown in the above photo 5 will facilitate engine service and overhaul. Consumable parts (such as gaskets) and replacement parts must also be on hand.

MAINTENANCE CHART

This chart should be considered strictly as an example for general lubrication and maintenance periods. You must take into consideration that weather, terrain, geographical locations, and a variety of individual uses all tend to demand that this time schedule may have to be altered to match the machine's environment.

The schedule is oriented to the average pleasure rider who rides approximately 80% of the time on city streets and secondary roads. For the rider who spends 10 – 12 hours per week riding hard in the dirt, the periods must be reduced drastically. This is most especially important in such critical areas as lubrication. Air cleaners, for example, should be cleaned and re-oiled every 100 – 150 miles under hard usage. And yet, the average rider need only clean his every month or 1,000 miles, whichever comes first.

ITEM	PERIOD
CONTROLS (lube and/or adjust)	1,000/monthly
SUSPENSION (lube and/or change oil)	5,000/bi-annually
WHEELS (inc. spokes, pressure)	1,000/monthly
DECARBONIZE ENGINE & EXHAUST	2,000-4,000 (as nec'y)
AIR INTAKE (filter, etc.)	1,000/monthly
FUEL SYSTEM (petcock, tank, carb, clean/adj.)	2,000/quarterly
BATTERY (ck. level, chg. as nec'y.)	1,000/monthly
IGNITION SYSTEM (ck. timing, re-set, replace parts as nec'y.)	2,000/or as nec'y.
TRANSMISSION (ck. 500/weekly) refill (10W-30)	2,000/bi-annually
DRIVE CHAIN (ck. 250/weekly, adj. as nec'y.) Lubricate/clean	500/monthly
SPARK PLUG (ck. 1,000 clean/regap as nec'y.) Replace	2,000-4,000/bi-annually
NUTS AND BOLTS (before every trip) DIRT: 100/daily	STREET: 250/weekly

CHAPTER 2 YAMAHA AUTOLUBE
(Separate Automatic Lubrication System)

2-1 What is Yamaha Autolube?

Conventional 2-stroke engines are lubricated by oil pre-mixed in gasoline, but YAMAHA's Autolube furnishes an automatic, separate lubrication system. That is, the oil in a separate oil tank is automatically regulated by the oil pump and fed to the engine according to engine speed and load.

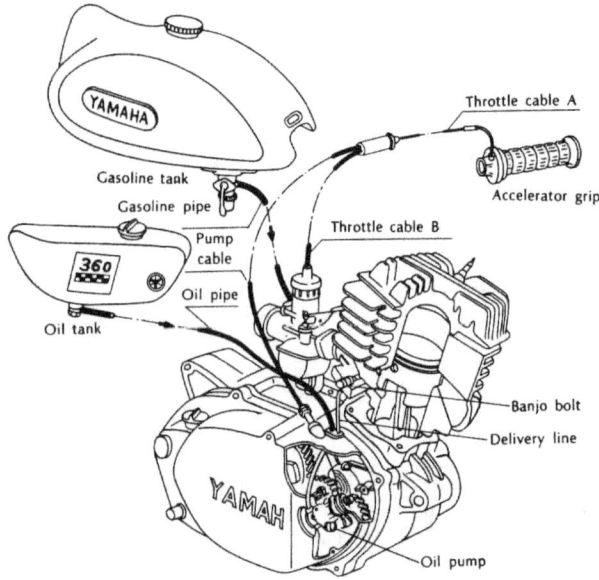

Fig. 2-1-1

2-2 Features of Yamaha Autolube

The oil pump is driven by the engine through a reduction gear, and is connected to the carburetor throttle cable controlled by the accelerator grip.

The oil pump automatically regulates the volume of lubricating according to engine speed and throttle valve opening, thus pumping the optimum amount of oil for engine lubrication under any operating condition.

This "automatic separate lubrication" does not merely eliminate disadvantags in the conventional pre-mix system, but it further improves the performance and efficiency of 2-stroke designs by eliminating certain oil-starvation condition wihch formerly existed.

A) The Autolube feeds an optimum amount of lubricating oil to the engine under any operating condition, thus featuring:
- Less oil consumption.
- Less carbon accumulation.
- Less exhaust smoke.
- Improved lubricating efficiency.

B) The Autolube simplifies fuel supply, thus featuring:
- Using straight gasoline directly in the gas tank.
- Less fuel contamination.

C) The Autolube improves the reliability of lubrication, thus eliminating:
- Special care concerning oil/fuel mixing ratio.

2-3 Handling the Oil Pump

The oil pump is a precision-machined assembly. Make no attempt to disassemble it. When you remove the oil pump from the engine, protect it from dust, dirt, etc., and after reinstalling it, bleed and adjust the pump correctly. Proper handling will keep the pump free from trouble.

The oil pump is simillar in both mechanism and construction to other Autolube systems. The only difference is the employment of a 5.5∅ plunger because of larger consumption of oil by a 250c.c. single cylinder engine.

1 Checking Minimum Pump Stroke

a Checking

1) Fully close the accelerator grip.

2) Turn the oil pump starter plate in the direction of the arrow marked on the plate. Then measure the gap between the adjustment pully and the adjust-

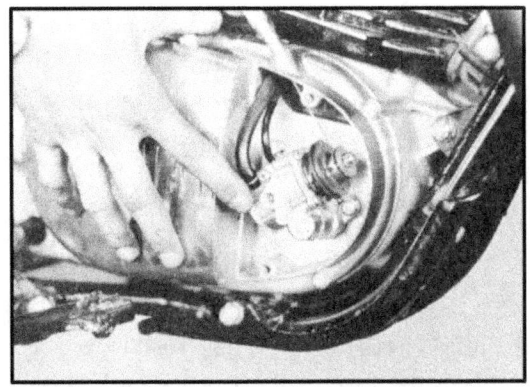

Fig 2-3-1

ment plate. Keep the gap as wide as possible by observing it with the eye.

3) Insert a feeler gauge (0.15mm.) into the gap.
   When the gap allows it to enter ......Stroke is correct.
   When the gap does not allow Stroke...... is insufficient.

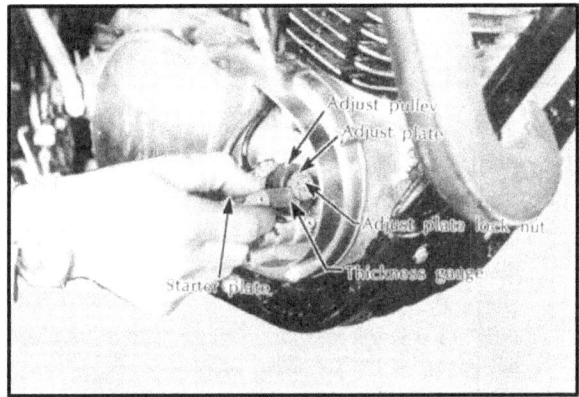

Fig 2-3-2

b Adjustment

1) Remove the adjustment plate lock nut, and then remove the adjustment plate.

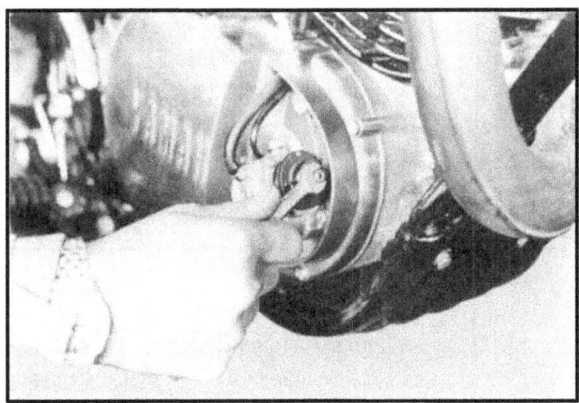

Fig 2-3-3

2) Install a 0.1mm adjustment shim where the adjustment plate was. (Fig. 2-3-4)

3) Reinstall the adjustment plate lock nut, and measure minimum stroke. When the gap allows a 0.20 mm. feeler gauge to enter but does not allow a 0.25mm, the stroke is correctly adjusted.
   Minimum stroke adjustment limite...0.15mm. or less
   stroke adjustment toleance......0.20 to 0.25mm.

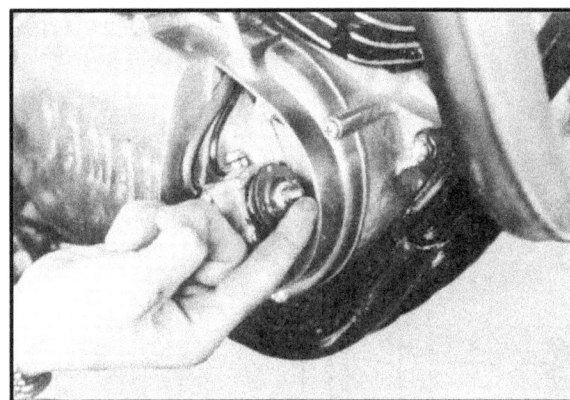

Fig 2-3-4

stroke adjustment toleance......0.20 to 0.25 mm.

2. Carburetor and Autolube Cable Adjustment

Perform the preceeding steps in section 2-3-1 to check minimum stroke, and adjust it if incorrect. Then adjust the Autolube and carburator cables.

a Throttle Cable Adjustment

1) To adjust the throttle cable free play with the engine at idle, begin by removing all slack from throttle cable B in Fig. 2-3-5

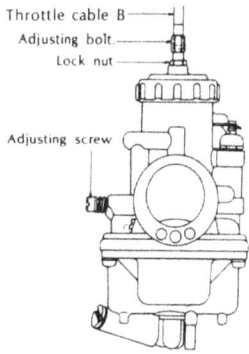

Fig 2-3-5

To remove all the free play from the throttle cable, loosen or tighten the throttle cable adjustment screw (see below) until all slack has been taken up. Next, screw the cable adjuster until there is 1mm free play (1/32") in the cable at the top the carburetor.

2) The next adjustment is at the throttle grip. Loosen the look nut and screw the adjuster in or

YAMAHA AUTO LUBE - Handling of the Oil Pump

out, whichever is necessary to get 0.5-1.0mm of free play at the cable end. (see Fig.2-3-6.)

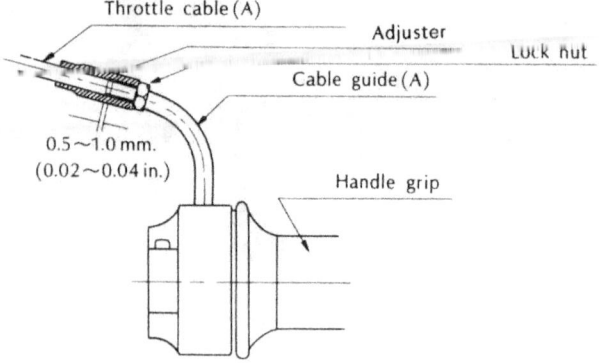

Fig 2-3-6

Fig 2-3-8

Pull the outer part of the throttle grip to check the play of throttle cable A. If the play is excessive or insufficient, adjust the free play with the adjustment screw.

b Auto lube Cable Adjustment

1) Adjust the pump cable so that the marking (arrow) on the Autolube pump adjustment pulley is aligned with the guide pin (see Figs. 2-3-7 & 8.)

Begin by fully closing the accelerator grip, then slowly turning it back again so that the slack in the throttle cable is completely taken up. Next, adjust the pump cable so that the marking on the pump adjustment pulley will be aligned with the guide pin, as shown in Fig. 2-3-7. Thf point of adjustment is at the end of the cable, just before it enters the case. Loosen the lock nut screw the the adjustor in or out, whichever direction is necessary to obtain the correct adjustment.

3 Bleeding

When the pump has been removed or the Autolube oil has run out, air will enter the pump. The air will cause an irregular flow of oil after the pump is mounted again or the oil is refflled. In order to prevent such an irregular flow of oil, bleed the pump in the following manner.

1) Remove the bleeder bolt.

Fig 2-3-9

2) Next, rotate the starter plate in the direction of the arrow marked on the plate. Continue turning the plate until no air remains, and tighten the bleeder bolt. To facilitate this bleeding, fully open the accelerator grip and rotate the starter plate. As the plunger stroke becomes greater, the air can be quickly bled. (Fig 2-3-10)

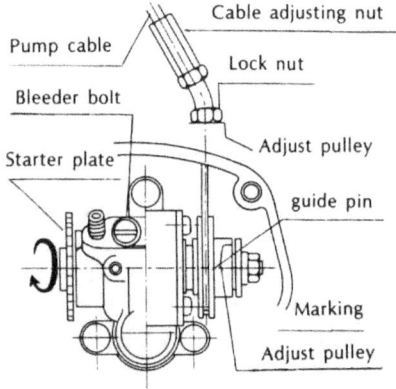

Fig 2-3-7

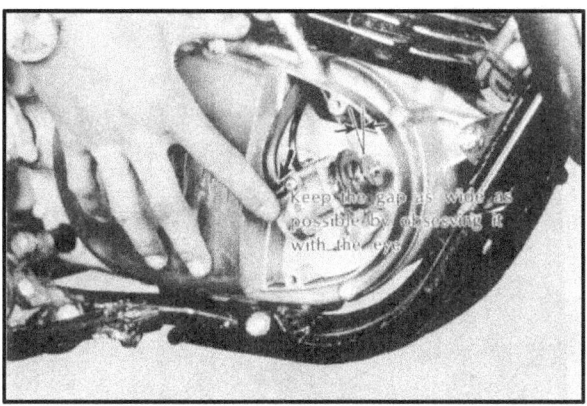

Fig 2-3-10

CHAPTER 3 5-PORT CYLINDER INDUCTION SYSTEM

3-1 Construction and Features Design of the 5-port Induction System

The 2 additional transfer passages are placed to the immediate rear of the standard transfer ports. These two additional ports run from the bottom of the cylinder up to the same height as the standard transfer ports. These additional ports are designed to direct the fresh charge at the area containing the remaining exhaust gases. As the fresh fuel charge enters the combusion area, the remaining exhaust gas is forced out the exhaust port leaving the combustion area with an uncontaminated full fresh fuel charge.

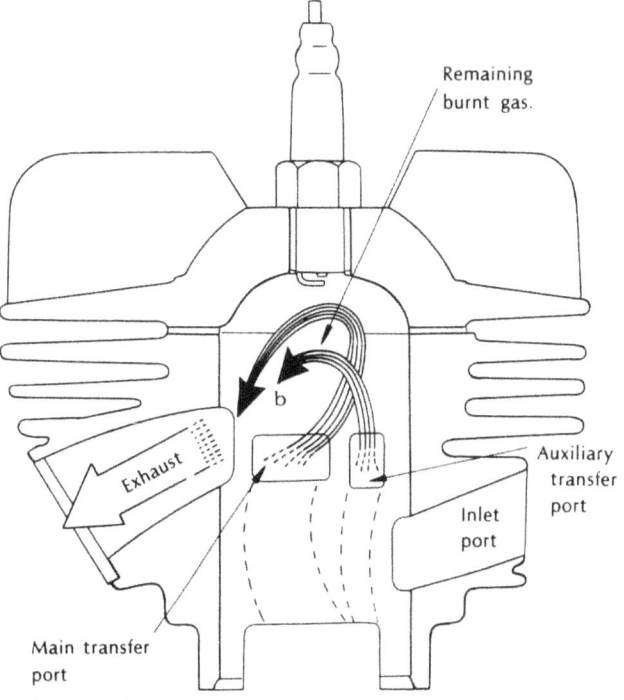

Fig 3-2-1

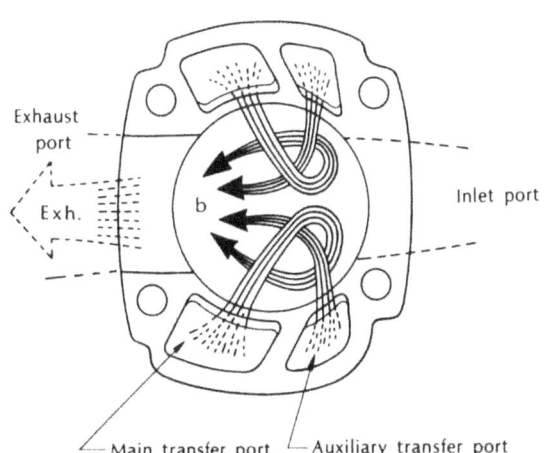

Fig 3-2-2

CHAPTER 4 ENGINE

The DT1-E 250cc Enduro engine has been designed with emphasis on both low speed trail riding and high speed road riding. The incorporation of the evenly spaced five-speed transmission and five-port induction system insure complete riding versatility for the owner. The width, height, and weight of the engine has been kept at a bare minimum to insure ease of handling in the roughest terrain.

Disassembly and assembly of the engine and its components should be done in the following manner and order. This will insure correct maintenance and service work for the owner and mechanic.

Preparation for disassembly of the engine :

1) All dirt, mud, dust, and foreign material should be thoroughly removed from the exterior of the engine assembly before removal and disassembly. This will prevent any harmful foreign material from entering the interior of the engine assembly.
2) Before engine removal and disassembly, be sure you have proper tools and cleaning equipment so you can perform a clean and efficient job.
3) During disassembly of the engine, clean and place all parts in trays in order of disassembly. This will ease and speed assembly time and insure correct installation of all engine parts.

4-1 Engine Removal

1. Start the engine and warm it up for a few minutes, then turn off the engine and drain the transmission oil.

   Volume of oil 1,000c.c. (1.0qt.)
   (Fig-4-1-1) (SAE10W/30)

Fig. 4-1-1

2. Remove the muffler.
   1) Remove the two springs and two bolts.

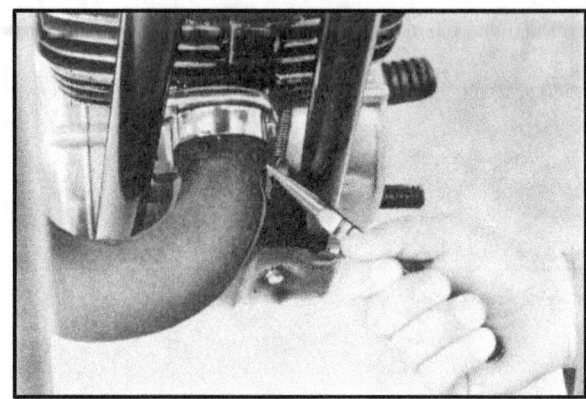

Fig 4-1-2

2) Remove the muffler holding bolts.
   (Figs. 4-1-3 and 4)

Fig 4-1-3

ENGINE - Engine Removal

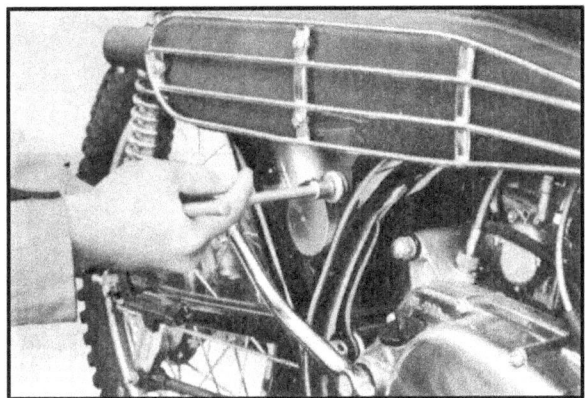

Fig 4-1-4

3 Remove the change pedal.

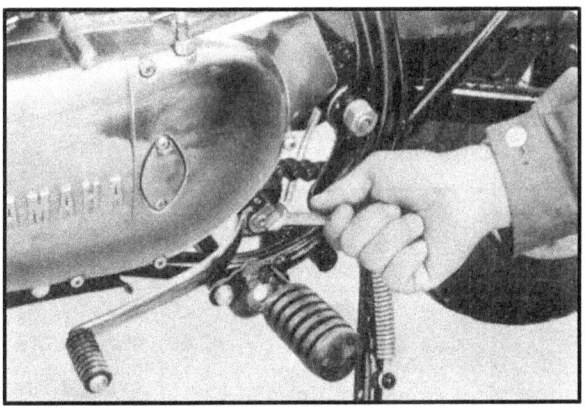

Fig 4-1-5

4 Remove the dynamo cover

Fig 4-1-6

5 Dicsonnect the master link and remove the chain.

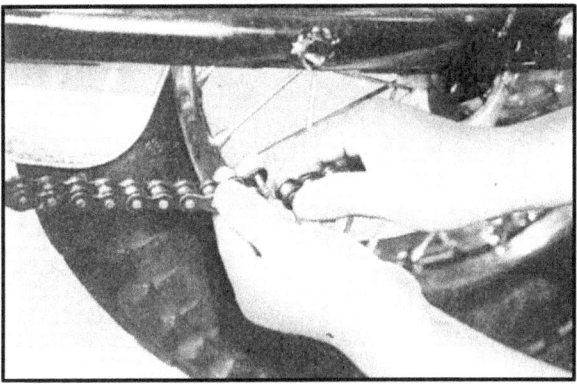

Fig 4-1-7

6 When replacing the chain, be sure the master link is facing in the correct direction.

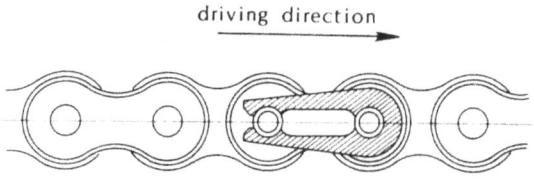

Fig 4-1-8

After replacing, adjust the chain free play to 25 mm. (1 in.) up and down at the center of the lower section with the rear wheel on the ground, with the rider in position.

6 Remove the pump cover and pump cable.

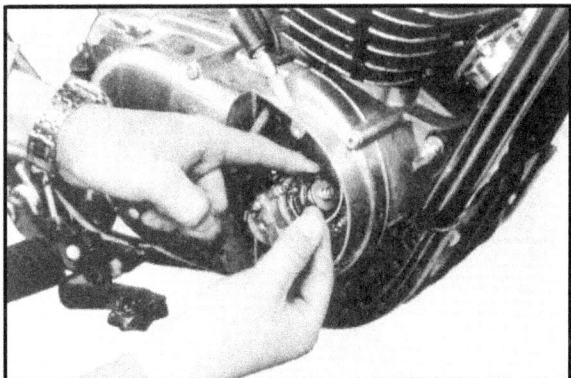

Fig 4-1-9

ENGINE - Engine Removal

7 Remove the tachometer cable.

Fig 4-1-10

8 Remove the carbureter trottlle valve.

Fig 4-1-11

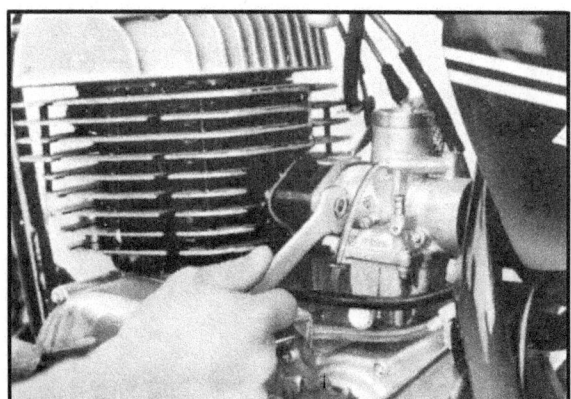

Fig 4-1-12

9 Disconnect the oil line and be sure to plug the hole to prevent oil from flowing out.

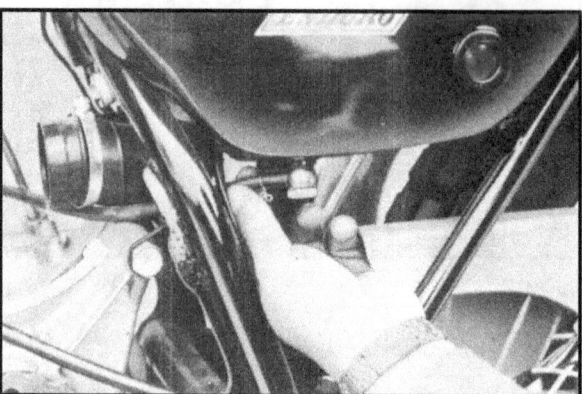

Fig 4-1-13

10 Disconnect the fuel line at the bottom of the fuel tank.

Fig 4-1-14

11 Remove the four engine mounting bolts.

Fig 4-1-15

ENGINE - Engine Removal, Cylinder Head

Fig 4-1-16

12 Remove the engine from the frame

Fig 4-2-1

Fig 4-1-17

Fig 4-2-2

2 Removing Carbon Deposits

Carbon deposits on the combustion chamber dome and piston crown will result in an increase in the compression ratio, as well as preignition and engine overheating.

Scrape the dome and piston crown clean.

4-2 Cylinder Head

The cylinder head is bolted on the cylinder with special nuts.

1 Removing

Remove the four special nuts from the top of the cylinder head, and then the head and gasket. Reverse the sequence for reinstallation. Replace the gasket if damaged.

Cylinder head tightening torque is 3.5~4.0kg-m (25.3~28.9ft-lbs.)

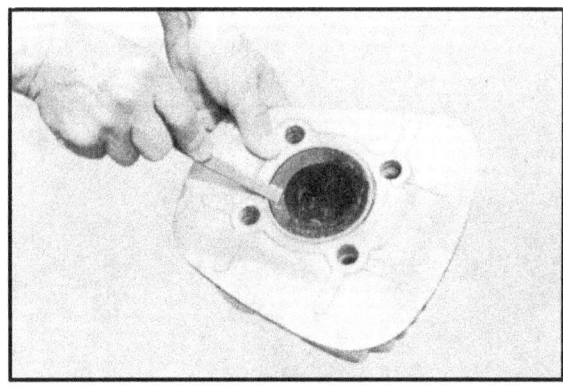

Fig. 4-2-3

ENGINE - Cylinder

4-3 Cylinder

1 Removing the Cylinder

1) Remove the oil delivery line banjo bolt from cylinder.

Fig 4-3-1

2) Remove the cylinder by striking it lightly with a plastic or rubber hammer

Fig 4-3-2

3) Always replace the cylinder base gasket when reassembling cylinder.

Fig 4-3-3

2 Checking the Cylinder for Wear

1) Measure the amount of cylinder wall wear with a sylinder bore measuring micrometer or cylinder gauge. (Measure it at four depths by positioning the instrument at right angles to the crankshaft.) If the difference between the maximum and minimum diameter exceeds 0.05mm (0.0019") rebore and hone the cylinder.

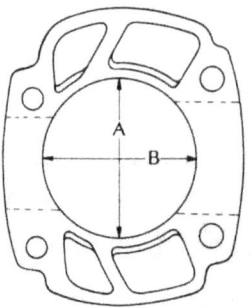

Fig 4-3-4

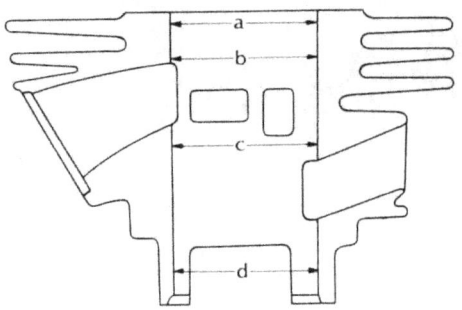

Fig 4-3-5

2) The minimum clearance between the piston and the cylinder is 0.040-0.045mm (0.0016" to 0.0018")

3 Cylinder Recondlitioning

1) Pistons are available in 0.25 and 0.50 mm (0.010" and 0.020") oversizes.
2) Cylinder should be rebored and honed to the diameter of the oversize piston plus the minimum allowable clearance. (5-3-2)
3) The error between the maximum and minimum diameters after honing should be no more than 0.04mm (0.0015")

ENGINE - Cylinder, Piston pin

4. Removing Carbon Deposits

Scrape off the carbon accumulation in the exhaust port of the cylinder with a hacksaw blade dulled at one end.

Fig 4-3-6

5 Installing the Cylinder

Put your fingers at each end of the piston ring, expand the ring, and slip it onto the piston. Align both ends of the ring with the knock pin in each ring groove. Then insert the piston into the cylinder. Take care not to damage the bottom of the cylinder with the rings.

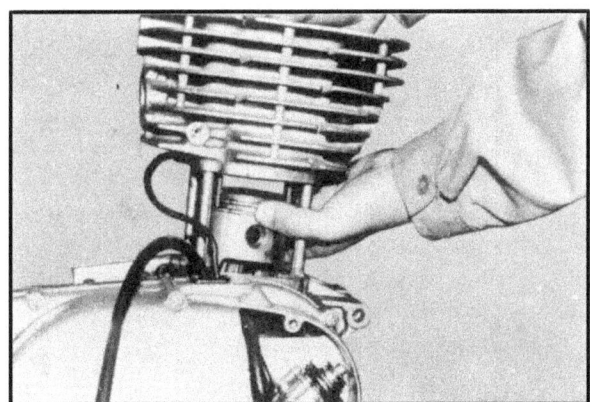

Fig 4-3-7

4-4 Piston Pin

1 Pulling out the Piston Pin

Remove the clips at ends of the piston pin both with needle nose pliers, and press out the piston pin with a finger or a slot-head screwdriver.

Note: Before removing the piston pin clips, cover the crankcase with a clean rag, so you will not accidentally drop the clip or other foreign particles into the crankcase.

Fig 4-4-1

2 Piston-to-Piston Pin Fit

The piston pin should fit snugly in its bore so that it drags a little as you turn it. If the pin is loose, replace the pin and/or the piston.

If the pin has step-wear in its center, replace the needle bearing as well as the piston pin. Check the small end of the connecting rod for wear by inserting the piston pin and bearing.

Fig 4-4-2

ENGINE · Piston Ring, Piston

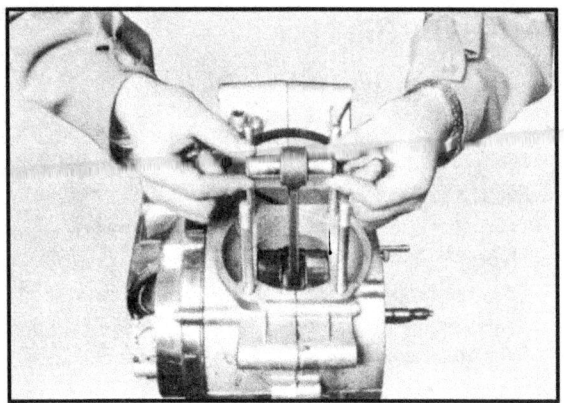

Fig 4-4-3

4-5 Piston Ring

1 Removing the Piston Rings

Put your thumbs at each end of the piston ring and pull the piston ring ends apart. Remove the ring by moving the ring off the piston on the other side of the ring ends.

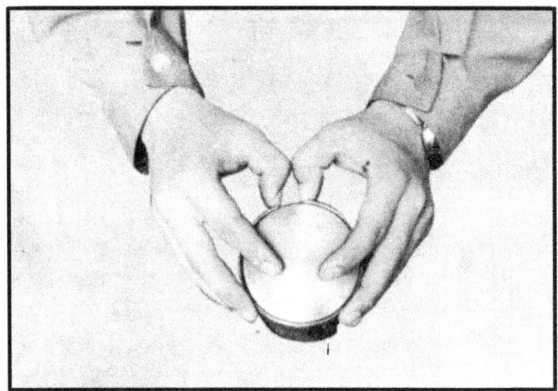

Fig 4-5-1

2 Installing the Piston Ring

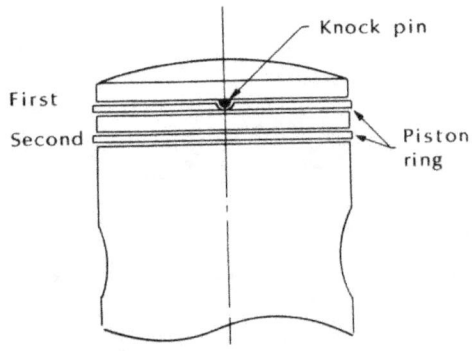

Fig 4-5-2

First fit the No.2 ring over the piston, and then the No.1 ring, and align their end gaps with the locating pin in each ring groove. (Fig. 4-5-2) The printing on all rings must face up to position the gap properly at the pin.

3 Checking the Piston Rings

1) Measurering piston ring wear
   Put the ring into the cylinder so that the ring is parallel to the cylinder bottom edge, and then measure the end gap with a feeler gauge. (Fig. 4-5-4)

Fig 4-5-3

The end gap should be between 0.2 and 0.4 mm. (0.008-0.015 in.) for both No.1 and No.2 rings. (0.4 – 0.5 mm. (0.016 – 0.019 in.) with GYT kit.)

2) Removing carbon
   Carbon on the piston rings and in the ring in grooves will make the rings stick in the piston, thus causing gas blow-by. Remoe the rings from the piston, and clean the carbon from the rings and ring grooves.

4-6 Piston

The piston is made of a high-silicon alnminum alloy

1. Checking and Correcting the Piston to Cylinder Wall Clearance

1) Measuring piston clearance
   Piston clearance is the difference between the minimum cylinder bore diameter and the maximum outside diameter of the piston.

18

As described in 4-3, Cylinder, piston clearance should be 0.040-0.045 mm. (0.0016-0.0018 in.)

To determine the maximum piston diameter, measure the piston with a micrometer at right angles to the skirt 10 mm. (3/8 in.) from its bottom edge. (Fig. 4-6-1)

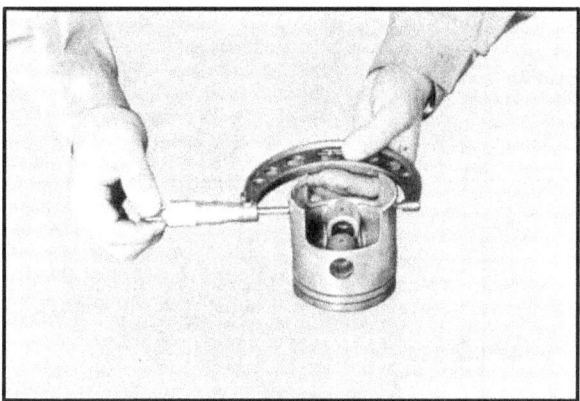

Fig 4-6-1

2) Checking and correcting scratches on the piston

A piston showing signs of seizure will result in noise and loss of engine power. It will also cause damage to the cylinder wall.

If a piston that has seized is used again without correction, another seizure will develop at the same area. Lightly sand the seizure "high spot" on the piston with #400 sandpaper until smooth (Fig. 4-6-2)

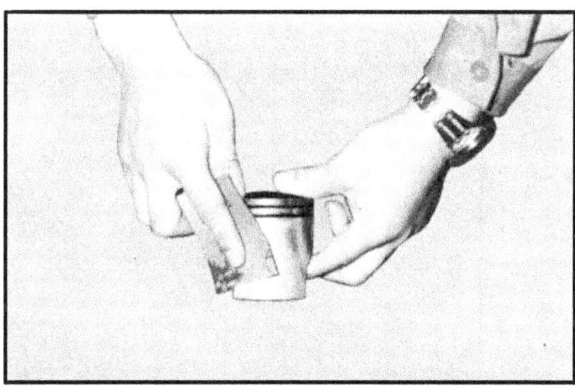

Fig 4-6-2

3) Removing Carbon

Remove carbon accumulations on the piston head with screwdriver or a saw-blade. (Fig. 4-6-3)

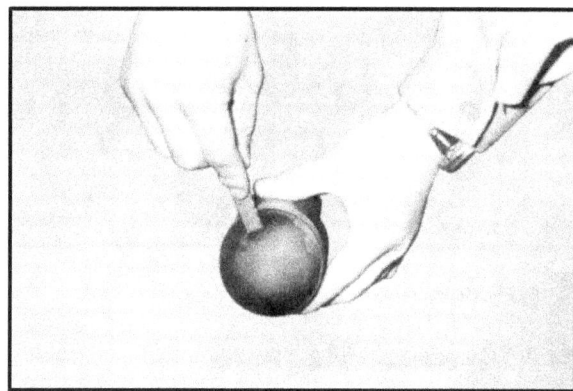

Fig 4-6-3

Carbon and gum accumulations in the piston groove will result in piston ring seizure. Remove all carbon from the ring groove (Fig. 4-6-4)

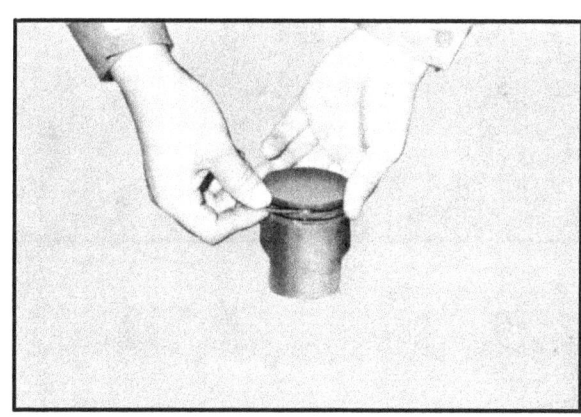

Fig 4-6-4

2 Piston Installation Direction

Install the piston with the arrow mark on the head pointing forward (toward the exhaust port of the cylinder.)

ENGINE - Flywheel Magneto

Fig 4-6-5

4-7 Flywheel Magneto

1. Remove the dynamo cover

Fig 4-7-1

2. Remove the nut using a flywheel magneto holding tool.

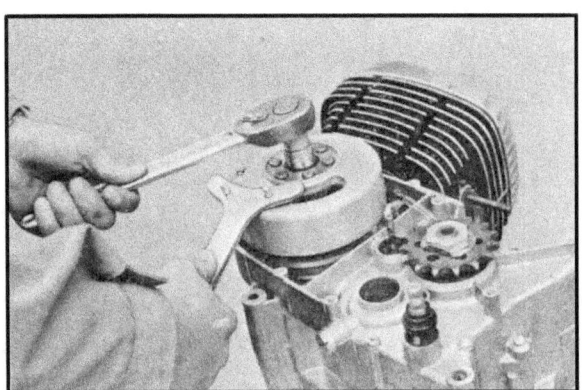

Fig 4-7-2

3. Install the flywheel magneto puller
   (It has a left-head thread)
   After the puller is secure, tighten the push screw and the flywheel will break loose.

Fig 4-7-3

4. Remove the three screws holding the flywheel neto base to the crankcase, and remove the flywheel magneto base.

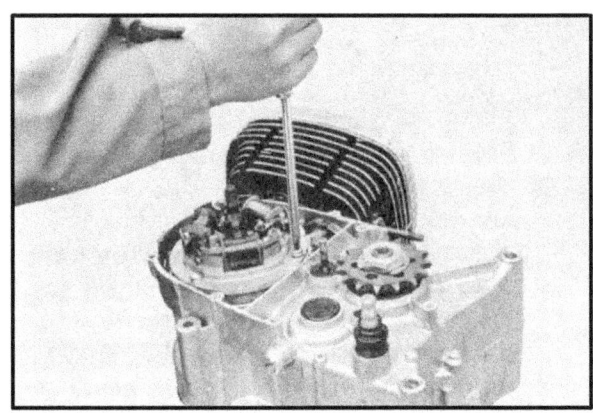

Fig 4-7-4

5. Remove the woodruff key.
   It is advisable to place the woodruff key on the flywheel magnets (using its magnetic force) while the key is removed for engine service.

ENGINE - Crankcase Cover (R.H.)

4-8 Crankcase Cover (R. H.)

1 Removal

1) Remove the kick crank mounting bolt and the crank.

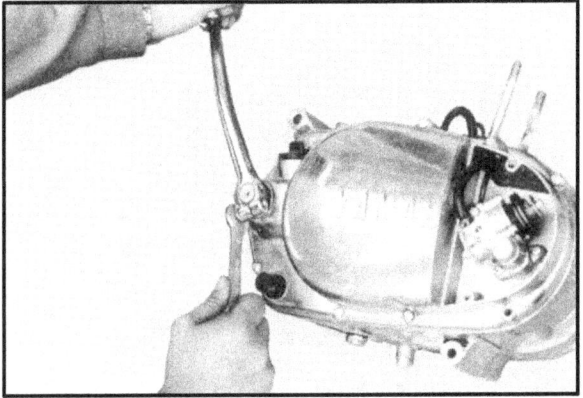

Fig 4-8-1

2) Remove the pan head screws holding the crankcase cover, and then remove the case cover. (The cover can be removed without taking off the oil pump.)

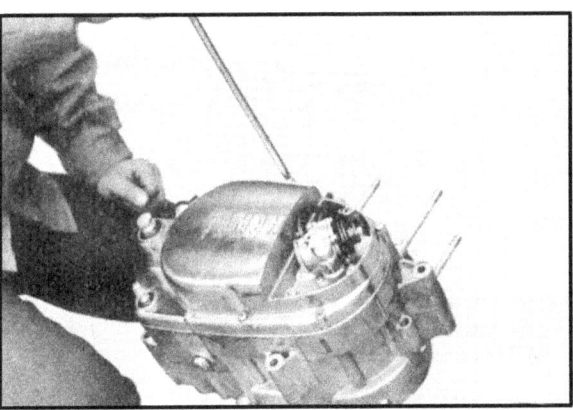

Fig 4-8-2

3) Remove the crankcase cover gasket and replace it, if damaged.

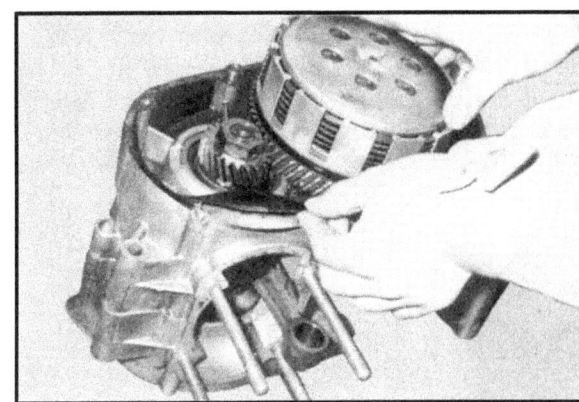

Fig 4-8-3

2 Installation

Spread YAMAHA Bond No.5 over the mating surface of the right-hand crankcase. Place the crankcase cover gasket on the crankcase, apply Yamaha Bond No.5 and install the right-hand crankcase cover. Be sure to apply YAMAHA Bond No.5 to the mating surface; otherwise, the crankcase will leak.

Note:

When installing the crankcase cover (R) make sure that the pump drive gear (made from synthetic resin) is correctly engaged with the primary drive gear.

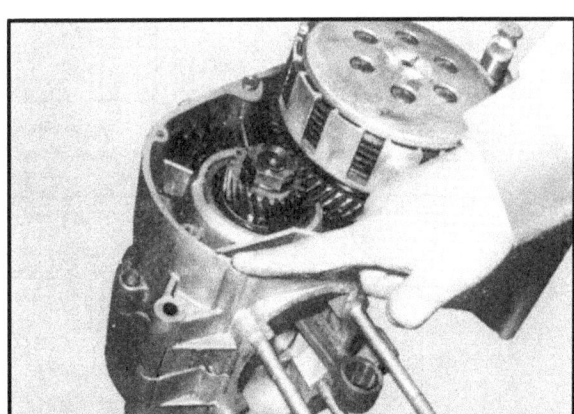

Fig 4-8-4

4-9 Clutch

The clutch is a wet, multi-disc type, consisting of six molded cork friction plates and seven clutch plates in the clutch housing mounted on the transmission main axle. To disengage the clutch, an inner push rod system is employed. The primary driven gear coupled with the clutch housing is meshed with a kick pinion gear allowing starting by kicking the starter with the clutch disengaged or engaged. A shock absorber consisting of coil springs is between the primary driven gear and the clutch housing.

The primary drive gear has 21 teeth, and the primary driven gear 65 teeth.
(Primary reduction ratio.........65/21 = 3.095)

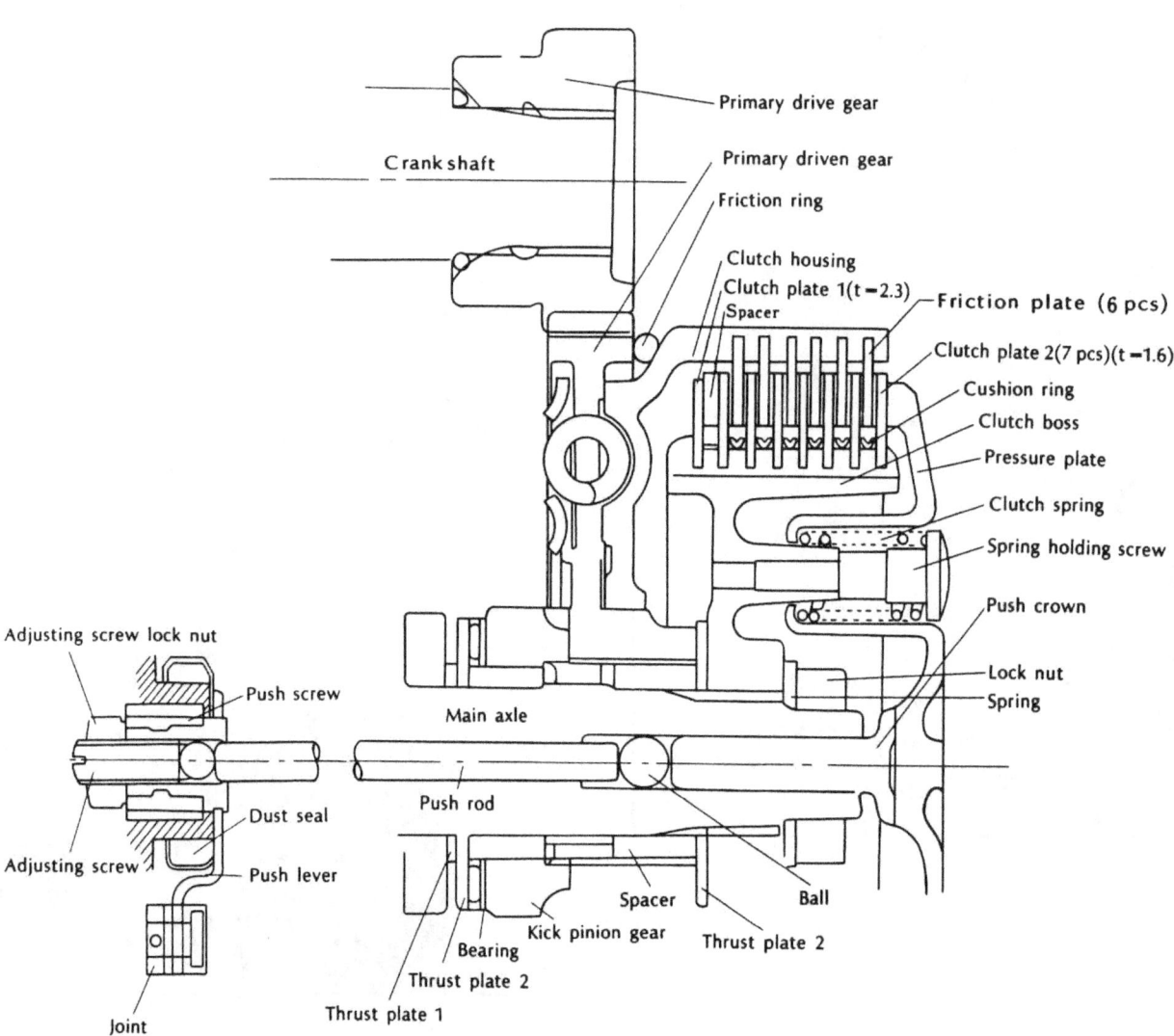

Fig 4-9-1

ENGINE - Clutch

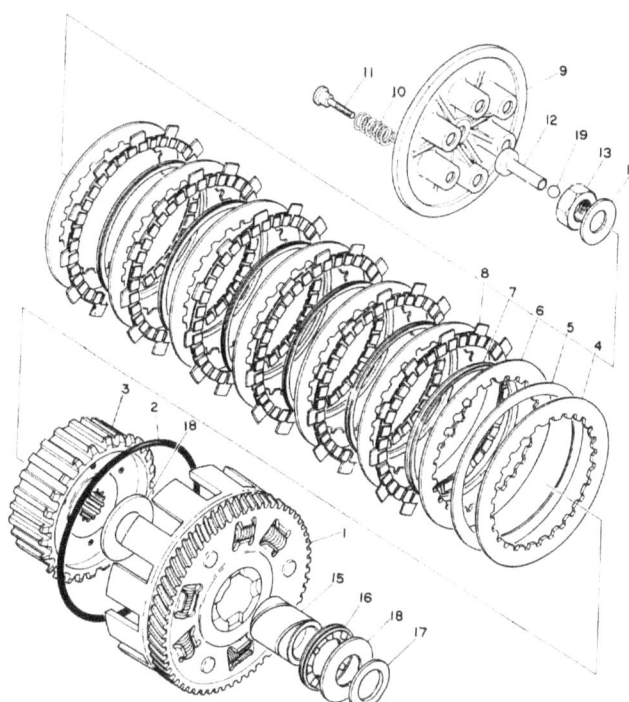

1. Primary driven gear complete
2. O-ring (Friction ring)
3. Clutch boss
4. Clutch plate 1
5. Spacer
6. Clutch plate 2
7. Cusion ring
8. Friction plate
9. Pressure plate
10. Clutch spring
11. Spring holding screw
12. Push crown
13. Lock nut
14. Spring
15. Specer
16. Thrust bearing
17. Thrust plate 2
18. Thrust plate 1
19. Ball

Fig 4-9-2 Clutch assy exploded view

1 Removing the Pressure Plate

Remove the six clutch spring holding screws, and take out the pressure plate and push crown.

Fig 4-9-4

Fig 4-9-3

23

ENGINE - Clutch

2 Removing the Clutch Boss

Install the clutch holding tool (same as R5, YDS5, YM2) on the clutch boss. Loosen the lock nut, and then remove the clutch boss.

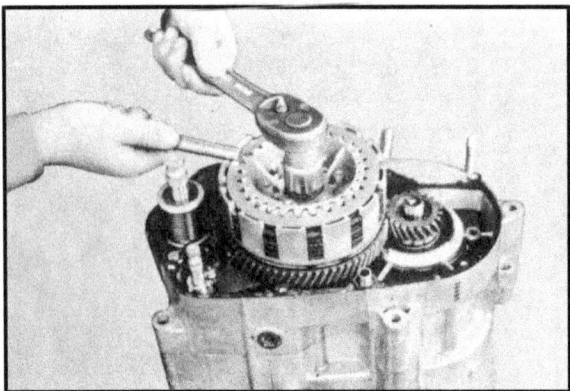

Fig 4-9-5

3 Checking the Clutch Spring

If the free length of the spring is 1 mm. (0.04 in.) or more shorter than the standard free length, replace it.

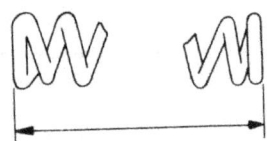

Free length 36.4 mm. (1.433 in.)

Fig 4-9-6

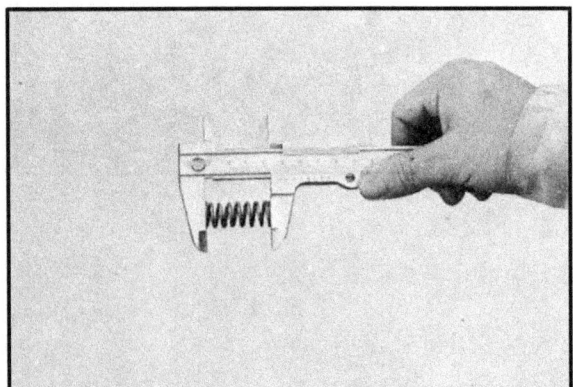

Fig 4-9-7

4 Check the Friction Plates

Inspect the friction plates for wear. Replace them if wear equals 0.3 mm. (0.012 in.) or more.

Standard thickness 3.0 mm. (0.118 in.)

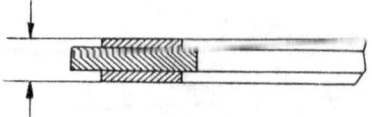

Fig 4-9-8

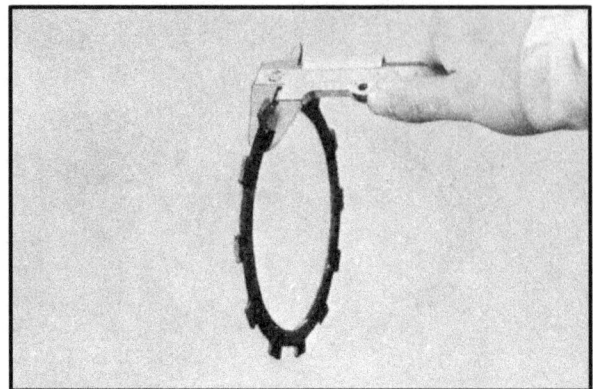

Fig 4-9-9

5 Clutch Housing Assembly (integrated with the primary driven gear).

A rubber friction ring is placed on the outside of the clutch between the primary driven gear and the clutch housing in order to reduce gear noise at low engine speeds.

1) Inspection

Insert the primary gear retaining collar (spacer) in the primary driven gear boss and check it for radial play.

If any scratches are found, replace it so it will not impair clutch action.

Fig 4-9-10

If the play is excessive (allowable clearance is between 0.009~0.048 mm.) replace the gear retaining collar because it will cause excessive noise.

6 Checking the Primary Gear Retaining Collar (Spacer)

Place the primary gear retaining collar around the main axle and again check it for radial play. If play exists (allowable clearance is between 0.020~0.062 mm.) replace the gear retaining collar. Replace any collar with step-wear on its outer surface.

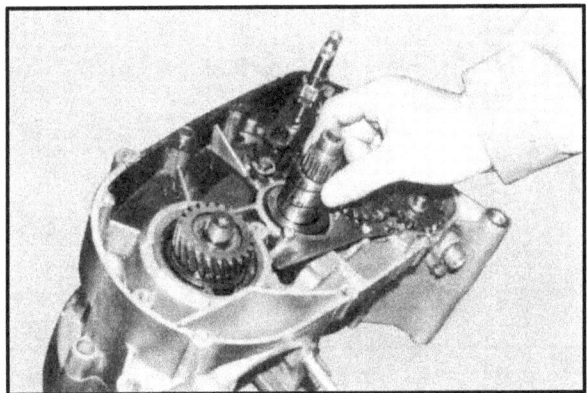

Fig 4-9-11

7 Fitting Cushion Rings

A cushion ring is installed between each of the clutch plates and the friction plates to insure even engagement and complete disengagement of the plates. When fitting cushion rings, be sure they are flat and not twisted.

Fig 4-9-12

8 Checking the Push Rod

Remove the push rod and roll it over a surface plate. If the rod is bent, straighten or replace it.

Fig 4-9-13

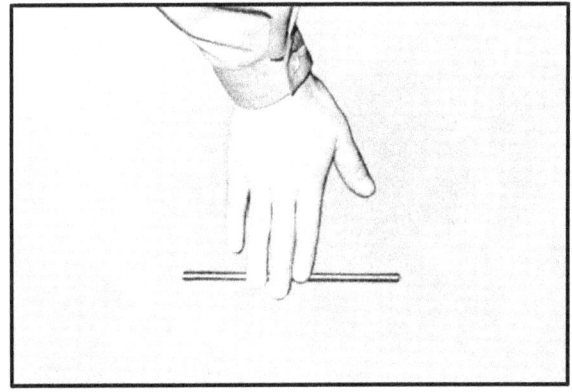

Fig 4-9-14

9 Caution on Re-assembling the Clutch

On both ends of the primary gear spacer are thrust washers and thrust bearings. If these washers and bearings are incorrectly installed, or omitted, the clutch boss will rub against the primary driven gear, impairing clutch action. The thrust bearing assembly fits on the primary retaining collar, but it may slip out of place when installing clutch boss. Therefore, apply grease to both surfaces of the bearing to make it stick to the gear retaining collar.

Befor fitting the clutch boss, install the clutch plates, friction plates, etc., and then install the clutch boss.

ENGINE - Adjusting the Clutch

Correct

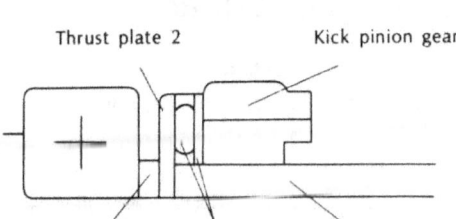

Fig 4-9-15

Incorrect

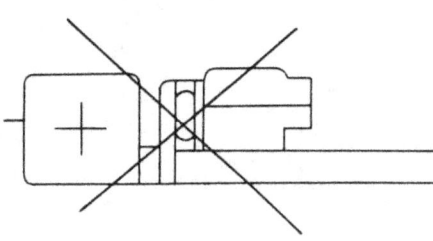

Fig 4-9-6

10 Adjusting the Clutch

1) Adjusting the Push Screw
Remove the clutch adjustment cover and loosen the push screw lock nut. Rotate the push screw in to a lightly seated position, and back it off 1/4 turn to get the proper spacing. The tighten the lock nut.

Fig 4-9-17

2) Adjusting the Clutch Cable Tension
The clutch cable becomes slackend after, being used for a long time. Occasionally the cable must be adjusted so that the play of the clutch handle is from 2 to 3 mm. (1/16-1/8 in.)

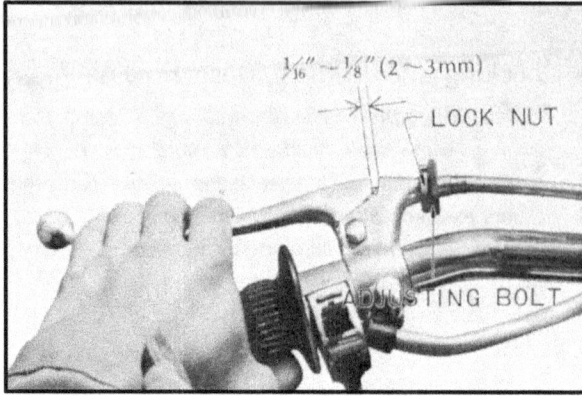

Fig 4-9-18

4-10 Primary Drive Gear

A Removal

Feed a rolled-up rag between the teeth of the primary drive gear and the primary driven gear to lock them, and then loosen the primary drive gear lock nut.

Fig 4-10-1

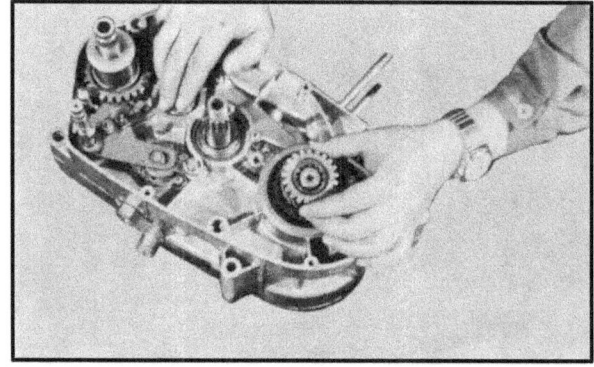

Fig 4-10-2

4-11 Kick Starter Mechanism

The kickstarter employs the primary kick system. To start the engine, you just kick the starter with the clutch disengaged or engaged. The ability to start the engine with the clutch disengaged can be a great advantage when racing. The kick gear is driven the tame as the YR1. When the kick shaft rotates, the ratchet wheel is disengaged from the ratchet wheel guide and meshes with the kick gear. The rotation of the kick gear is transmitted through the idler gear to the kick pinion that is engaged with the primary driven gear.

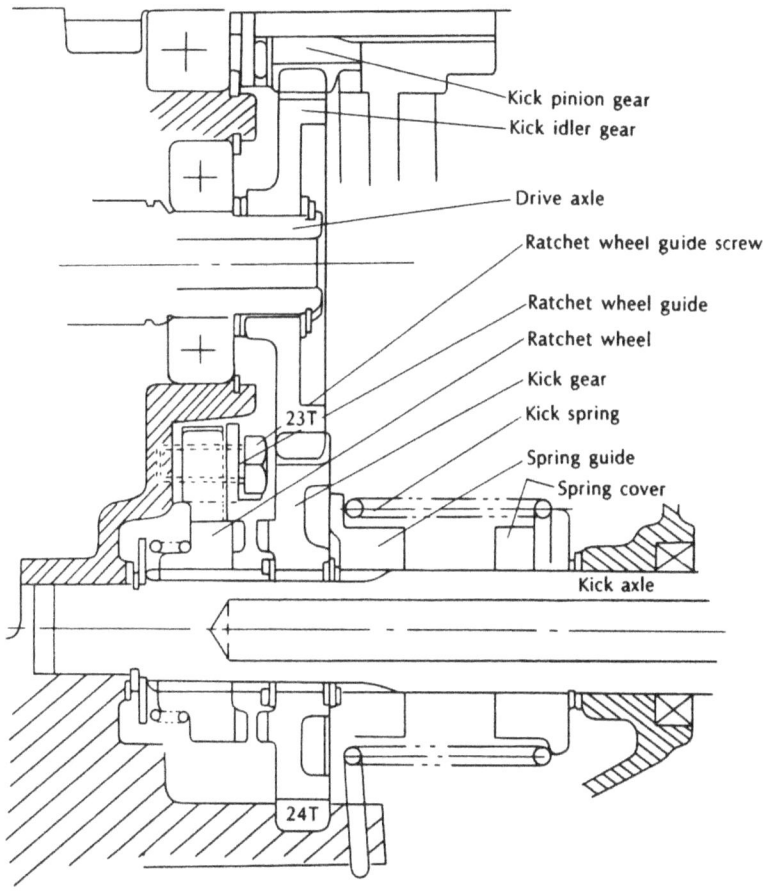

Fig 4-11-1

ENGINE - Kick Starter Mechanism

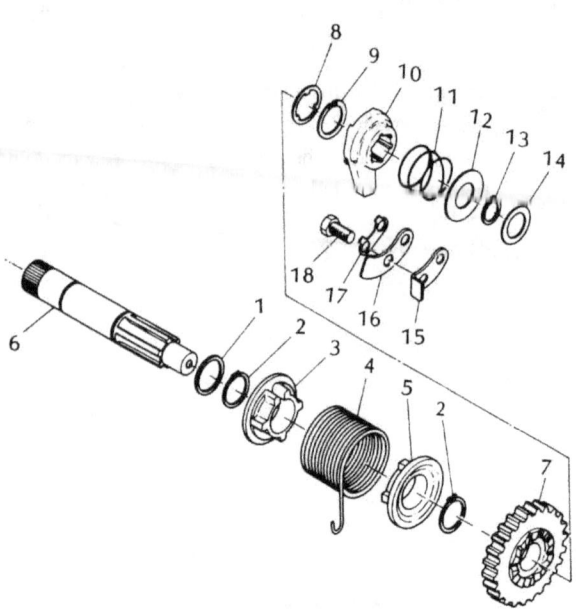

1. Shim 2
2. Circlip
3. Spring cover
4. Kick spring
5. Spring guide
6. Kick axle
7. Kick gear
8. Washer
9. Clip
10. Ratchet wheel
11. Ratchet wheel spring
12. Spring cover
13. Circlip
14. Shim 1
15. Stopper
16. Ratchet wheel guide
17. Lock washer
18. Ratchet wheel guide screw

Fig 4-11-2

1 Removal

1) Remove the kick spring.

2) Then remove the kick starter assembly.

Fig 4-11-3

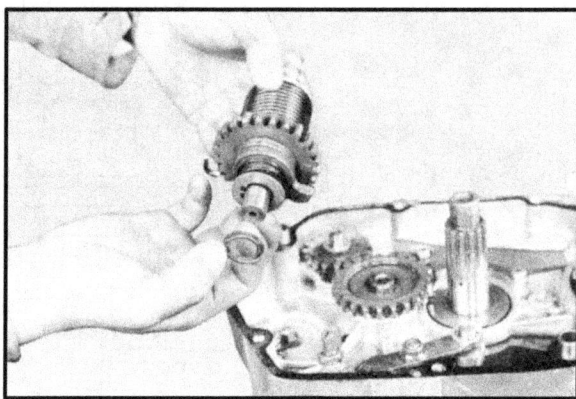

Fig 4-11-4

2 Reverse the sequence for reinstallation.

Notes on Assembling

1) Align the marking on the kick starter axle with that of the ratchet wheel.
2) When installing the kick starter assy in the crankcase, slide the rachet wheel pawl over the ratchet wheel guide toward the stopper attached to the case. Make sure that the pawl is in close contact with the stopper. Then pull the spring forward and hook it on the stopper.

ENGINE - Starter Mechanism, Shift Mechanism

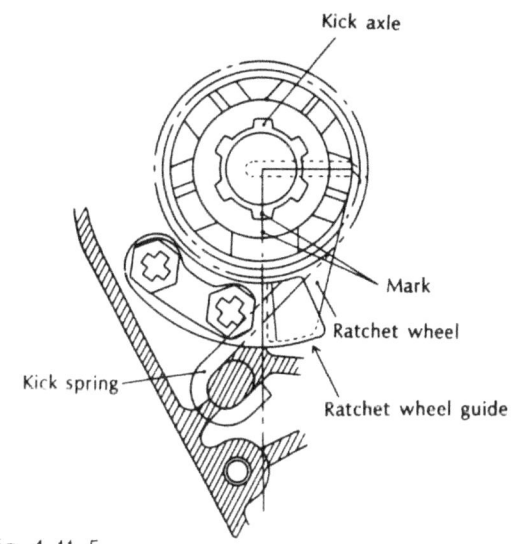

Fig 4-11-5

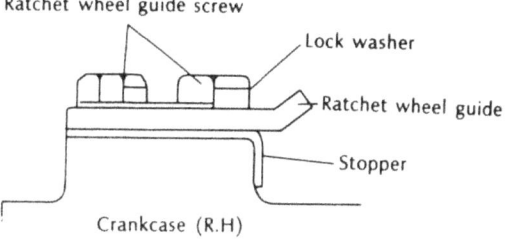

Fig 4-11-6

3 Removing the Kick Ideler Gear

Remove the circlip with clip pliers, and then the kick idler gear can be easily removed.

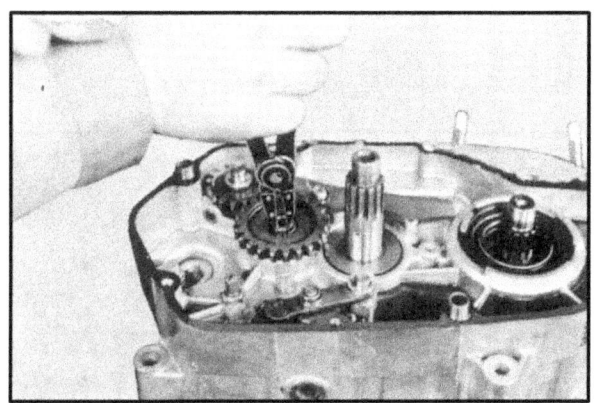

Fig 4-11-7

4 Removing the Tachometer Drive Gear

The tachometer drive gear is engaged with the kick idler gear to convey the revolutions per minute of the crankshaft to the tachometer through the tachometer cable.

Remove the clip with pliers and the tachometer drive gear can be removed.

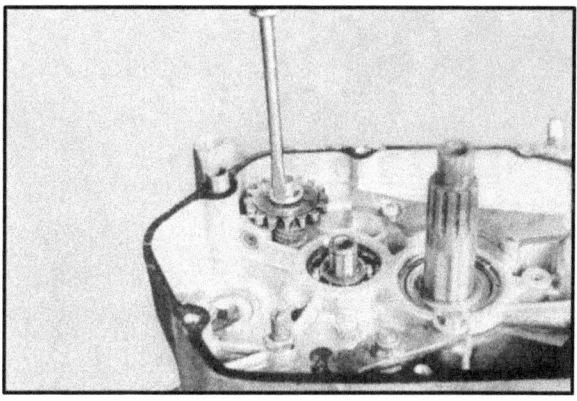

Fig 4-11-8

1. Drive gear axle
2. Circlip
3. Shim
4. Drive gear
5. Primary gear

Fig 4-11-9

4-12 Shift Mechanism

The DT1-E has been designed to allow the owner to convert it to an optimum output competition machine by installing Yamaha's GYT parts. Therefore, the machine in standard form has been constructed to assure smooth and accurate gear shifting by using an already proven shifting mechanism.

The shift cam drum has one shift fork and two other shift forks are installed on a guide bar located parallel to the cam drum. The three shift forks slide back and forth in the slotted guides that are grooved in the shift drum. A safety device has been provided to prevent the shifter from by-passing the next gear when a quick or hard shift is made. This provides dependability and assurance for correct shifting for the desired gear even under

ENGINE · Shift Mechanism

the roughest conditions such as comperition racing. A see-saw type shifting arrangement is used that enables the rider to shift quickly and easily down for the lower gears and up for the higher gears. Neutral position is located between first and second gears.

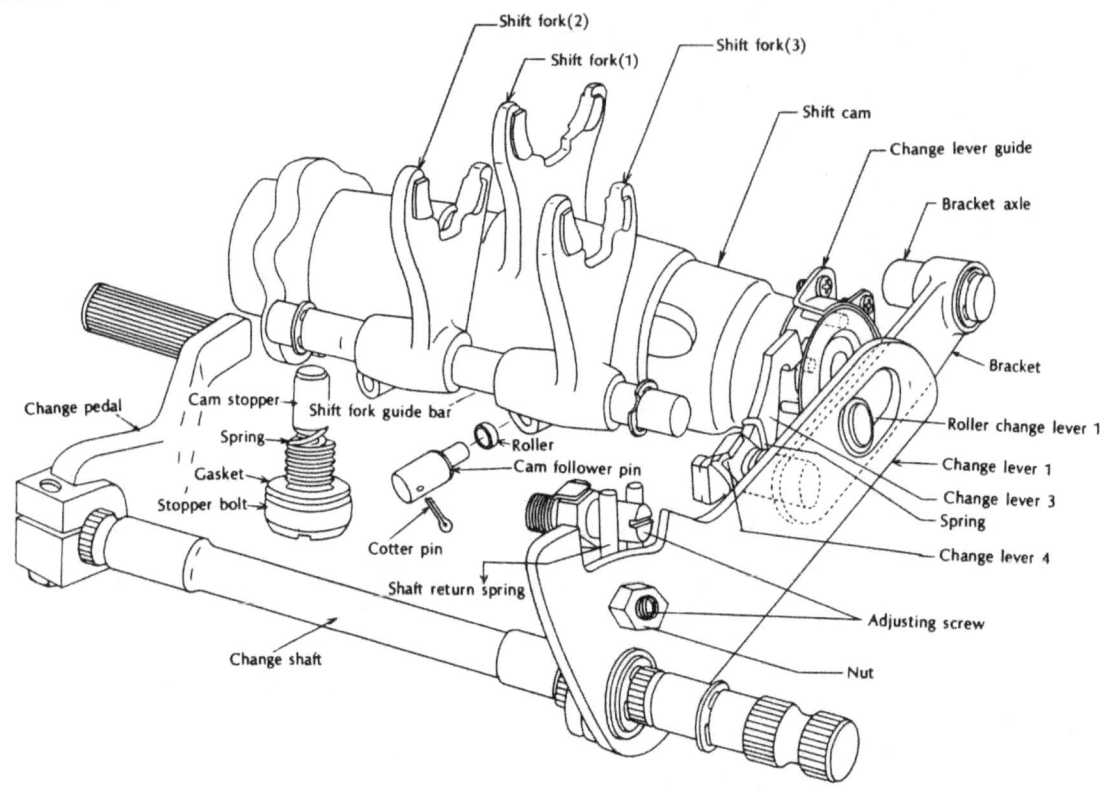

Fig 4-12-1

1 Removing the Change Axle Assembly

1) Remove the change axle sealing boot.

2) Pull out the change shaft assembly.

Fig 4-12-2

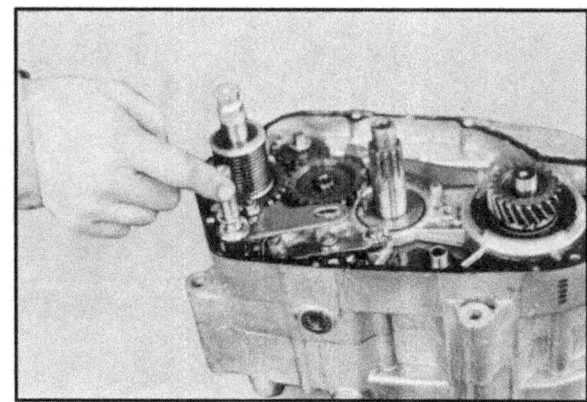

Fig 4-12-3

2 Checking the Gear Shift Parts

1) Check the gear shift return spring A broken or fatigued gear shift return spring will impair the return action of the shifting mechanism.

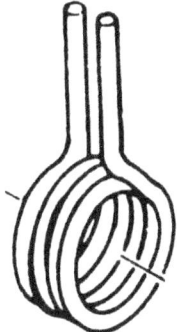

Fig 4-12-4

3 Removing the Change Lever 3 and 4

Remove 'E' clip with slot-head screwdriver, and the change lever can be removed.

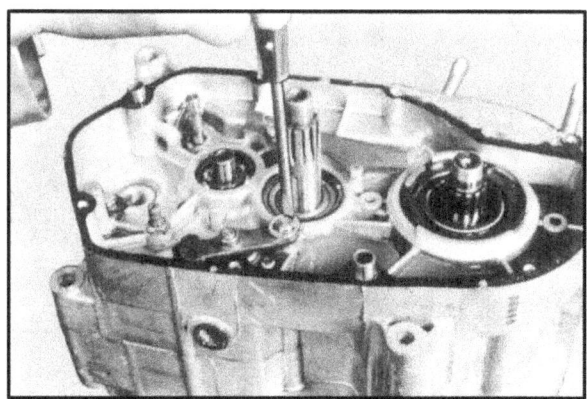

Fig 4-12-5

4 Checking the Change Lever Spring

Check for a fatigued or broken change lever spring. A faulty change lever spring may result in an imporper shifting sequence.

5 Gear Change Adjustment

1) Fully move the gear change lever up and down and turn the adjusting bolt (eccentric bolt) on the case so that the clearance (a) will become equal to the clearance (a') (a) is the clearance between the bent part of change lever 3 and the stopper (shaded area in the drawing) and (a') is the clearance between the bent part of the stopper. The stopper is a device for preventing the shifter from overrunning the correct position. After the adjustment, lock the adjusting screws with the lock nut.

2) Next turn the adjusting screw (eccentric screw) on change lever 4 so that the clearance (b) will become even with the clearance (b') on each gear position.
(b) is the clearance between the pin and change lever 4. After the adjustment, lock the adjusting screw with the lock nut.

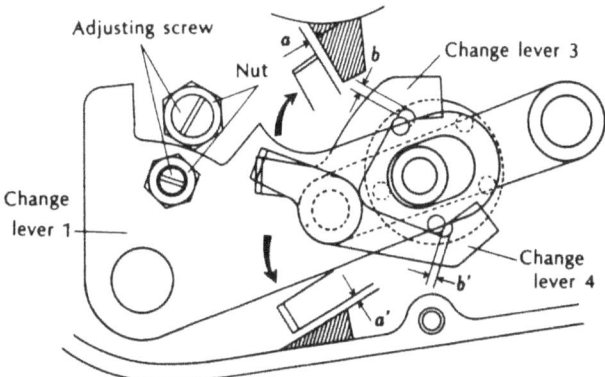

Fig 4-12-6

4-13 Drive Sprocket

1 Removal

1) Straighten the bent edge of the lock washer with a blunt-ended metal punch.

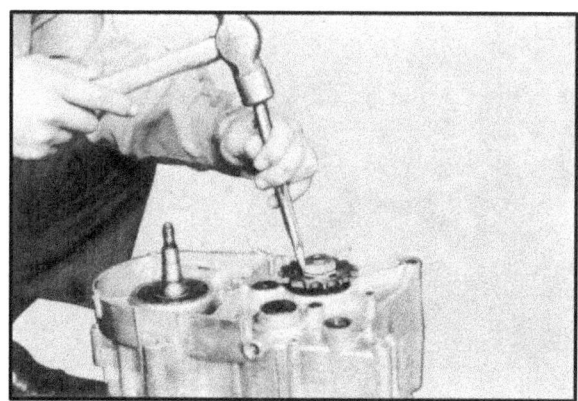

Fig 4-13-1

2) Keep the drive sprocket from turning with the holding tool, and remove the flywheel magneto

ENGINE - Drive Sprocket, Crankcase

sprocket nut.

If the flywheel magneto puller is not available, shift the transmission to low gear, and fit a wrench on the sprocket nut. Then tap the handle of the wrench with a hammer and the shock will loosen the nut.

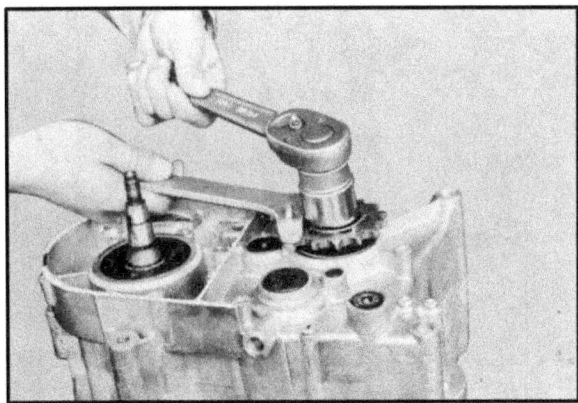

Fig 4-13-2

2 Inspection

A worn drive sprocket will result in excessive chain noise, and shorten the life of the chain. Check the sprocket for worn teeh, and replace if it is worn.

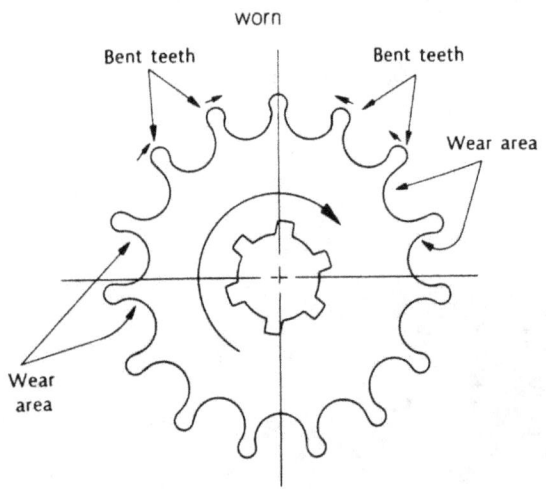

Fig 4-13-3

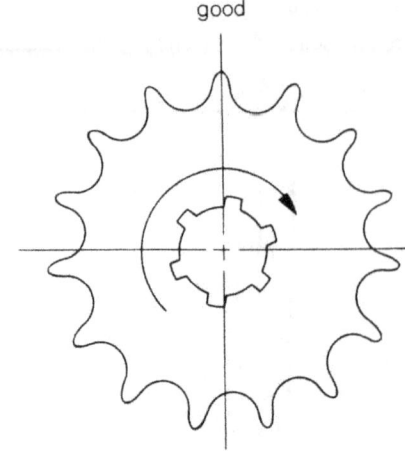

Fig 4-13-4

4-14 Crankcase

1 Separating

1) Remove neutral stopper.

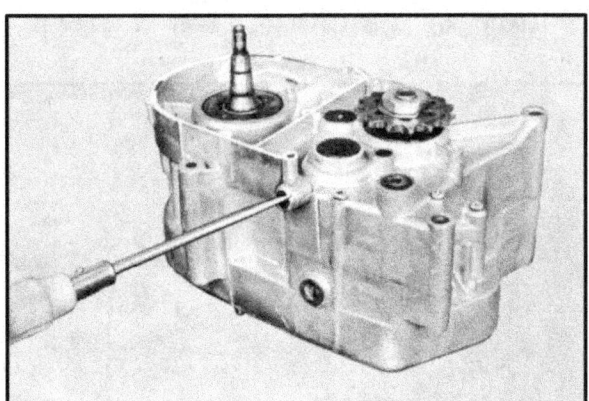

Fig 4-14-1

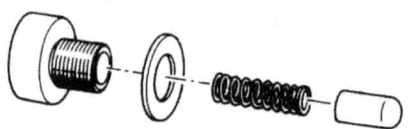

Fig 4-14-2

ENGINE - Crankcase

2) Remove the change lever guide

Fig 4-14-3

3) Remove the pan head screws from the left crankcase.

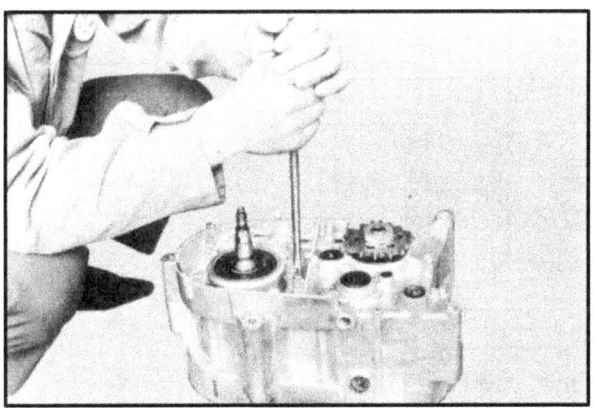

Fig 4-14-4

4) Install the crankcase separating tool on the right crankcase. Divide the crankcase while tapping the main axle and the crankcase alternately with plastic tip hammer.

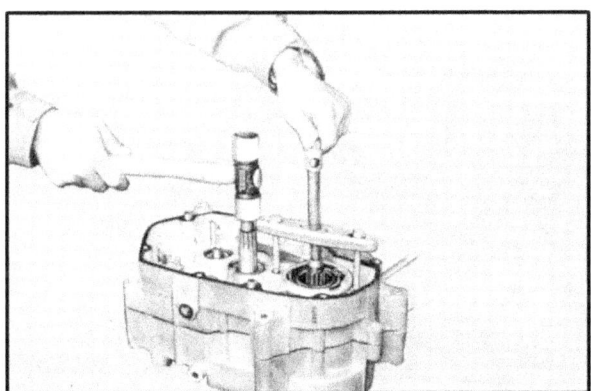

Fig 4-14-5

Note:

Fully tighten the bolts of the crankcase dividing tool, and keep the tool in a horizontal position. The crankcase is designed to split into two halves, right and left.
Only one drain plug is provided for both the transmission and clutch housings. Both housings can be drained at the same time by removing the drain plug.

2 Reassembling

When reassembling the crankcase, be sure to apply YAMAHA BOND No.5 to the mating surfaces of both halves.

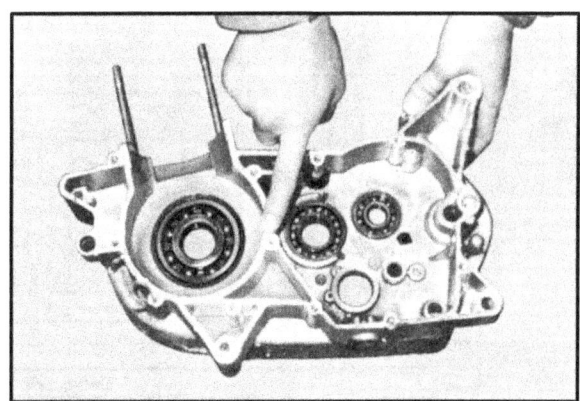

Fig 4-14-6

ENGINE - Transmission Assembly

4-15 Transmission Assembly

The constant mesh wide ratio 5-speed transmission makes it possible to fully utilize the performance of the engine throughout the entire speed range from low to high. The top pinion is similar in type to the third gear wheel, and the third gear pinion is similar to the top gear wheel. For layout of the transmission and related part, refer to Fig. 4-15-1 and 2. The primary reduction ratio is 65/21 = 3.095. Therefore the total reduction ratios will be :

Primary reduction ratio × Transmission gear reduction × Secondary reduction ratio = Total reduction ratio.

1st 65/21 × 38/15 × 44/14 = 24.644
2nd 65/21 × 34/19 × 44/14 = 17.408
3rd 65/21 × 30/23 × 44/14 = 12.689
4th 65/21 × 26/26 × 44/14 = 9.728
5th 65/21 × 23/30 × 44/14 = 7.458

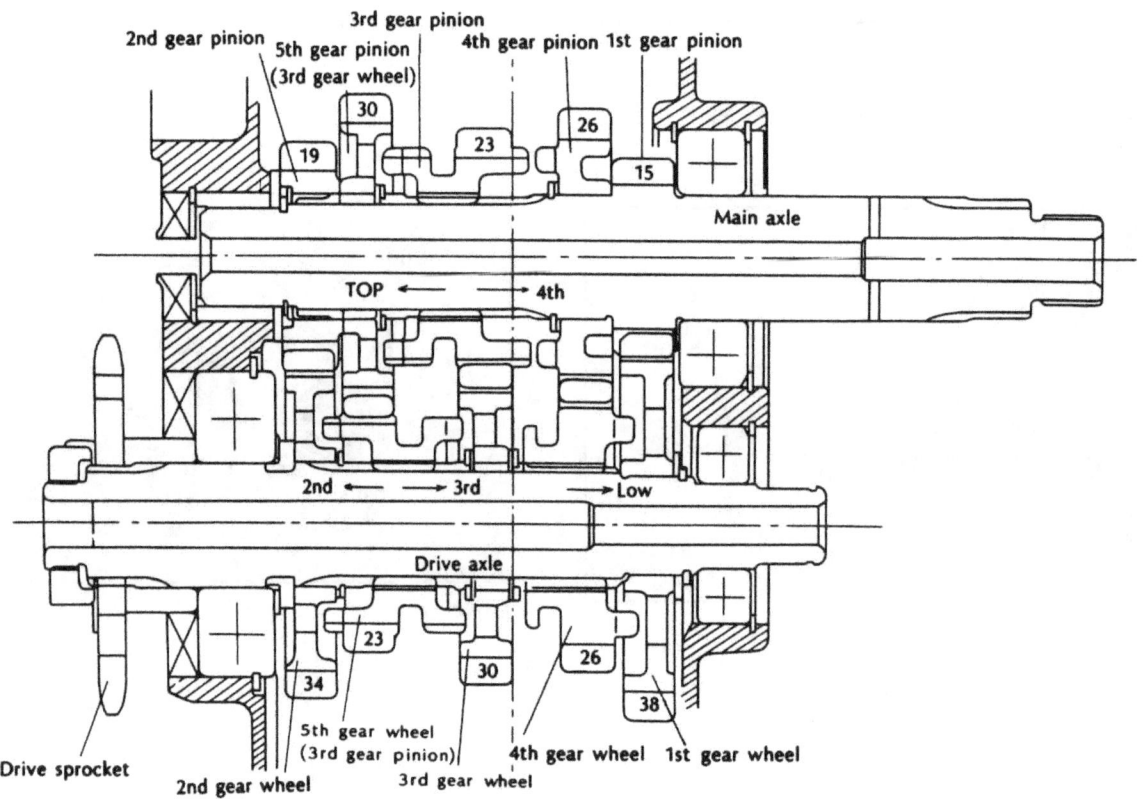

Fig 4-15-1

ENGINE - Transmission Assembly

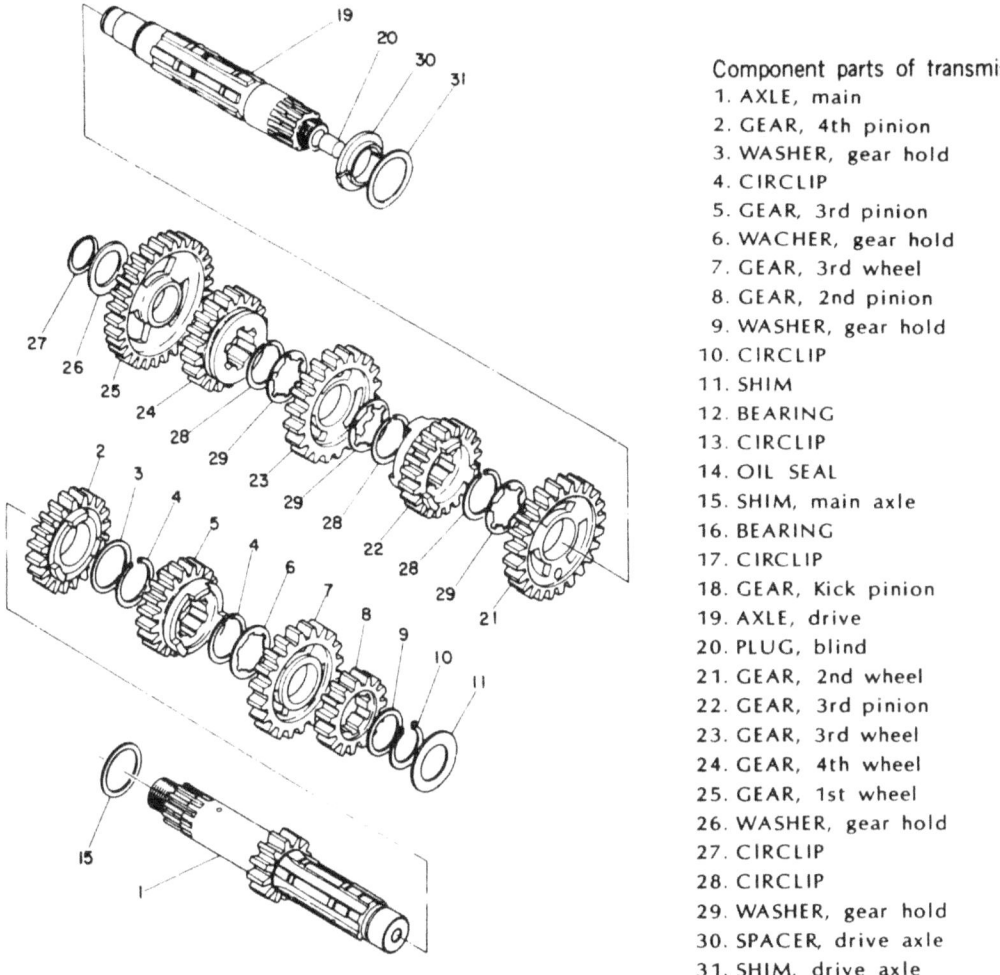

Component parts of transmission
1. AXLE, main
2. GEAR, 4th pinion
3. WASHER, gear hold
4. CIRCLIP
5. GEAR, 3rd pinion
6. WACHER, gear hold
7. GEAR, 3rd wheel
8. GEAR, 2nd pinion
9. WASHER, gear hold
10. CIRCLIP
11. SHIM
12. BEARING
13. CIRCLIP
14. OIL SEAL
15. SHIM, main axle
16. BEARING
17. CIRCLIP
18. GEAR, Kick pinion
19. AXLE, drive
20. PLUG, blind
21. GEAR, 2nd wheel
22. GEAR, 3rd pinion
23. GEAR, 3rd wheel
24. GEAR, 4th wheel
25. GEAR, 1st wheel
26. WASHER, gear hold
27. CIRCLIP
28. CIRCLIP
29. WASHER, gear hold
30. SPACER, drive axle
31. SHIM, drive axle

Fig 4-15-2 Component parts of transmission

1. Removal

Remove the transmission and shifter as an unit.

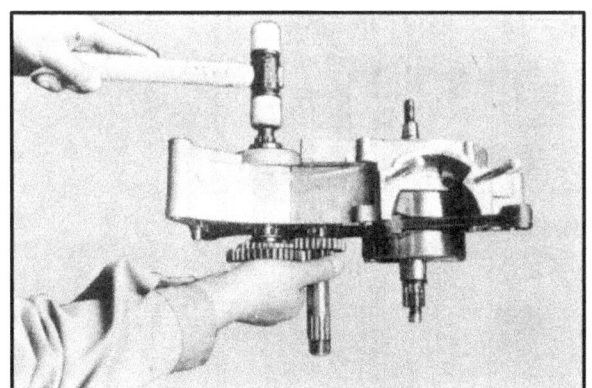

Fig 4-15-3

2 Reinstallation

Reinstall the transmission and shifter as an unit in the left crankcase half after they are sub-assembled. They can not be installed separately. The transmission unit must be in neutral during installation.

4-16 Crankshaft

The crankshaft requires the highest degree of accuracy in engineering and servicing of all the engine parts. The crankshaft is also more susceptible to wear, and therefore, it must be handled with special care.

To increase the inertia force of the crank, the diameter of the crankshaft is increased to 30 mm. (1.18 in.) the thickness of the flywheel to 26 mm. (1.02 in.) and its diameter to 110 mm. (4.33 in.)

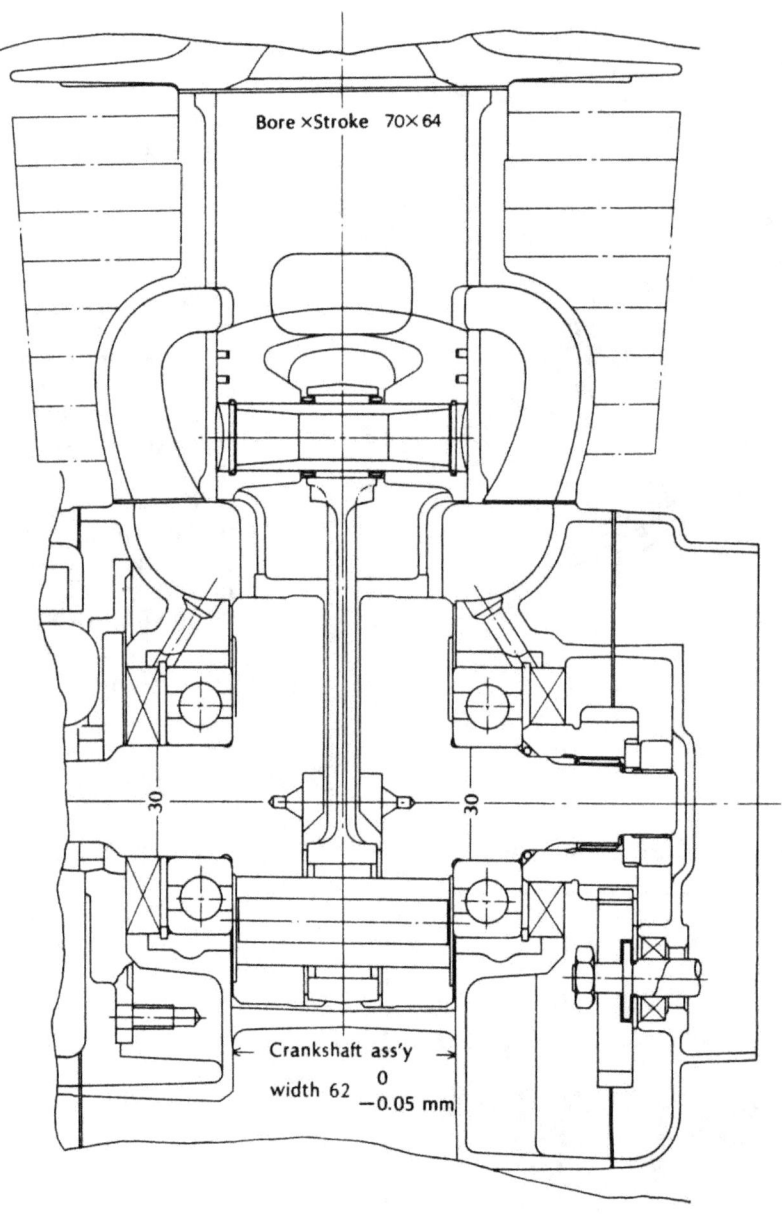

Fig 4-16-1

ENGINE · Crankshaft

Crankshaft component parts

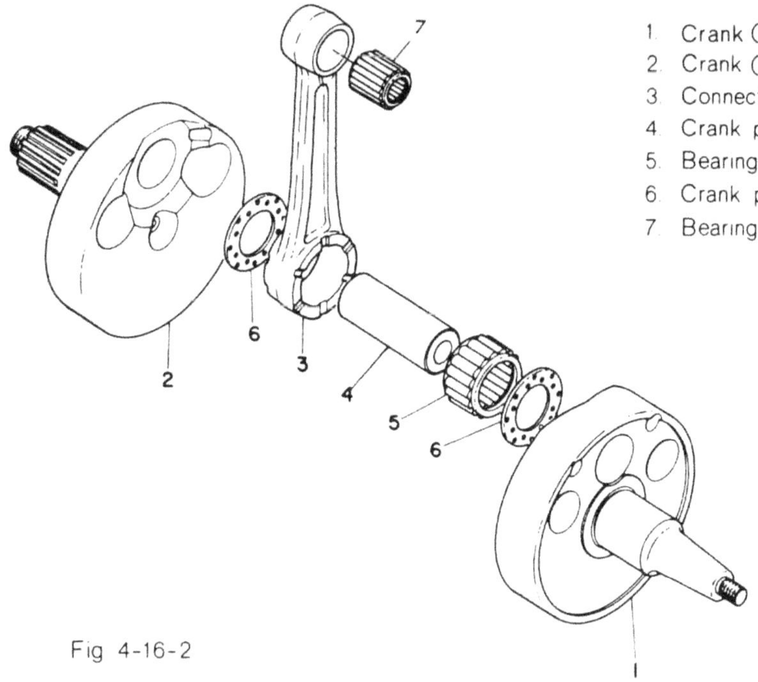

1. Crank (L.H.)
2. Crank (R.H.)
3. Connecting rod
4. Crank pin
5. Bearing
6. Crank pin washer
7. Bearing

Fig 4-16-2

1 Removing the Crankshaft Assembly

Remove the crankshaft assembly with the crankcase separating tool.

Note:
Fully tighten the bolts of the crankcase dividing tool, and keep the tool in parallel with the crankcase surface.

Note:
1) The crankshaft setting tool is the same as those used for YG1, and YF1.
2) The crank fitting spacer is required because the crankshaft is larger in diameter. The oil seal is larger in outside diameter than crankshaft setting tool body.

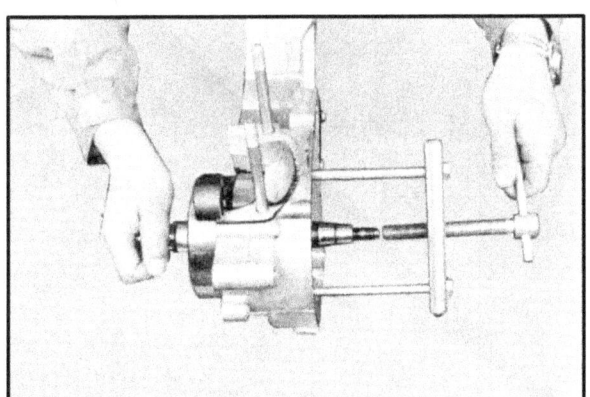

Fig 4-16-3

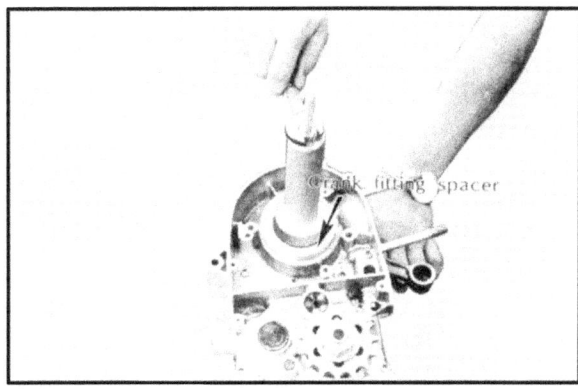

Fig 4-16-4

2 Installing the Crankshaft Assembry

Install the crankshaft assembly by using the crankshaft setting tool and the crank fitting the spacer. Hold the connecting rod at top dead center at with one hand while turning the handle of the setting tool with other.

ENGINE - Crankshaft

3. Inspection and Servicing

1) Checking the crankshaft components

Check connecting rod axial play at small end (to determine the amount of wear of crank pin and bearing at large end) (Fig. 4-16-5)	Small end play should not exceed 2 mm.(0.078 in.)	If small end play exceeds 2 mm, disassemble the crankshaft, check connecting rod crank pin and large end bearing. Replace defective parts. Small end play after reassembly should be within 0.8-1.0 mm.(0.031~0.04 in.)
Check the connecting rod for axial play at large end. (Fig. 4-16-6)	Move the connecting rod to one side and insert a feeler gauge. Large end axial play should be within 0.4—0.5 mm.(0.019 in.)	If excessive axial play is present, (0.6 mm or more) disassemble the crankshaft and replace any worn parts.
Check accuracy of the crankshaft ass'y runout. (Misalignment of parts of the crankshaft) (Fig. 4-16-7)	Dial gauge readings should be within 0.03 mm. (0.0012 in.)	Correct any misalingment by tapping the flywheel with a brass hammer and by using a wedge.

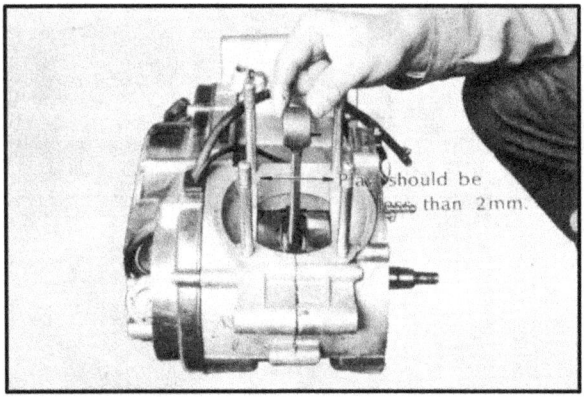

Fig. 4-16-5

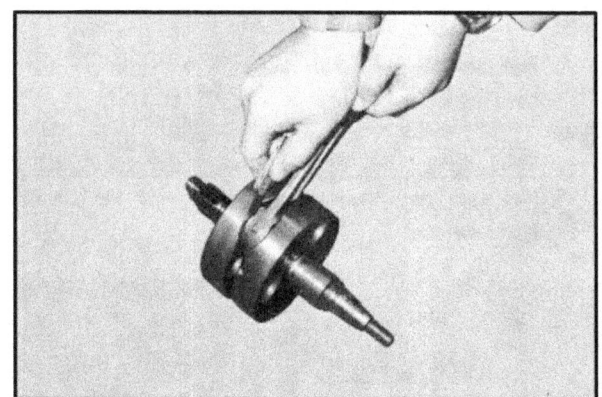

Fig. 4-16-6

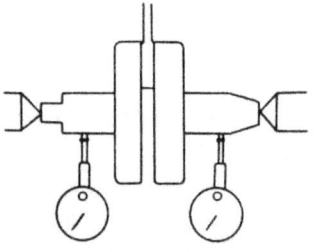

Fig 4-16-7

4-17 Bearings and Oil Seals

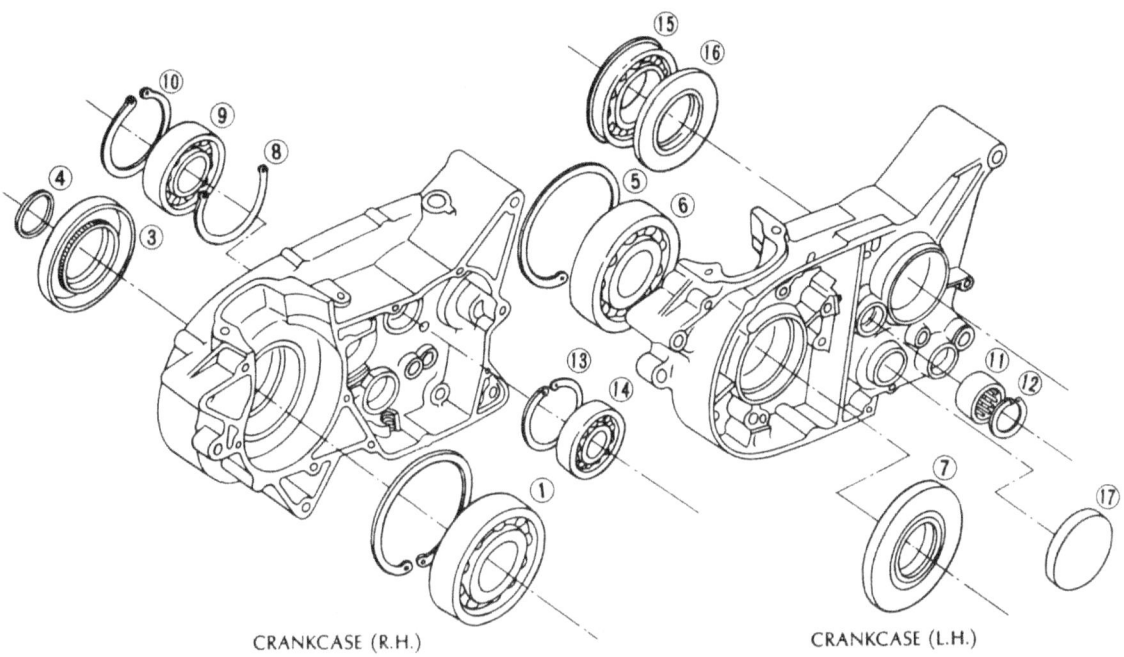

Fig. 4-17-1

1. Bearing 6306
2. Circlip R-72
3. Oil seal SW42-72-10
4. O-ring 3.2-24.5
5. Circlip R-72
6. Bearing 6306
7. Oil seal SW30-72-10
8. Circlip 25.1-31-0.3
9. Bearing 6205
10. Circlip
11. Bearing 20-26-16
12. Circlip 25.1-31-0.1
13. Circlip
14. Bearing 6203
15. Bearing 6305NR
16. Oil seal SD-35-62-6

ENGINE - Bearings and Oil Seals

1) Removal and Installation

1) Removal

   a. Pry the oil seals out of place with a slot head screwdriver.

   Always replace the oil seals when overhauling the engine.

   Note: Place a piece of wood under the screwdriver to prevent damage to the case.

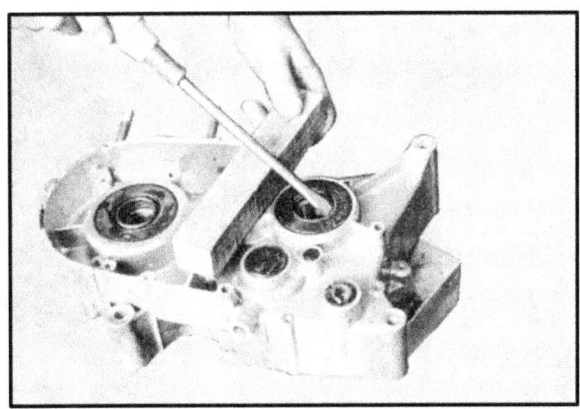

Fig. 4-17-2

   b. Remove the bearing with a bearing puller.

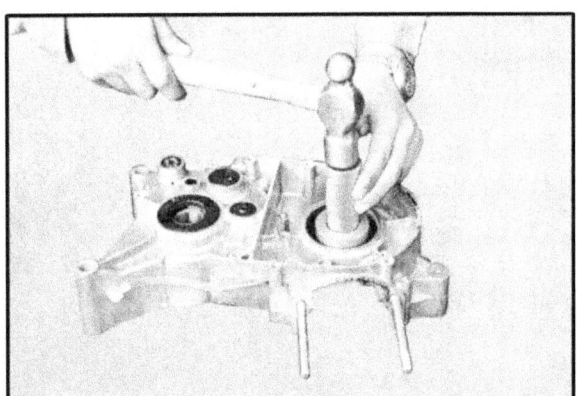

Fig. 4-17-3

2) Installation

Install bearings and oil seals with their stamped manufacturer's marks or numerals facing out ward. (In other words, the stamped letters must be on the exposed view side.)

The crankshaft bearing circlip should be installed so that the circlip end gap is aligned with the arrow marked on each of the crankcase halves.

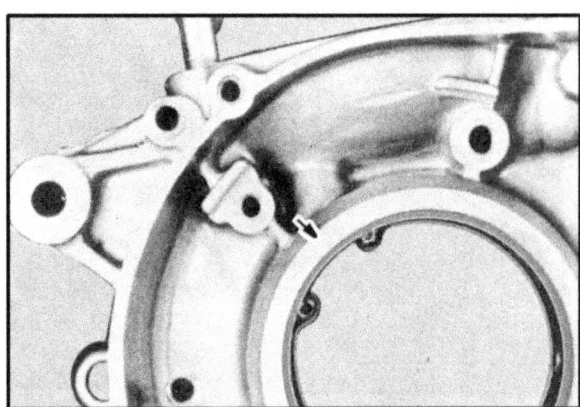

Fig. 4-17-4

ENGINE - Carburetor

4-18 Carburetor

The standard DT1-E is equipped with a VM 26 SH (26 mm.) carburetor that is equipped with a built-in starter jet.

The carburetor is bolted to a 30 mm. thick bakelite insulator that is between the carburetor and cylinder. This insulator provides more than adequate heat insulation. The carburetor floats have been specially designed to keep the float level from fluctuating due to vibration or shock. The main jet is installed in such a manner to provide quick and easy replacement from the outside by merely removing the jet holder on the bottom left side of the carburetor float bowl.

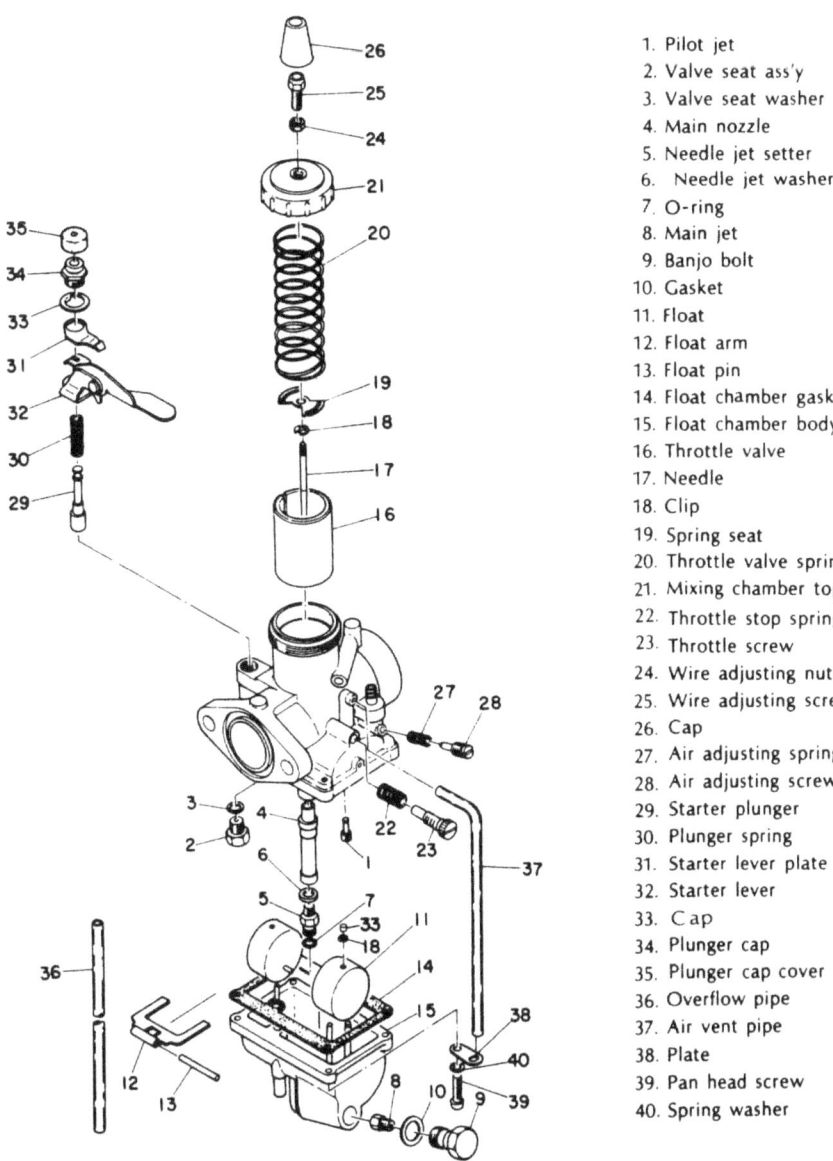

1. Pilot jet
2. Valve seat ass'y
3. Valve seat washer
4. Main nozzle
5. Needle jet setter
6. Needle jet washer
7. O-ring
8. Main jet
9. Banjo bolt
10. Gasket
11. Float
12. Float arm
13. Float pin
14. Float chamber gasket
15. Float chamber body
16. Throttle valve
17. Needle
18. Clip
19. Spring seat
20. Throttle valve spring
21. Mixing chamber top
22. Throttle stop spring
23. Throttle screw
24. Wire adjusting nut
25. Wire adjusting screw
26. Cap
27. Air adjusting spring
28. Air adjusting screw
29. Starter plunger
30. Plunger spring
31. Starter lever plate
32. Starter lever
33. Cap
34. Plunger cap
35. Plunger cap cover
36. Overflow pipe
37. Air vent pipe
38. Plate
39. Pan head screw
40. Spring washer

Fig. 4-18-1 Exploded diagram of carburetor

1. Checking the Carburetor

1) Float

Remove the float and shake it to check if gasoline is inside. If fuel leaks into the float while the engine is running, the float chamber fuel level will rise and make the fuel mixture too rich. Replace the float if it is deformed or leaking.

ENGINE - Carburetor

2) Float valve

Replace the float valve if its seating end is worn with a stop or if it is scrached. Check the float valve spring for fatigue. Depress the float vallve with your finger, and make sure that it properly seats against the valve seat when released. If the float valve spring is weakened, fuel will overflow, flooding the float chamber while the gas is on.

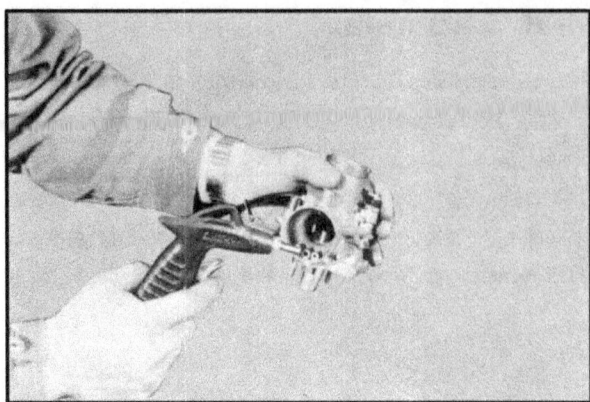

Fig. 4-18-4

3) Overflowing

If fuel overflows, check the carburetor as described in 1) and 2) above. If neither 1) nor 2) cures the overflowing, it may be caused by dirt or dust in the fuel preventing the float valve from seating properly. If any dirt or dust is found, clean the caburetor, petcock and gas tank.

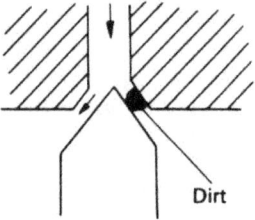

Fig. 4-18-2

2. Float Level Adjustment

The carburetor float level is checked by the Yamaha factory during assembly and testing. But rough riding, worn needle valve, or bent float arm can cause the float level to fluctuate. If the float level raises, this will cause a rich ful/air mixture that can cause poor performace and spark plug fouling. If the float level decreases, this can cause a lean fuel/air mixture that can result in engine damage.

If the machine is subjected to continuous rough riding or many miles of travel, the float level should be checked and set regularly and in the following manner.

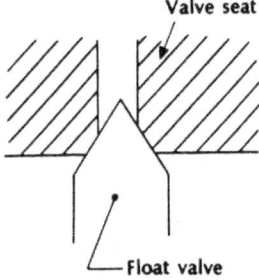

Fig. 4-18-3

4) Cleaning the carburetor

Disassemble the carburetor, and wash all its parts in a suitable solvent. Then blow all the parts off with compressed air. All jets and other delicate parts should be cleaned by blowing compressed air through them.

Carburetor float setting:
(with needle spring unloaded)

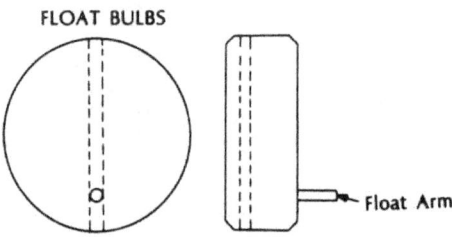

When replacing the float bulbs, place float arm towards the bottom side of float bowl.

Fig. 4-18-5

ENGINE - Carburetor, Air Cleaner

1) Remove the float chamber body, and turn over the mixing body. Let the float arm rest on the needle valve with the spring fully expanded.
2) Then measure the distance "A" from the float arm lever to the float chamber joint surface.
   Standard measurement of A. 15.8 mm (0.622 in)
3) When the A distance measured is less than recommended bend the tang tang up. If it is greater, bend the tang down (with carburetor body upside down.)

3. Ide Mixtur-Idle speed **Adjustment**

Turn the idle mixture screw in until lightly seated, then back it out 1½ turns no more or no less. There is no need to experiment. This is a factory setting that can be set with the engine stopped. No further adjustment is required.

Engine idle speed is set by warming up the engine completely and then screwing the idle speed screw in or out, whichever direction is necessary for the engine to idle between 1,200 and 1,300 rpm.

Carburetor float setting:
(with needle spring unloaded)

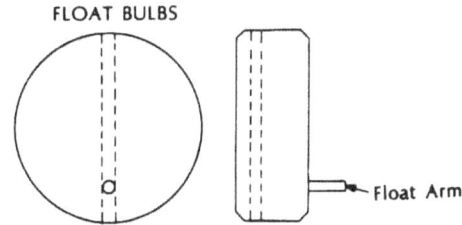

FLOAT BULBS

Float Arm

When replacing the float bulbs, place float arm towards the bottom side of float bowl.

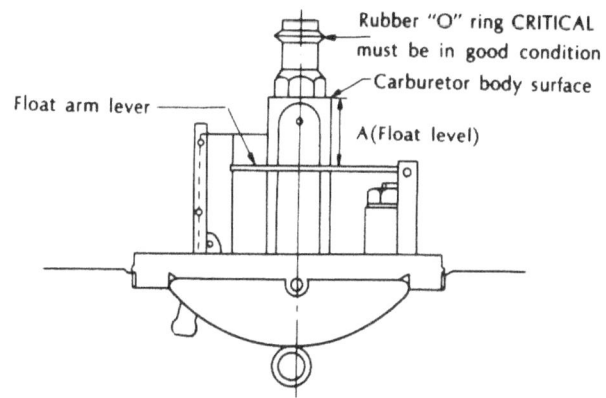

Rubber "O" ring CRITICAL must be in good condition
Carburetor body surface
Float arm lever
A (Float level)

Set at center line.
Carburetor body must be held upside down when setting float level.

Fig. 4-18-6

4. Carburetor Setting Table

Name of Parts	Abbreviation	Specifications
Main jet	M.J.	160
Needle jet	N.J.	0-2
Jet needle	J.N.	5D1-3 stages
Pilot jet	P.J.	35
Starter jet	G.S.	60
Throttle valve cut away	C.A.	2.5
Air screw setting	A.S.	1½
Idling speed	—	1,300 ±100 r.p.m.
Float level	F.L.	15.8 mm (0.622 in.)

4-19 Air Cleaner

1. Removal

To remove the air filter, open the seat cover and remove four air cleaner mounting screws. Then the element can be removed.

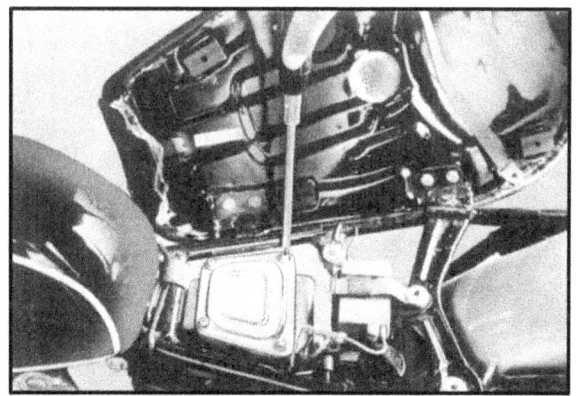

Fig. 4-19-1

ENGINE - Air Cleaner

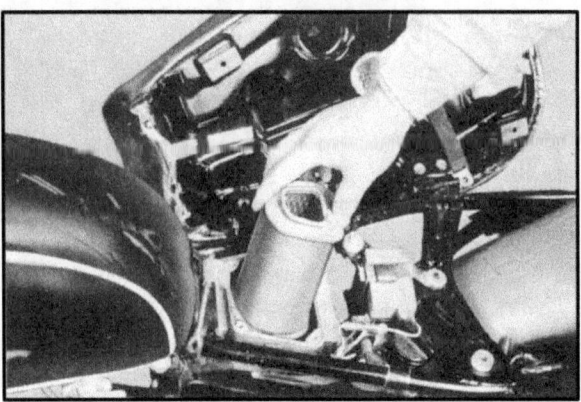

Fig. 4-19-2

2. Cleaning

Wash the foam filter thoroughly in solvent until all dirt has been removed. Squeeze all the solvent out. Pour oil onto the filter (any grade of 20 or 30 wt) work it completely in, and then squeeze out the surplus oil. The filter should be completely impregnated with oil, but not "dripping" with it.

CHAPTER 5 CHASSIS

The Yamaha DT1-E has been designed for versatility and a combination of uses. It is equipped with all necessary street legal equipment to insure pleasurable road or street riding. This machine can be quickly converted to a competion machine and therefore has been engineered to have a minimum weight factor. Yet with the reduction in weight; rigidity, strength, and safety have been incorporated in the design of the frame to provide an unexcelled competition machine.

5-1 Front Wheel

The 19" front wheel is equipped standard with a 3.25-19" Trials Universal tire. This tire gives the rider assurance of maximum performance and safety for both road riding and trail riding.
To insure against tire slippage on the rim, a tire bead lock had been installed in the wheel. The front wheel brake size is 150mm.x 30mm. (5.9 x 1.18 in.) A labyrinth seal is installed between the wheel hub and brake plate to provide a seal against dust water.

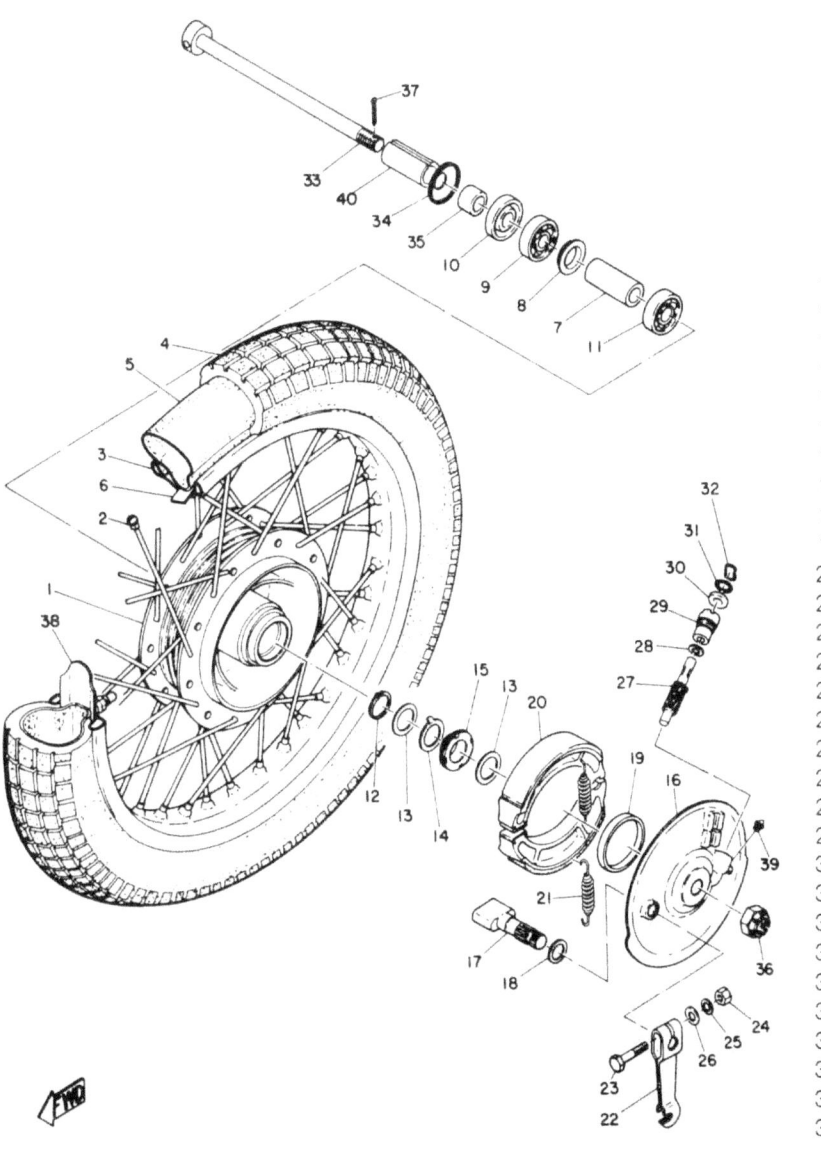

1. Hub
2. Spoke set
3. Rim
4. Front tire
5. Tube
6. Rim band
7. Bearing spacer
8. Spacer flange
9. Bearing
10. Oil seal
11. Bearing
12. Circlip
13. Thrust washer 2
14. Meter clutch
15. Drive gear
16. Brake shoe plate
17. Cam shaft
18. Cam shaft shim
19. Oil seal
20. Brake shoe complete
21. Brake shoe return spring
22. Cam shaft lever
23. Bolt
24. Nut
25. Spring washer
26. Plane washer
27. Meter gear
28. Thrust washer 1
29. Bushing
30. Oil seal
31. O ring
32. Stop ring
33. Wheel shaft
34. Hub dust cover
35. Wheel shaft collar
36. Shaft nut
37. Spring washer
38. Bead spacer
39. Grease nipple

Fig 5-1-1   Construction

CHASSIS – Front Wheel

1 Removal

1) Disconnect the brake cable at the front brake lever.

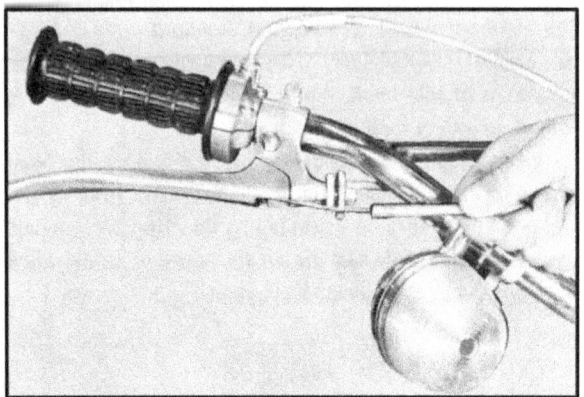

Fig 5-1-2

2) Disconnect both the brake cable and speedmeter cable from the front wheel hub plate.

Fig 5-1-3

4) Remove the front wheel nut.

Fig 5-1-4

3) Loosen the front wheel axle lock nuts.

Fig 5-1-5

5) Pull out the front wheel axle by simultaneously twisting and pulling on the axle.

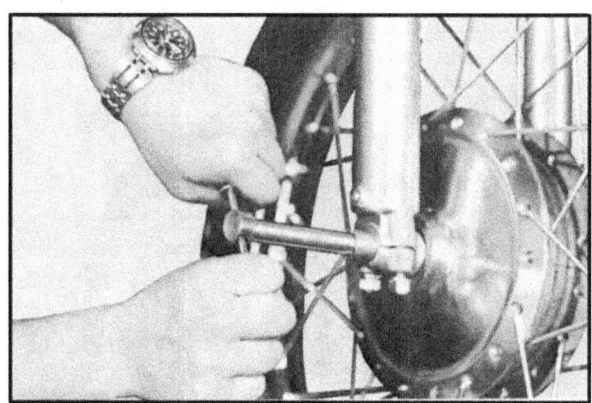

Fig 5-1-6

6) Raise the front of the machine and set it on a box. Then remove the wheel assembly.

Fig 5-1-7

2 Checking

1) Run out of the rim
   As show in Fig. 5-1-8, measure the runout of the rim with a dial gauge. Runout limits 2mm. (0.07 in.) or less

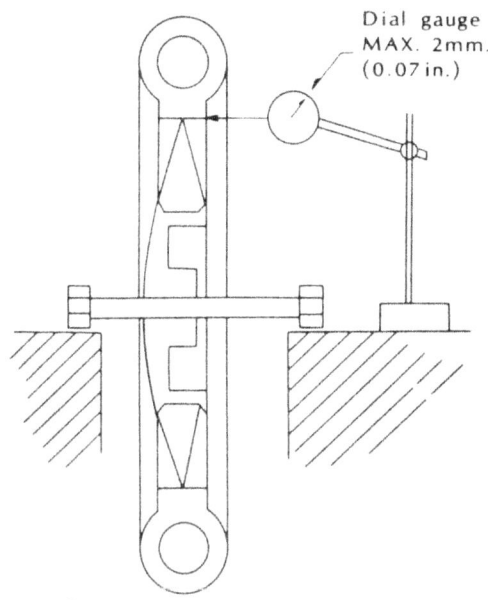

Fig 5-1-8

2) Brake shoe
   Measure the outside diameter at the brake shoe with slide calipers. If it measures less than 146 mm (5.75 in.), replace it. Smooth out a rough shoe surface with sandpaper or hand file.

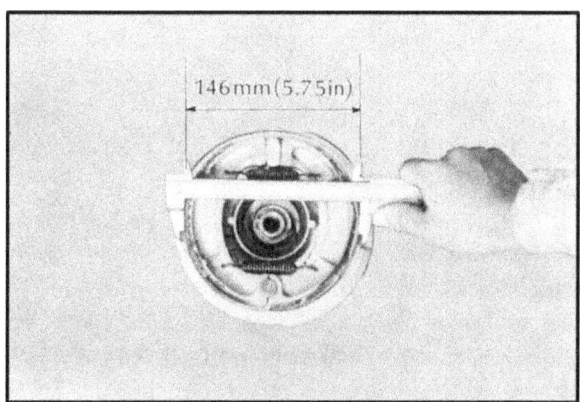

Fig 5-1-9

3) Brake drum
   Oil or scratches on the inner surface of the brake drum will impair braking performance or result in abnormal noises. Clean or smooth out the surface with a rag soaked in laquer thinner or with sandpaper.

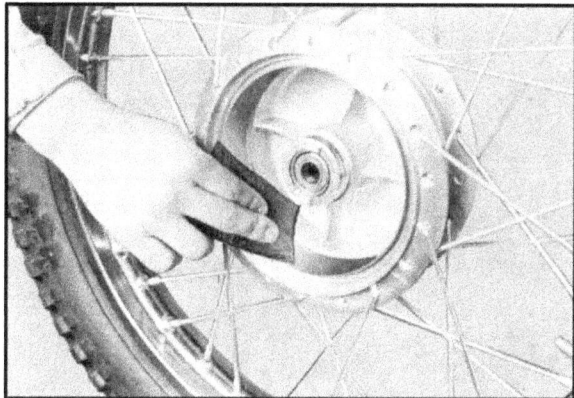

Fig 5-1-10

4) Check the spokes. If they are loose or bent, replace or tighten them. If the machine is ridden in rough country often or raced the spokes should be checked regularly.

5) Repairing the brake shoe
   If the brakes shoe has uneven contact with the brake drum or scratches, smooth out the surface with sandpaper or hand file.

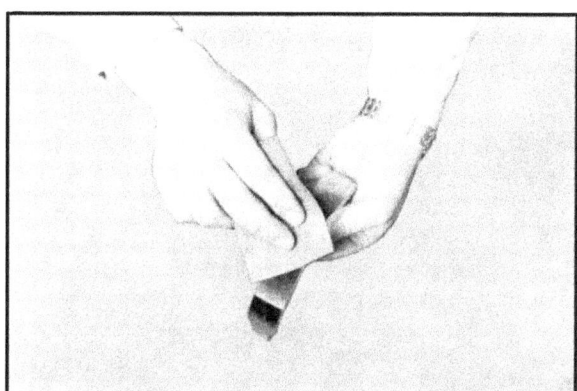

Fig 5-1-11

6) If the tire is excessively worn replace the tire
7) Check the tires for damage regularly
8) If the bearings allow excessive play in the wheel or if it does not turn smoothly, replace the bearing

CHASSIS - Front Wheel, Rear Wheel

Replacing the Wheel Bearing

a First clean the outside of the wheel hub.
b Insert the bent end of the special tool (as shown in Fig. 5-1-13) into the hole located in the center of the bearing spacer, and drive the spacer out from the hub by tapping the other end of the special tool with a hammer. (Both bearing spacer and spacer flange can easily be removed.)
c Then push out the bearing on the other side.
d To install the wheel bearing, reverse the above sequence. Be sure to grease the bearing before installation and use the bearing fitting tool (furnished by Yamaha).

d) Remove the circlip.
e) Push out the clutch hub bearing toward the sprocket side by the use of the bearing fitting tool.
f) To install the clutch hub bearing, reverse the above sequence. Before installation, grease the bearing and oil seal.

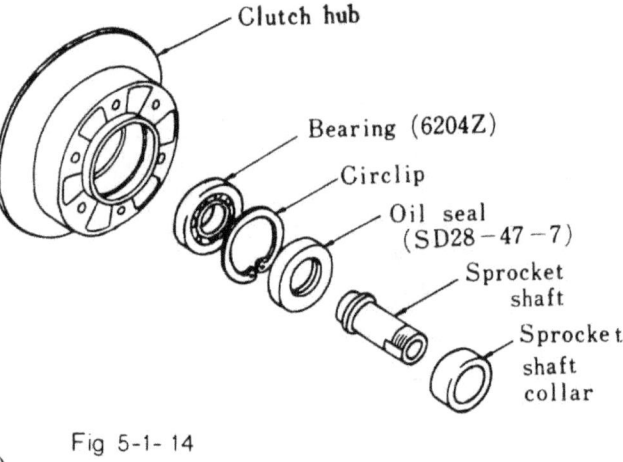

Fig 5-1-14

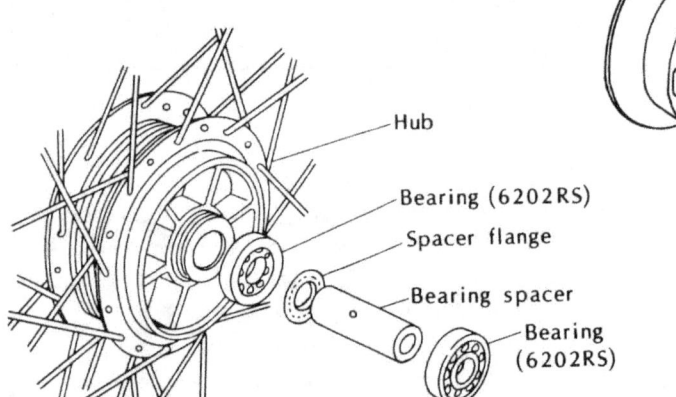

Fig 5-1-12

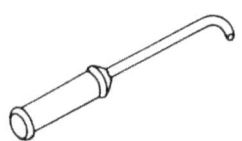

Insert the bent end of the special tool into the hole located in the center of the bearing spacer.

Fig 5-1-13

Replacing the Clutch Hub Bearing

a First remove the sprocket shaft by pushing it out toward the other side.
b) Remove the sprocket shaft collar. (It can easily be pulled out with your hand.)
c) Remove the oil seal. Exercise care not to damage the oil seal.

9) Replace a bent or damaged front wheel axle.
10) If the tooth surface of the helical speedometer drive gear is excessively worn replace it.
11) Check the lips of the seals for damage or warpage. Replace if necessary.

5-2 Rear Wheel

The rear wheel is 18-in. size, and the rear tire is the 4.00-18 Trials Universal. It is also good for road riding. Two rim locks are provided to prevent tire slippage in the rim. The single leading shoe type brake is of the 150mm. x 30mm. size. A labyrinth seal between the wheel hub and the brake plate is provided to prevent water and dust leakage. The brake tension bar is of link design to minimize the shifting of the brake cam lever position when the rear swing arm is moving up and down. The rear fender is steel, and rubber mounted on the frame. It is also wide enough to protect the engine unit from dust and water.

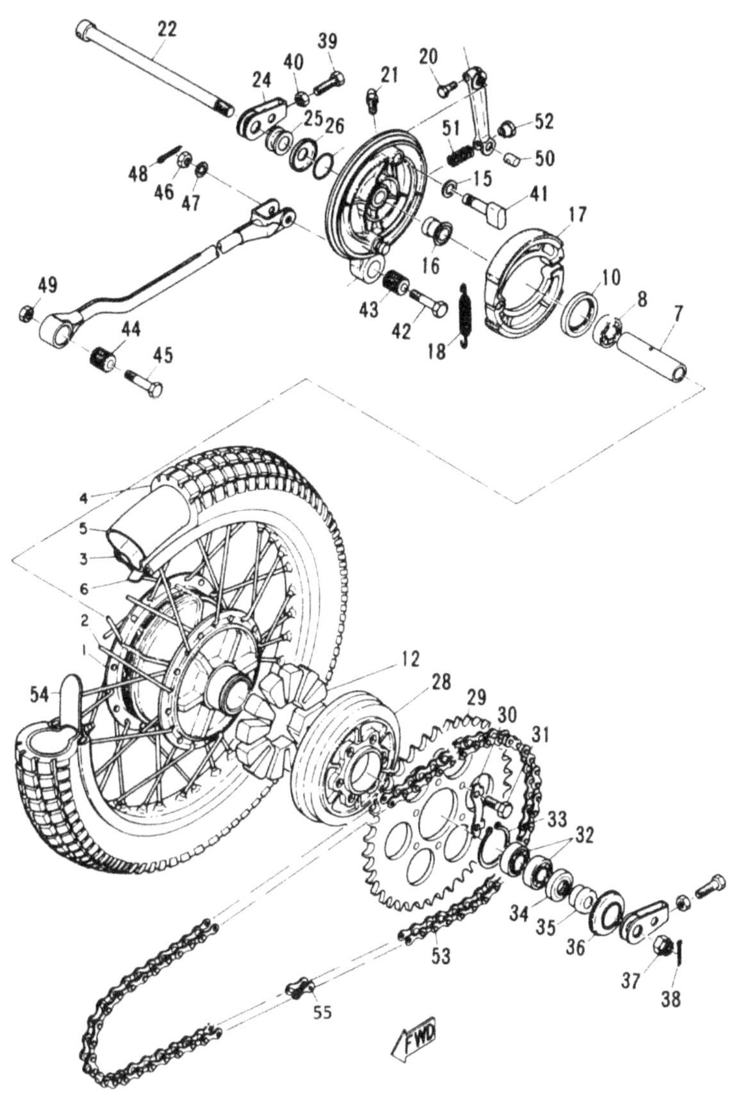

CHASSIS - Rear Wheel

1. Hub
2. Spoke set
3. Rim
4. Rear tire
5. Tube
6. Rim band
7. Bearing spacer
8. Spacer flange
19. Bearing
10. Oil seal
11. O-ring
12. Clutch damper
13. Brake shoe plate
14. Shaft cam
15. Cam shaft shim
16. Shaft bushing
17. Brake shoe complete
18. Return apring
29. Cam shaft lever
20. Bolt
21. Grease nipple
22. Wheel shaft
23. Shaft collar
24. Chain puller
25. Wheel shaft collar
26. Plate dust cover
27. Sprocket shaft
28. Hub clutch
39. Sprocket wheel gear
30. Lock washer
31. Fitting bolt
32. Bearing
33. Circlip
34. Oil seal
35. Sprocket shaft collar
36. Dust cover
37. Sprocket shaft nut
38. Cotter pin
49. Chain puller bolt
40. Nut
41. Blind plug
42. Pan head screw
43. Spring washer
44. Tension bar
45. Tension bar bolt
46. Nut
47. Spring washer
48. Cotter pin
59. Tension bar clip
50. Clevis pin
51. Rod spring
52. Adjusting nut
53. Chain
54. Bead spacer
55. Link, master

Fig. 5-2-1 Rear Wheel Construction

1. Removal

1) Remove the tension bar and brake rod from the rear shoe plate.

Fig. 5-2-2

Fig. 5-2-3

49

CHASSIS - Rear Wheel

2) Disconnect the master link of the chain and remove the chain.

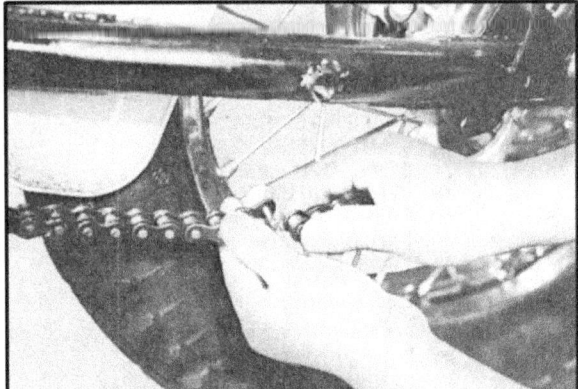

Fig. 5-2-4

3) Loosen the chain tension adjusting nuts and bolts on both right and left sides.

Fig. 5-2-5

4) Remove the rear wheel shaft nut.

Fig. 5-2-6

5) Pull out the rear wheel shaft by striking it with a plastic tip hammer.

Fig. 5-2-7

6) Remove the right-hand chain puller and distance collar.

Fig. 5-2-8

7) Lean the machine to the left and remove the rear wheel assembly.

Fig. 5-2-9

CHASSIS · Rear Wheel

Replacing Tires

1) Removal

a. Remove the valve cap and lock nut (12 mm.) from the tire valve, and deflate the tire.

b. Loosen the bead spacer lock nut (10 mm.) Two bead spacers are provided for the rear wheel, and one for the front wheel.

c. Twist the bead spacer until it slips off the edge of the wheel rim.

d. Remove the tire from the wheel rim by the use of two tire levers (Exercise care to avoid damaging the inner tube with the levers.)

It is noted that to remove the inner tube, one side of the tire should be pried over the wheel rim.

2) Installation

a. Pull the bead spacer toward the wheel rim flange.

b. Replace the tube between the tire and the wheel rim, and half inflate the tube. Be sure that the valve stem is directed toward the wheel shaft. Install the tube in over the same side of the rim that the tube is removed from.

c. Mount the tire on the wheel rim by the use of tire levers. For this operation, it is advisable that the bead on one side of the tire be pushed in toward the rim flange.

d. To avoid pinching the tube between the tire and the rim, tap the tire with a hammer.

e. Tighten the bead spacer lock nut.

f. Tighten the tire valve lock nut, and inflate the tire to the recommended pressure, then install the valve cap.

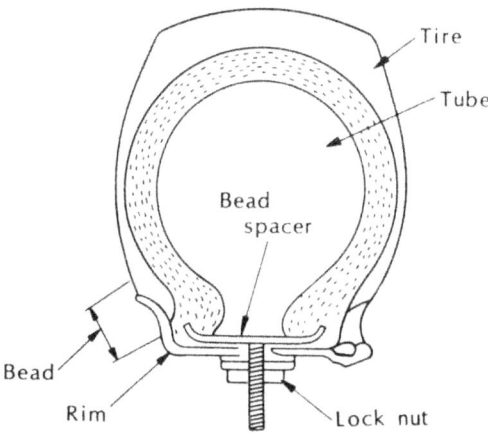

Fig. 5-2-11

2. Inspection

1) Run out of the rim

Check the rim for run out in the same way as the front wheel. Maximum limit of run out ...... 2 mm (0.07 in.) or less.

2) Brake shoe

Check the brake shoe in the same way as the front wheel. Minimum limit ...... 140 mm (5.75 in.)

3) Brake drum

Check the brake drum in the same way as the front wheel.

4) The spokes are measured in the same way as the front wheel. A loose spoke should be tightened.

5) If the bearing has a excessive play or it does not turn smoothly, replace it.

6) If the tire or the pattern is worn out, replace it.

7) If the lip of the oil seal is damaged or warped, replace it.

5-3 Rear Wheel Sprocket

A. Removal

1) Removing the sprocket

a. Bend the lock washer ears flat

Fig. 5-3-1

b. Remove the sprocket mounting bolts

Fig. 5-3-2

CHASSIS – Rear Wheel Sprocket

B. Checking

1) Checking

   Check the lock washer and hexagonal bolt for breakage and damage. If the lock washer is not bent over the hexagon bolt head or broken, or if the bolt is loose, the sprocket can become loose. Make sure that both lock washers and the mounting bolts are tight.

Fig. 5-3-3

CHASSIS - Tires and Tubes, Front Forks

5-4 Tires and Tubes

1) Normal tire pressure

   Thought tire pressure is the rider's choice the standard tire pressure is as follows.

   a. On-the-road riding

   Front............................13 lbs./in² (0.9 kg./cm²)

   Rear............................16 lbs./in² (1.1 kg./cm²)

   b. Off-the-road riding

   Front............................8.5 lbs./in² (0.6 kg./cm²)

   Rear............................10 lbs./in² (0.7 kg./cm²)

5-5 Front Forks

The DT1-E is equipped with competition designed telescopic double dampening front forks. These specially designed front forks provide excellent riding comfort along with handling superiority. The maximum stroke travel is almost 7 inches (175 mm.)

The combination of fork stability and long stroke travel provides safety and handling ease for the rider over even the roughest of terrain. This front fork design also reduces weight, eases maintenance, and gives functional and attractive appearance. The simplicity and dependability of the front forks is provided by the installation of the fork spring inside of the fork tube.

1. Removal

   1) Remove the front fender

      The light-weight aluminum front fender is rubber-mounted on the stay.

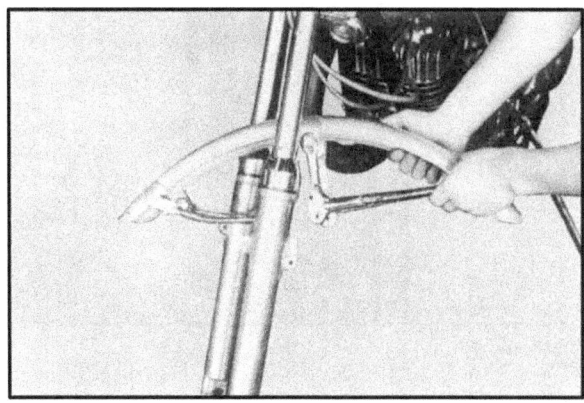

Fig. 5-5-1

2) Loosening the arrow marked bolt

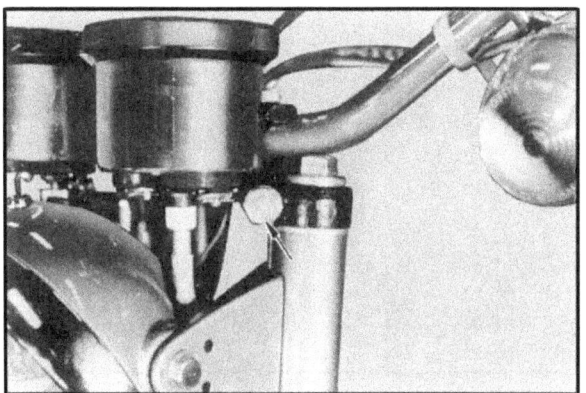

Fig. 5-5-2

3) Loosen the inner tube pinch bolts on the underbracket.

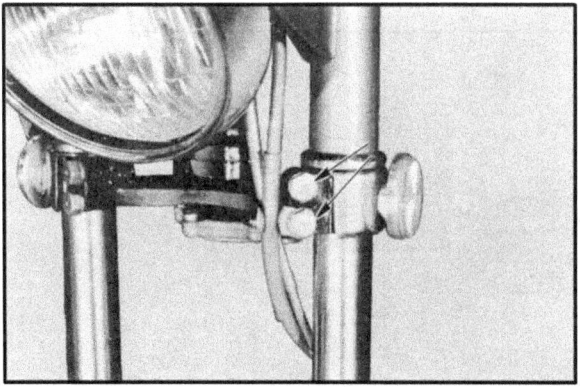

Fig. 5-5-3

CHASSIS - Front Forks

4) Pull the outer tube downward.

Fig. 5-5-4

3) The inner tube can be separated from the outer.

2. Disassembling the Inner and Outer Tubes

1) Drain the oil from the fork.

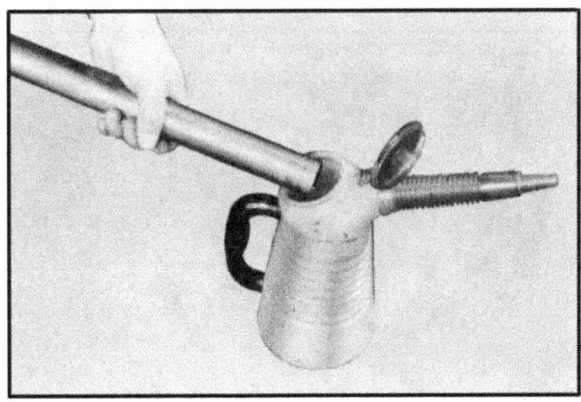

Fig. 5-5-5

2) Remove the special bolt (arrow marked) from the bottom of the outer tubes.

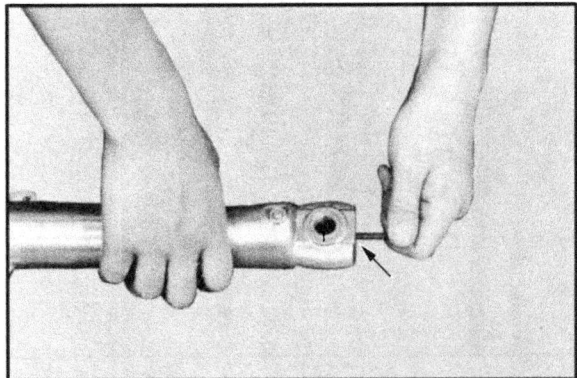

Fig. 5-5-6

CHASSIS - Front Forks, Rear Shocks

Front Fork Exploded View

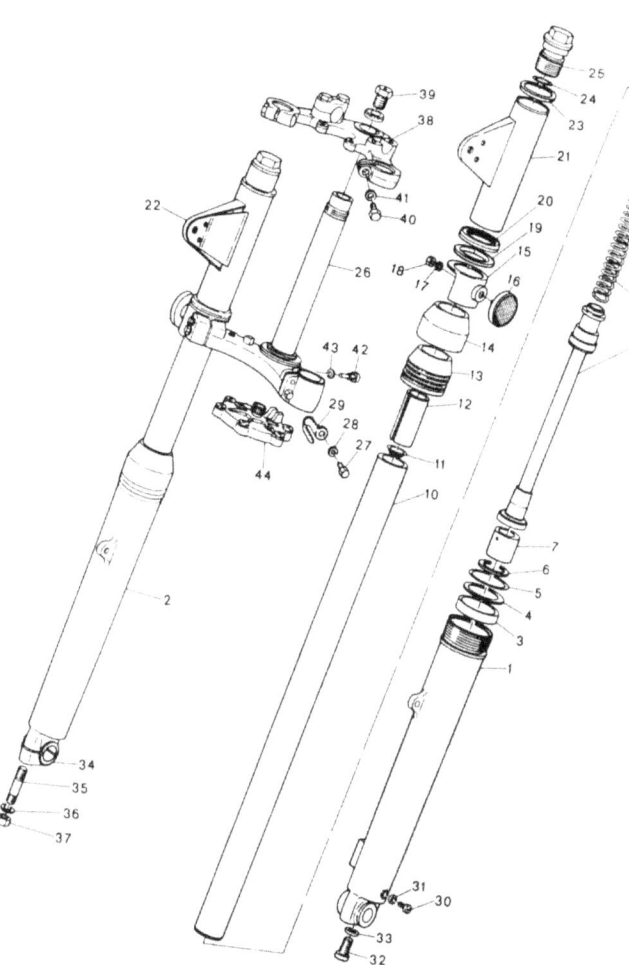

1. Tube, outer left
2. Tube, outer right
3. Oil seal
4. Washer, oil seal
5. Clip, oil seal
6. Circlip
7. Piston
8. Cylinder comp.
9. Spring, fork
10. Tube, inner
11. Seat, spring upper
12. Spacer
13. Seal, dust
14. Cover, dust seal
15. Cover, outer
16. Reflector
17. Washer, spring
18. Nut
19. Packing (lamp stay)
20. Guide, cover under
21. Cover, upper left
22. Cover, upper right
23. Guide, cover upper
24. Packing
25. Bolt, cap
26. Under bracket comp.
27. Bolt, under bracket
28. Washer, spring
29. Holder, wire
30. Plug, drain
31. Gasket, drain plug
32. Bolt
33. Packing
34. Holder, axle
35. Bolt, axle holder
36. Washer, spring
37. Nut
38. Crown, handle
39. Bolt, steering fitting
40. Bolt
41. Washer, spring
42. Bolt
43. Washer, spring
44. Handle damper assy

Fig. 5-5-9

3. Checking

1) Inner tube

Check the inner tube for bending or scratches. If the bend is slight, it can be corrected with a press. It is recommended, however, to replace the tube if possible.

2) Oil seal

When disassembling the front fork, replace the oil seal in the outer tube nut.

4. Assembling

1) For assembling the front fork, reverse the order of disassembling. Check if the inner tube slides in and out smoothly.

2) Installing the front fork on the frame.

a. Bring up the front fork to the correct position and tighten the under bracket mounting bolt.

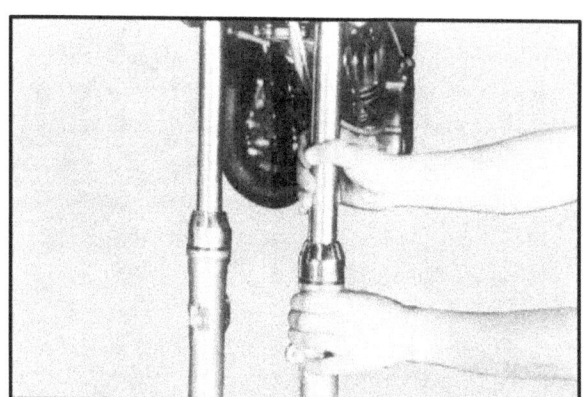

Fig. 5-5-10

b. Pour oil into the inner tube through the upper end opening. Front fork oil: Motor oil SAE 10W/30 175 c.c. (5.9 oz.) per fork leg.

c. Install the cap bolt.

5-6 Rear Shocks

The rear shocks have a maximum stroke of 90 mm. (3.54 in.) The rear cushion features superb damping and 3-position adjustable springs, that allow the rider to adjust the rear shocks to suit any riding condition.

CHASSIS - Rear Shocks

1. Checking the Condition of the Damping Units.

1) Remove the rear shock assembly.

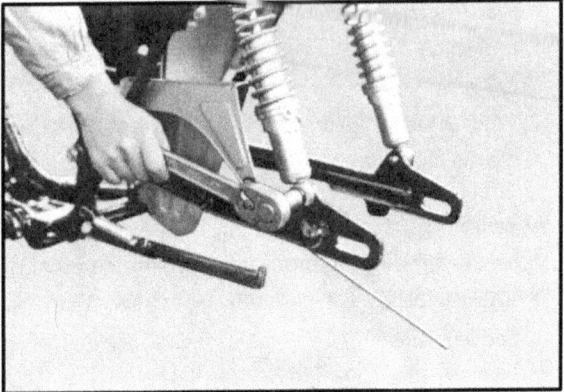

Fig. 5-6-1

2) Compress the shocks by applying weight as shown in Fig. 5-6-2, and release it.

If the shock quickly restores half-way and then slowly returns to the original position after it reaches 10 mm. (3/8 in.) before the original position, the rear shocks are in good condition. But if the cushion returns quickly to the original position, check the cushion for oil leakage, and replace the assembly if the oil leaks.

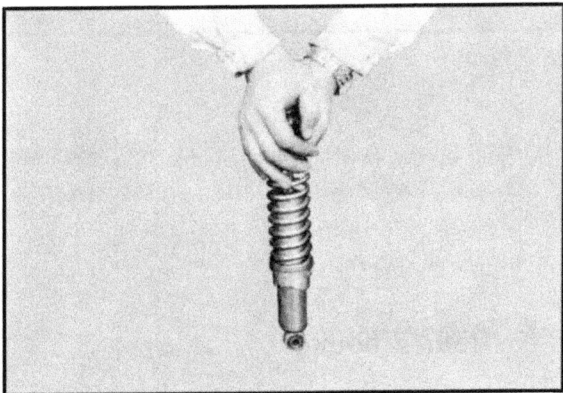

Fig. 5-6-2

1) Removing

1) Set the petcock lever at "Stop" position and disconnect the fuel line at the petcock.

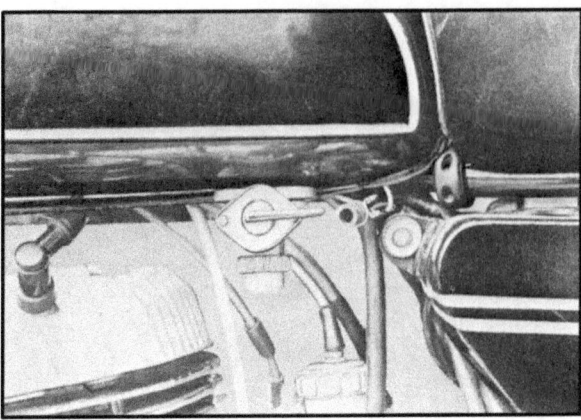

Fig. 5-7-1

2) Open the seat.
3) Remove the rubber band.

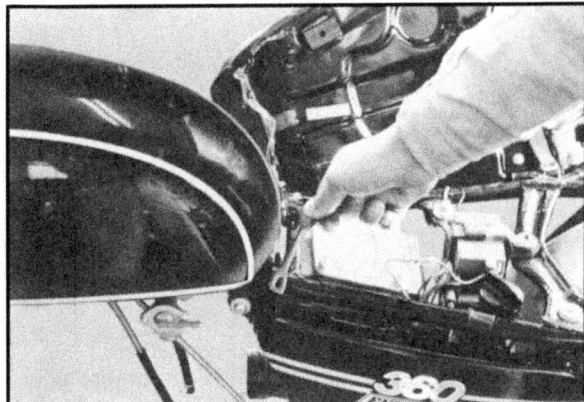

Fig. 5-7-3

5-7 Gas Tank

The gas tank has been shaped so that the rider can freely change his riding position. The front of the tank slips into the tank stay and the rear is held by rubber band. Tank capacity 9.5 litres (2.5 gals.)

4) Remove the gas tank.

Fig. 5-7-4

5-8 Rear Swing Arm

The rear swing arm is made of steel tube that improves the strength and torsional rigidity. The pivot employs permanent lubrication bearings.

1. Removing
1) Remove the chain case mounting bolts.

Fig. 5-8-1

2) Remove the rear swing arm shaft nut, pull out the shaft, and remove the rear swing arm.

Fig. 5-8-2

2. Checking
1) Check the play of the rear swing arm by shaking it from side to side as shown in Fig. 5-8-3, with the rear swing arm installed. If the play is excessive, replace the rear swing arm bushings or the rear swing arm shaft.

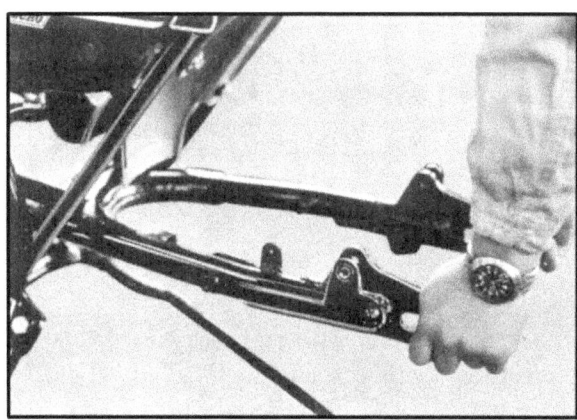

Fig. 5-8-3

2) Insert the bushing as indicated in Fig. 5-8-4, and check it for play. If the play is excessive, replace the bushing.

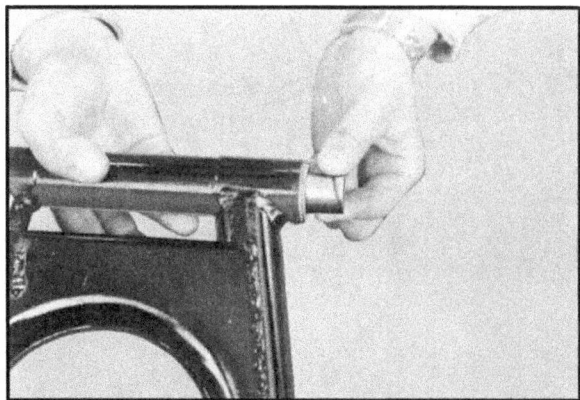

Fig. 5-8-4

CHASSIS - Steering Head

3) Grease the rear arm shaft periodically.

Replacing Rear Swing Arm Bushings

On motorcycles being habitually used for on-the-street riding, rear swing arm bushings should be replaced every 10,000 km. (6,000 miles.) The same may not apply to those used for racing or rough riding. Replacement should be made according to machine condition such as excessive play of the rear swing arm, or hard steering (wander, shimmy or rear wheel hop,) or upon request of the customer.

5-9 Steering Head

1. Sectional View of the Steering Head

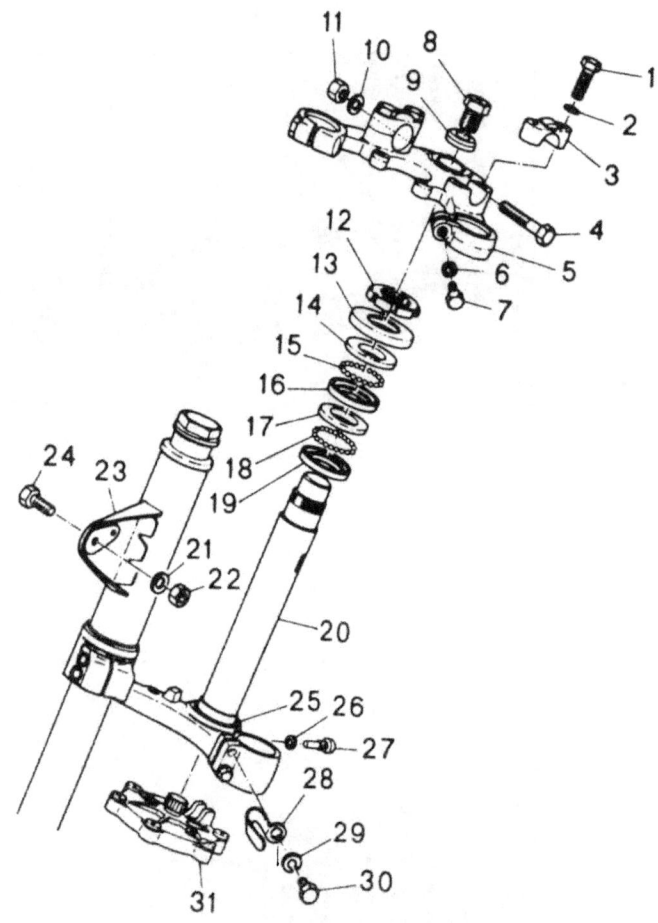

1. Bolt
2. Spring washer
3. Handle upper holder
4. Bolt
5. Handle crown
6. Spring washer
7. Bolt
8. Steering fitting bolt
9. Crown washer
10. Spring washer
11. Crown nut
12. Fitting nut
13. Ball race cover
14. Ball race (2)
15. Ball ($\frac{3}{16}$" ×22 pcs)
16. Ball race (1)
17. Ball race (2)
18. Ball ($\frac{1}{4}$" ×19 pcs)
19. Ball race (1)
20. Under bracket complete
21. Spring washer
22. Nut
23. Upper cover
24. Bolt
25. Dust seal
26. Spring washer
27. Bolt
28. Wire holder
29. Spring washer
30. Bolt
31. Oil damper

Fig. 5-9-1

2. Checking

1) Ball Races and Steel Balls

Check the ball races and steel balls for pitting or wear. Check them very carefully if the machine has been in long use. If they are worn or cracked, replace all of them because defective ball races or steel balls adversely affect the maneuverability of the machine. Replace any ball race having scratches or streaks resulting from wear. Clean and grease the balls and races periodically.

Note: Do not use a combination of new balls and used races or vice versa. If any of these are found defective, replace the whole ball and race assembly.

5-10 Oil Tank, Battery Box and Tool Box

The oil tank is located on the left side under the seat. It is designed to be as narrow as possible so that it will not contact the rider's lower limbs when he stands upright on the footrests. To fill the autolube oil tank, life the seat and the tank cap will be exposed. Oil tank capacity......1.6 litres.(1.7 qts.)

The battery box and the air cleaner case is located right under the seat.

5-11 Frame

The double cradle-type frame is made of high tension steel tubes that provide strength, rigidity and light weight. Other dimensional features include higher ground clearance, narrower width, and longer wheelbase.

The engine is bolted to the frame at four positions. The caster is measured at 60.50°

5-12 Handlebars

The upswept type longer handlebars are ideal for motocross events and are provided with deep-cut pattern grips to prevent hand slippage. The lever holder is provided with an adjusting screw for the play of clutch cable and brake cable.

The meter bracket is mounted on the ends of the handle crown, to carry the speedometer on its left side and the tachometer on its right side.

5-13 Miscellaneous

The footrest is made of a single steel tube extending under the lower part of the frame, and bolted to the frame. The engine guard is bolted to the frame to protect the entire crankcase........covering from the exhaust system to the drain plug.

Chapter 6 Electrical System

6-1 Construction

The Yamaha D11-E Electrical System is designed to facilitate lightweight, functional operation and simplicity.
Yet with these features, the Ignition System and Lighting System facilitate dependable engine operation and all necessary lighting equipment. A 6 volt battery is used in conjunction with the flywheel magneto. All of the light bulbs have been increased in size to insure sufficient night riding visibility.

6-2 Table of component Parts

Parts	Manufacturer	Model & Type
Flywheel magneto	Mitsubishi Elec.	FZA-IBL
Spark plug	NGK	B-8ES
Headlight	Koito Mfg.	6V, 35W/35W
Speedometer	Nippon Seiki	
Tachometer	Nippon Seiki	
Handle switch	Asahi Denso	ACS
Main switch	Asahi Denso	TIM
Ignition coil	Mitsubishi Elec.	HP-E
Horn	Nikko Kinzoku	MF-6
Battery	Nippon Battery	MV1-6D
Rectifier	Mitsubishi Elec.	DS10HJ1
Fuse	Osachi Mfg.	10A
Stop switch	Niles. Parts	SH40E
Taillight	Stanley Elec.	6V, 5.3W/17W

6-3 Connection Diagram

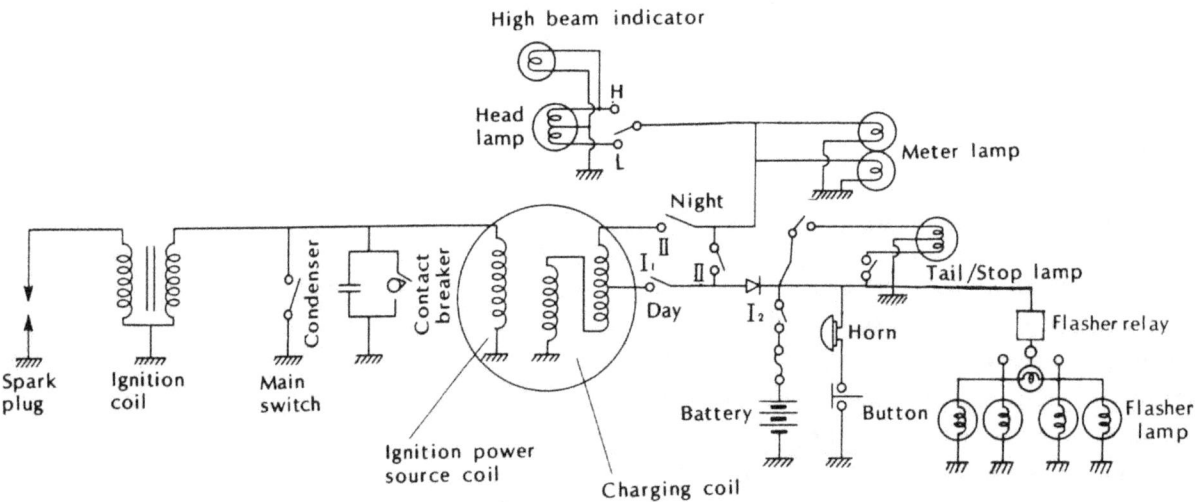

Fig. 6-3-1

ELECTRICAL SYSTEM - Ignition System, Ignition Timing, Ignition Coil

6-4 Ignition System—Function and Service

1. Function

The ignition system consists of the components as shown in Fig. 6-4-1. As the flywheel rotates, the contact breaker points begin to open and close, alternately. This make-and-break operation develops an electromotive force in the ignition power source coil, and produces a voltage in the primary coil. The ignition coil is a kind of transformer, with a 1:50 turn ratio of the primary to the secondary winding. The voltage (150-300 V) which is produced in the primary coil, is stepped up to 12,000-14,000 V by mutual-induction, and the the electric spark jumps across the spark plug electrodes.

Ignition Timing, 3.2 mm. B.T.D.C
Maximum ignition point gap 0.3 to 0.4 mm.
(0.012"—0.015")

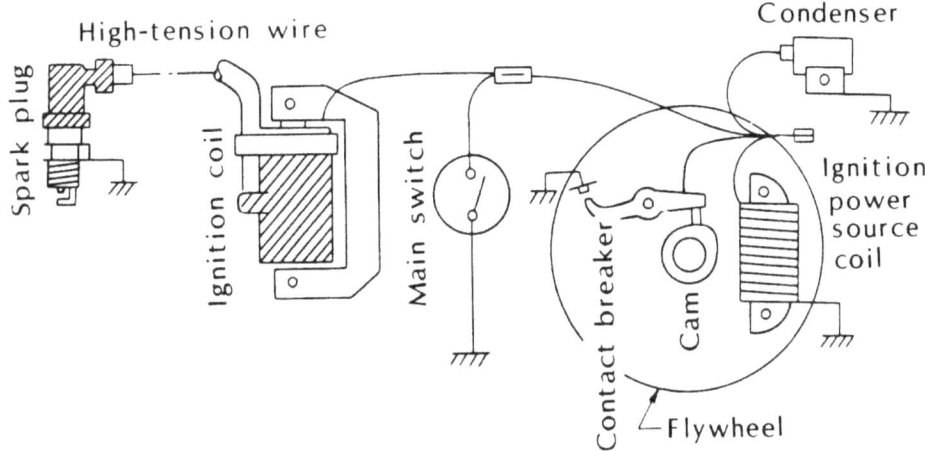

Fig. 6-4-2

6-5 Ignition Timing

The DT1-E cylinder head studs and cap nuts are of a different design because of the size and function of the cylinder. The cap nuts used have a large diameter and therefore a special adaptor is required to facilitate use of the dial indicator for ignition timing on the standard model. The cylinder head most be removed and the special dial indicator adaptor attached to the dial indicator stand.

The piston should be brought to T.D.C. and the dial indicator set at this position. The crankshaft should then be turned in reverse and the piston brought down below 3.2 mm. below T.D.C. The flywheels should then be rotated forward until the piston reaches 3.2 mm. below T.D.C. At this point the ignition points should just be opening. A low resistance point checker (100 Ohms or less) should be used to determine an opening and closing position of the ignition points.

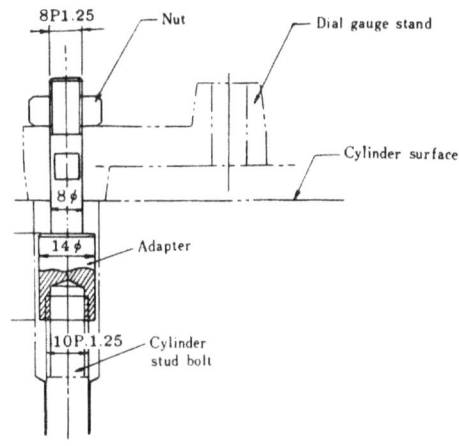

Fig. 6-5-1

6-6 Ignition Coil

Primary coil resistance value.........
0.6 Ω ± 10% (20°C or 68°F)
Secondary coil resistance value.........
5.8KΩ ±10% (20°C or 68°F)
(For measuring methods, refer to Fig. 6-6-1)

ELECTRICAL SYSTEM - Condenser, Charging System

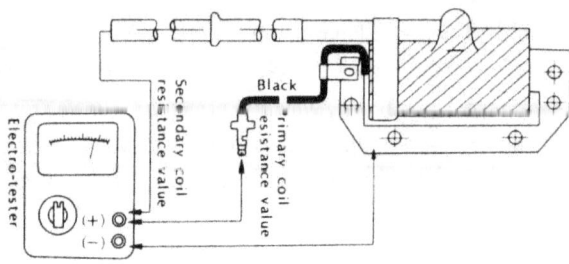

Fig. 6-6-1

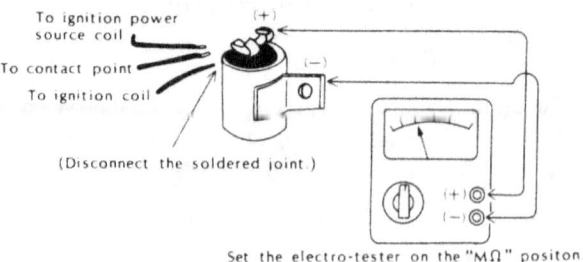

Fig. 6-7-1

Note: When measuring the secondary coil resistance value, disconnect the plug cap. Otherwise, the resistance of the 5KΩ noise suppressor incorporated in the plug will be added to the tester reading.

Spark Test:

Remove spark plug from cylinder head and reconnect the high voltage lead. Then ground the spark plug and see if it sparks as you crank the kickstarter.

If it sparks 7 mm. or so and has a white blue color, the ignition coil should be considered to be in good condition.

6-7 Condenser

The condenser instantly stores a static electric charge as the contact breaker points separate, and the energy stored in the condenser discharges instantly when the points are closed. If it were not for the condenser, an electrical charge would are across the separating contact points, causing them to burn.

The condenser minimizes the burning of the contact points, greatly affecting the flow of current in the primary winding of the ignition coil.

If the contact points show excessive wear, or the spark is weak (the ignition coil is in good condition) check the condenser.

Insulation resistance tests should be conducted by connecting the tester as shown in Fig 6-7-1. If the pointer swings fully and the reading is more then 3MΩ, the insulation is in good condition. If the insulation is punctured, the pointer will stay pointing the uppermost reading.

Note: After this measurement, the condenser should be discharged by connecting the positive and negative sides with a thick lead wire.

Capacity tests can be performed by simply setting the tester to the condenser capacity. The tester should be connected with condenser in the same way as in the case of the insulation resistance test. Before this mesaurement, be sure to set the tester correctly.

If the reading is within 0.22μF±10%, the condenser capacity is correct.

6-8 Charging System

The charging system consists of the fly wheel magneto (charging and lighting coils) rectifier, and battery.

1. Flywheel Magneto

As the flywheel rotates, an alternate current is generated in the charging and lighting coils and converted to a half-wave current by means of a silicon rectifier. This half-wave current charges the battery.

Charging Capacity (Daytime.)

Green lead: Charging begins at 2,500 r.p.m.
              2.0 A or less   at 8,000 r.p.m.
White lead: 0.15 A or more at 2,500 r.p.m.
              4.0 A or less   at 8,000 r.p.m.

ELECTRICAL SYSTEM - Charging System

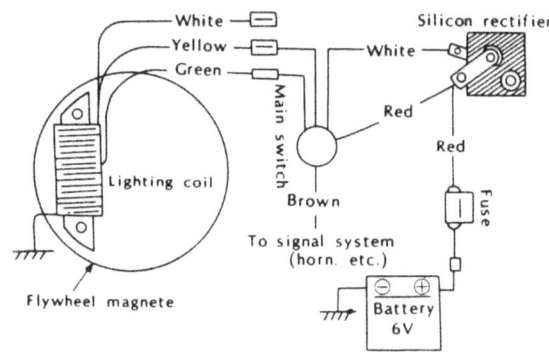

Fig. 6-8-1

Ligting Capacity (Night time)
(with normal loads and normal wiring.)
    5.8 V or more at 2,000 r.p.m.
    8.5 V or less at 8,000 r.p.m.

* The charging and lighting capacity is obtained when the battery is fully charged. If the battery is in a low state of charge and low in voltage, the charging rate will not be exactly the same as above. However, it is desirable that the figures are as close as possible.

2. Silicon Rectifier

The alternate current, which is generated by the flywheel magneto, is rectified and charged to the battery. For this rectification, a single-phase halfwave silicon rectifier is employed.

    Chracteristics: Rated output — 4A.
                      Rated peak inverse voltage 400V.

Polarity:

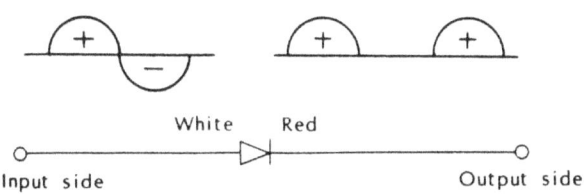

Fig. 6-8-2

1) Checking the Silicon Rectifier

For measurements, and ohmmeter can be used. However, this section discusses only the checking method by means of the ohmmeter.

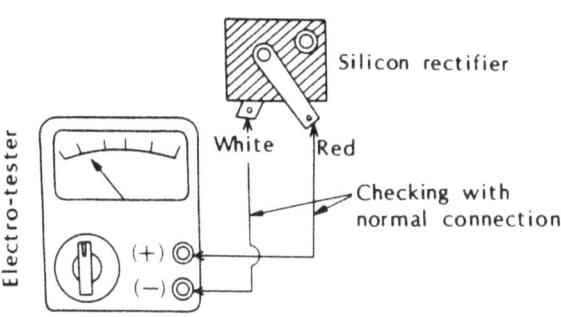

(Set the tester on "Resistance.")

Fig. 6-8-3

Checking with Normal Connection

Connect the tester's read(+) to the silicon rectifier's red terminal, and connect the tester's black lead (−) to the rectifier's white terminal.
Standard value: 9–10 Ω

If the tester's pointer will not swing back over from the scale, the rectifier is defective.

Checking with Reversed Connection

Connect the tester the other way around.
Standard value: If the pointer will not swing, the rectifier is in good condition.
If the pointer swings, the rectifiter is faulty.

3. Operational Note

The silicon rectifier can be damaged if subjected to overcharging. Special care should be taken to avoid a short circuit and/or incorrect connection of the positive and negative leads at the battery. Never connect the rectifier directly to the battery to make a continuity check.

6-9 Battery

The battery is a 6 volt—2 AH unit that is the power source for the horn, taillight, flasher light and stoplight. Because of the fluctuating charging rate due to the difference in engine R.P.M.s, the battery will lose its charge if the horn and stoplight are excessively used. The charging of the battery begins at about 2,500 R.P.M. Therefore, it is recommended to sustain engine R.P.M.s at about 2,500 to 3,500 R.P.M. to keep the battery charged properly. If the horn and stoplight are used frequently the battery water should be checked regularly as the continuing charging will dissipate the water.

If the battery will not retain a charge (and the battery is in good condition) the white wire of the flywheel magneto can be connected to the green wire of the wiring harness. This will increase the charging rate but if the machine is ridden for long periods of time with this wiring connection, the battery can be overcharged and damaged.

1) Checking

1) If sulfation occurs on plates due to lack of the battery electrolyte, will show and white accumulations the battery should be replaced.
2) If the bottoms of the cells are filled with corrosive material falling off plates, the battery should be replaced.
3) If the battery shows the following defects, it should be replaced.

* The voltage will not rise to a specific value even after long hours charging.
* No gassing occurs in any cell.
* The 6 V battery requires a charging currnt of more than 8.4 volts in order to supply current at a rate of lamp per hour for 10 hours.

2. Service Life

The service life of a battery is usually 2 to 3 years, but lack of care as described below will shorten the life of the battery.

1) Negligence in re-filling the battery with electrolyte.
2) Battery being left discharged.
3) Overcharging by rushing charge.
4) Freezing
5) Filling with water or sulfuric acid containing impurities when re-filling the battery.

3. Storage

If any motorcycle is not going to be used for a long time, remove the battery and have it stored by a battery service shop. The following instructions should be observed by shops equipped with chargers.

1) Recharge the battery.
2) Store the battery in a cool, dry place, and avoid temperatures below 0°C. (32°F)
3) Recharge the battery before mounting it on the motorcycle.

4. Service Standards
Battery: MV 1-6D (Nippon Battery)

Battery Spec.	6V-2AH	
Electrolyte-Specific gravity and quantity	1.26-1.27, 110 c.c.	At full charge
Initial charging current	0.2 A for 25 hours	Brand new motorcycle
Charging current	0.2 A for 13 hours (Charge until specific gravity reaches 1.26-1.27)	When discharged
Refilling of electrolyte	Distliled water up to the max. level line.	Once a month

6-10 Checking the Main Switch
(removed from the chassis)

Key "O" position Off)
Black — Switch body

Key "I" position (for day)
Green ↔ White
Red ↔ Brown

Key "II" position (for night)
Yellow ↔ White
White ↔ Blue
Red ↔ Brown

If the readings on the above six meaurements are nearly 0Ω, and no short-circuit is noticed between the terminals, as well as between the lead terminal and the switch body, the main switch is in good condition.

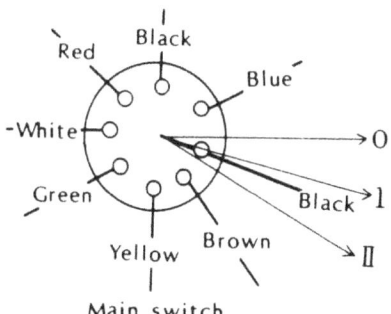

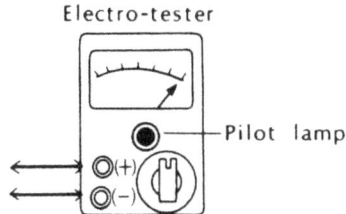

(Switch on the tester and use an ohmmeter.)

Fig. 6-10-1

6-11 Spark Plug

The life of a plug and its discoloring vary, according to the habits of the rider. At each periodic inspection, replace burned or fouled plugs with suitable ones according to the color and condition of the bad plugs. One machine may be ridden only is urban areas at low speeds, whereas another may be ridden for hours at high speeds, so confirm what the present plugs indicate by asking the rider how long and how fast he rides, and recommend a hot, standard, or cold plug accordingly.

It is actually economical to install new plug every 3,000 km (2,000 miles) since it will tend to keep the engine in good condition and prevent excessive fuel consumption.

1. **How to "read" spark plug (condition)**
   1) Best...... When the porcelain around the center electrode is a light tan color.
   2) If the electrodes and porcelain are black and somewhat oily, replace the plug with a hoter-type for low speed riding.
   3) If the porcelain is burned white and/or the electrodes are partially burned away, replace the plug with a colder-type for high speed riding.

2. **Inspection**
   INSTRUCT THE RIDER TO:
   Inspect and clean the spark plug at least once a month or every 1,000 km. (500 miles) Clean the electrodes of carbon and adjust the electrode gap to 0.5-0.6 mm. (0.023 in.) Be sure to use standard B-8ES plug as replacements to avoid any error in reach.

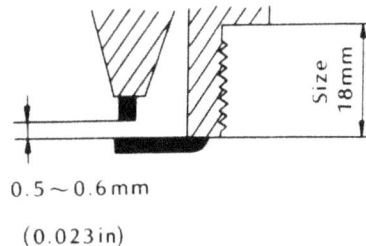

Fig. 6-11-1

6-12 Lighting and Signal Systems

The lighting and signal systems consist of the horn, flasher light and stoplight (power source-battery) and the headlight, taillight, meter lamps, high beam indicator, speedometer and tachometer (power source-flywheel magneto)

ELECTRICAL SYSTEM - Lighting and Signal System

1. Headlight
The headlight has two 6V, 35W bulbs, and a 6V, 1.5W high beam indicator on its top. A beam direction adjusting screw is fitted on the right side of the light rim so that the horizontal direction of the beam can be adjusted.(not vertical)

2. Taillight and Stoplight
A 6V, 5.3W taillight and a 6V, 17W stoplight are mounted.

3. Horn
The horn is a 6V, flat type, and has a tone-volume adjusting nut on its back. After adjustment is made, apply paint or lacquer to the nut for water proofing purposes.

4. Speedometer
A circular type speedemeter is rubber-mounted on the bracket.It has a built-in trip meter and odometer. For illumination, a 6V, 3W bulb is provided.

5. Tachometer
An independent tachometer is mounted separately from the speedometer. The revolutions per minute of the crankshaft are conveyed from the kick idler gear through the gear unit to the tachometer. The meter lamp is of the 6V, 3W type.

Note: Use bulbs of the correct capacity for the headlight, meter lamp and high-beam indicator which are directly connected to the flywheel magneto. If large capacity bulbs are used, the voltage will drop, giving a poor light. On the contrary, if smaller capacity bulbs are used, the voltage will rise, shortening the life of bulbs. Avoid the use of a 12V bulb, because shorter service life will result. When the headlight beam switch is operated to change the beam from one to the other, the headlight is designed to keep both bulbs burning,during the change-over. This is to protect other light bulbs, meter lamps, taillight, etc., from burning out as a result of turning off the headlight, though temporarily.

If one of these light bulbs burns out while the machine is running, it will overload other bulbs and shorten their service life. In this case, reduce the engine speed and replace the burnt bulb as quickly as possible.

CONVERSION FOR COMPETITION - List of GYT Parts

Chapter 7 Conversion for Competition

The Yamaha Enduro 250 DT1-E is easily converted into a high performance competition machine by using GYT parts.
GYT: Genuine Yamaha Tuning

7-1 List of GYT Parts

The following alternate parts for racing are available through authorized Yamaha dealers.

No.	Parts No.	Parts Name	Quantity	Remarks
1	● 214-11111-70	Head, cylinder	1	
2	▲ 94700-00016	Plug, spark	1	NGK B-10E(N)
3	● 214-11311-70	Cylinder	1	
4	● 214-11631-70	Piston	1	
5	● 214-11611-70	Ring, Piston	1	
6	● 214-14101-70	Carburetor ass'y	1	
7	▲ 161-15426-00	Cover, oil pump	1	
8	▲ 214-17819-00	Cap, housing	1	
9	● 214-17461-40	Sprocket, drive	1	14 Teeth
10	▲ 214-25446-10	Gear, sprocket wheel	1	46 Teeth
11	▲ 214-25448-10	Gear, sprocket wheel	1	48 Teeth
12	● 214-14610-70	Muffler	1	
13	● 214-14763-01	Spacer, rubber	1	
14	● 214-14764-00	Spacer, rubber	1	
15	● 214-14793-61	Plate, outer	1	
16	152-25139-00	Plug, blind	1	
17	94127-21071	Tire, front	1	2.75-21-4PR
18	94227-21031	Tube	1	〃
19	94327-21024	Band, rim	1	〃
20	94416-21038	Rim	1	〃
21	214-25196-10	Spoke, inner	1 set	〃
22	214-25197-10	Spoke, outer	1 set	〃
23	214-25101-70	Front wheel ass'y	1 set	3.25-19-4PR

●Included in GYT Kit   ▲Not included in GYT Kit
●▲The above parts are also sold individually.

CONVERSION FOR COMPETITION · GYT Competition Parts

Installation of the Yamaha GYT Parts and removal of unnecessary equipment, such as lighting, quickly transforms the DT1-E Trail into a competition proven racing machine. After installation of the highly tuned GYT parts, the DT1-E engine will gain optimum output at midrange and top end.

1. **Specifications (comparison of GYT Parts to standard parts.)**

    1) Cylinder Head. Volume and shape of combustion chamber changed to increase top end performance. Spark plug hole moved to center of the head.
    2) Cylinder. Chrome plated cylinder liner inside of aluminum cylinder body. Port timing changed to increase performance. Intake port diameter increase.
    3) Piston. Material changed to Lowex for increased reliability. One cast iron piston ring. Design of piston changed to match port timing of cylinder.
    4) Carburetor. Size increased to 30 mm venturi (VM 30 SH.) Main jet size increased to 200.
    5) Exhaust system. Tuned exhaust (expansion chamber) to give maximum performance.
    6) Spark plug. Heat range and type of plug changed to B-10E(N).
    7) Oil Pump. Removed to facilitate installation of GYT cylinder.

2. **Check engine condition before installation of GYT Parts.**

    After installation of the GYT parts, the engine will be set-up for optimum output. Therefore, to insure reliability, performance, and engine safety, the critical engine compoents should be checked and set to recommended standards before installation of GYT parts.

    1) Remove the engine from the frame and disassemble engine. (Refer to section 5 Engine.)
    a. Check the crankshaft assembly, crank bearing, connecting rod, connecting rod big end and small end bearings, and set to recommended standards or replace faulty parts as necessary.
    b. Oil seals. It is suggested to replace all of the oil seals upon engine disassembly for installation of GYT parts to insure against the slightest possible leakage.
    c. Replace all gaskets and O rings upon assembly of the engine and use recommended sealant.

3. **Installation of GYT Parts.**

    1) Install a cap housing cover over the tachometer drive opening in the right-hand crankcase if the tachometer is removed from the machine.
    2) Assemble cylinder head, cylinder, and piston with new gaskets.
    3) Assemble VM 30SH carburetor with 10 mm thick insulator on cylinder.

    Carburetor Specifications

Name of Part	Abbreviation	Specifications
Main jet	M. J.	#200
Needle jet	N. J.	O-2
Jet needle	J. N.	5DP 7-3 stages
Throttle valve cut away	C. A.	3.5
Air screw setting	A. S.	1
Starter jet	G. S.	#60
Float level	F. L.	24.0 mm (0.945 in)

4) If the oil pump is removed, install an oil pump cover plate on the crankcase, installing a 6 mm bolt in the inlet hole on the cylinder intake port. Follow the oil manufacturer's recommendation for fuel/oil ratio.

A 15:1 fuel/oil ratio should be mixed in the gas tank when the Autolube pump is removed.

If the oil pump is retained, a 30:1 fuel/oil ratio could be mixed in the gas tank in conjunction with the Autolube pump.

5) Secondaey sprocket ratio will have to be determined by the owner depending on the type of riding or competition conditions to be encountered.

The gearing should be reduced if thes machine is to be raced on a short or extremely rough course. If the secondary drive sprocket is changed, be sure to bend the lock washer ears up after installation of the gear.

6) After installation of the GYT parts, thoroughly check the condition of the engine components. The engine should be considered in new condition. Start the engine and run between 4,000 and 5,000 R.P.M. for 5 to 10 minutes. Let the engine cool and repeat this procedure several times.

Remove the spark plug and make a reading as to the spark plug heat range, main jet size and jet needle position. Adjust as necessary and take the machine for a trial run. Remove the spark plug again and make another reading for spark plug heat range, main jet size and jet needle position.

7-3 Addittional Modification

All of the unnecessary equipment such as lighting, mirrors, etc., should be removed if the machine is to be raced. Removal of the speedometer and/or tachometer will be optional with the rider and depend on the type of riding to be done.

Further modification, such as gear ratio, tire changes, suspension changes or modification, installation of 21 in. front wheel, etc., is part of personalization and up to the owner.

7-4 Specifications(GYT)

Piston Clearance	0.045–0.050 mm
Spark plug	Standard B-10E(N)
Ignition Timing	B.T.D.C. 2.3 mm
Secondary reduction	Chain
Carburetor setting	Main Jet #200
	Needle Jet 0-2
	Pilot Jet #80
	Cut away 3.5
	Number of turns back off air screw 1
Float level	24.0 mm (0.945 in)
Fuel Mixing ratio	If the AUTOLUBE is in use 30:1 If not 15:1
Gear Oil amount	1,000 c.c. (1.0 qt)
Oil Pump	
Minimum stroke	0.20–0.25 mm
Maximum stroke	1.85–2.05 mm

7-5 Setting the Ignition Timing

1) Install the dial gauge in the cylinder head.
   Note: On the special racing head the spark plug hole is centered and parallel to the cylinder bore.

2) Roughly aligns the red mark on the rotor with the pointer attached to the stationary plate.

3) Check to see if the points are clean and not pitted. They can be smoothed with #400 sandpaper or with an oil stone.

4) Connect a tester to the points and ground so that the exact opening and closing of the points can be measured.

5) Rotate the rotor so that the piston will be lowered 2.3 mm B.T.D.C. At this point, loosen the breaker plate setting. Adjust the breaker plate so that the points just close. Then tighten the breaker plate.

7-6 Check and Service Prior to Racing

The following items should be checked and serviced before racing.

1) Check the cylinder, piston, and crankshaft ass'y for any defects.
2) Make sure that the carburetor is clean and correctly set.
3) Check ignition timing, lead wire connect on, and insulation.
4) Retighten screws, bolts and nuts in all parts.
5) Check the cables.
6) Clean the gas tank and petcock.
7) Adjust and oil the chain.
   Adjust the drive chain so that it has free play of approximately 1 in.(25 mm.) up and down at the center of the lower section with the rear wheel on the ground.

CONVERSION TABLE

LENGTHS

Multiply	By To Obtain	Multiply	By To Obtain
Milimeters(mm)	.03937 Inches	Kilometers(km.)	.6214 Miles
Inches(in.)	25.399 Mlimeters	Miles(mi.)	1.609 Kilometers
Centimeters(cm.)	.393707 Inches	Meters(m.)	3.281 Feet
Inches(in.)	2.54 Centimeters	Feet(ft.)	.3048 Meters

WEIGHTS

Kilograms(kg.)	2.20462 Pounds	Grams(g.)	.03527 Ounces
Pounds(lbs.)	.453592 Kilograms	Onces(oz.)	28.35 Grams

VOLUMES

Cubic centimeters(c.c.)	.061 Cubic inches	Imperial gallons	277.274 cu. in.
Cubic inches(cu. in.)	16.387 c.c.	Liters (l.)	1.057 Quarts
Liters (l.)	.26418 Gallons	Quarts (qt.)	.946 Liters
Gallons (gal.)	3.785 Liters	Cubic centimeters(c.c.)	.0339 Fluid ounces
U.S. gallons	1.2 Imperial gals.	Fluid ounces(fl. oz.)	29.57 c.c.
Imperial gallons	4.537 Liters.		

OTHERS

Metric horsepower(ps.)	1.014 bhp.	Foot-pounds(ft-lbs)	.1383 kg-m
Brake horsepower(bhp.)	.9859 ps.	Kilometers per liter(km/l)	2.352 mpg
Kilogram-meter(kg-m)	7.235 Foot-pounds	Miles per gallon(mpg)	.4252 km/l

GAS (FUEL) TO OIL RATIO CHART (U.S. Gallons)

Gas/Oil Ratio	12:1	15:1	20:1	24:1	28:1	30:1	36:1	40:1
Oil (qt.) per 1Gal. Gas	0.33	0.27	0.2	0.17	0.14	0.13	0.11	0.1
Oil (oz.) per 1Gal. Gas	10.7	8.5	6.4	5.3	4.6	4.3	3.6	3.2
Oil (qt.) per 5Gal. Gas	1.66	1.33	1.0	0.84	0.72	0.67	0.55	0.5
Oil (oz.) per 5Gal. Gas	53.5	42.67	32.0	26.6	22.8	21.32	17.8	16.0

TORQUE SPECIFICATIONS

Size	Kg/M	Ft.Lbs.	In.Lbs.
6mm	1.0	7	90
7mm	1.5	11	135
8mm	2.0	15	180
10mm	3.5-4.0	26-29	300-350
12mm	4.0-4.5	29-33	350-400
14mm	4.5-5.0	33-37	400-450
17mm	5.8-7.0	40-50	500-600

MILLIMETERS TO INCHES

	0	0.1	0.2	0.3	0.4	0.5	0.6	0.7	0.8	0.9
0		.0039	.0079	.0118	.0157	.0197	.0236	.0276	.0315	.0354
1	.0394	.0433	.0472	.0512	.0551	.0591	.0630	.0669	.0709	.0748
2	.0787	.0827	.0866	.0906	.0945	.0984	.1024	.1063	.1102	.1142
3	.1181	.1200	.1260	.1299	.1339	.1378	.1417	.1457	.1496	.1535
4	.1575	.1614	.1654	.1693	.1732	.1772	.1811	.1850	.1890	.1929
5	.1969	.2000	.2047	.2087	.2126	.2165	.2205	.2244	.2283	.2323
6	.2362	.2402	.2441	.2480	.2520	.2559	.2598	.2638	.2677	.2717
7	.2756	.2795	.2835	.2874	.2913	.2953	.2992	.3031	.3071	.3110
8	.3150	.3189	.3228	.3268	.3307	.3346	.3386	.3425	.3465	.3504
9	.3543	.3583	.3622	.3661	.3701	.3740	.3780	.3819	.3858	.3898
10	.3937	.3976	.4016	.4055	.4094	.4134	.4173	.4213	.4252	.4291

.01mm= .0004 .03mm= .0012 .05mm= .0020 .07mm= .0028 .09mm= .0035
.02mm= .0008 .04mm= .0016 .06mm= .0024 .08mm= .0031 .10mm= .0039

INCHES TO MILLIMETERS

	0	.01	.02	.03	.04	.05	.06	.07	.08	.09
0		.254	.508	.762	1.016	1.270	1.524	1.778	2.032	2.286
.1	2.540	2.794	3.048	3.302	3.556	3.810	4.064	4.318	4.572	4.826
.2	5.080	5.334	5.588	5.842	6.096	6.350	6.604	6.858	7.112	7.366
.3	7.620	7.874	8.128	8.382	8.636	8.890	9.144	9.398	9.652	9.906
.4	10.160	10.414	10.668	10.922	11.176	11.430	11.684	11.938	12.192	12.446
.5	12.700	12.954	13.208	13.462	13.716	13.970	14.224	14.478	14.732	14.986
.6	15.240	15.494	15.748	16.002	16.256	16.510	16.764	17.018	17.272	17.526
.7	17.780	18.034	18.288	18.542	18.796	19.050	19.304	19.558	19.812	20.066
.8	20.320	20.574	20.828	21.082	21.336	21.590	21.844	22.098	22.352	22.606
.9	22.860	23.114	23.368	23.622	23.876	24.130	24.384	24.638	24.892	25.146
1.0	25.400	25.654	25.908	26.162	26.416	26.670	26.924	27.178	27.432	27.686

.001″= .0254mm .003″= .0762mm .005″= .1270mm .007″= .1778mm .009″= .2286mm
.002″= .0508mm .004″= .1016mm .006″= .1524mm .008″= .2032mm .010″= .254 mm

VI. CONNECTION DIAGRAM (DT1B)

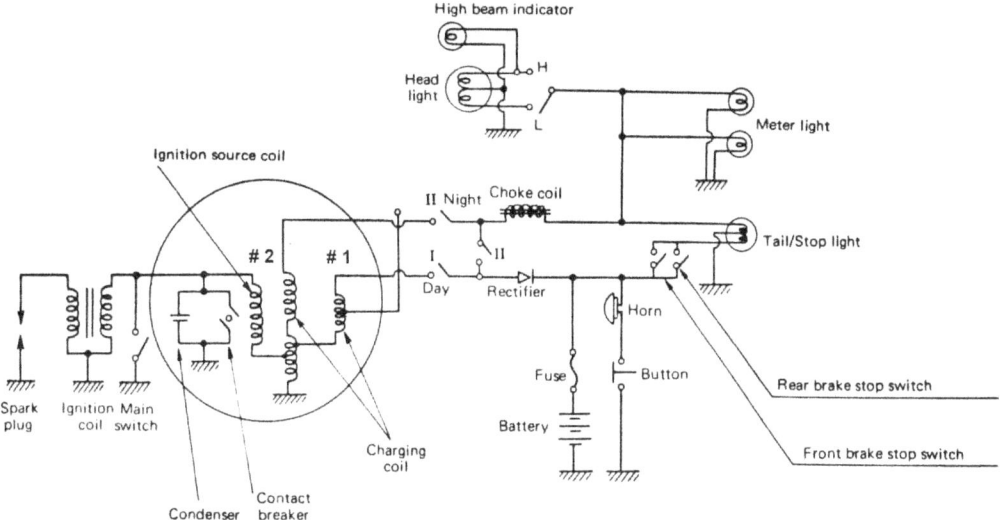

Basic connection diagram for DT1A (late), DT1B and DT1C. DT1A did not use choke coil. DT1C did not either. DT1C has different number of windings in lighting circuit coils but hook-up is basically the same. DT1S (1969½) is basically DT1B chassis, DT1C engine. With very few exceptions, color code for all models is the same.

6-2 Table of component Parts*

Parts	Manufacturer	Model & Type
Flywheel magneto	Mitsubishi Elec.	**FZC-1AIL**
Spark plug	NGK	B-8ES
Headlight	Koito Mfg.	6V, 35W/35W
Speedometer	Nippon Seiki	
Tachometer	Nippon Seiki	
Handle switch	Asahi Denso	ACS
Main switch	Asahi Denso	TIM
Ignition coil	Mitsubishi Elec.	HP-E
Horn	Nikko Kinzoku	MF-6
Battery	Nippon Battery	MV1-6D
Rectifier	Mitsubishi Elec.	DS10HJ1
Fuse	Osachi Mfg.	10A
Stop switch	Niles. Parts	SH40E
Taillight	Stanley Elec.	6V, 5.3W/17W

*Except for magneto lighting source coils above parts the same for entire DT1 Series (DT1B inc. choke coil).

6-3 Connection Diagram-DT1E

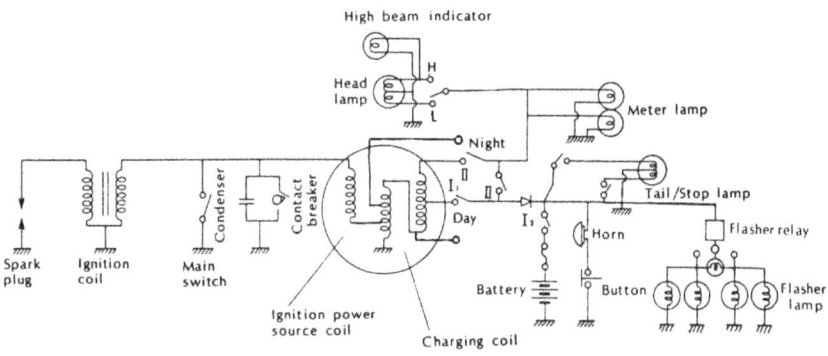

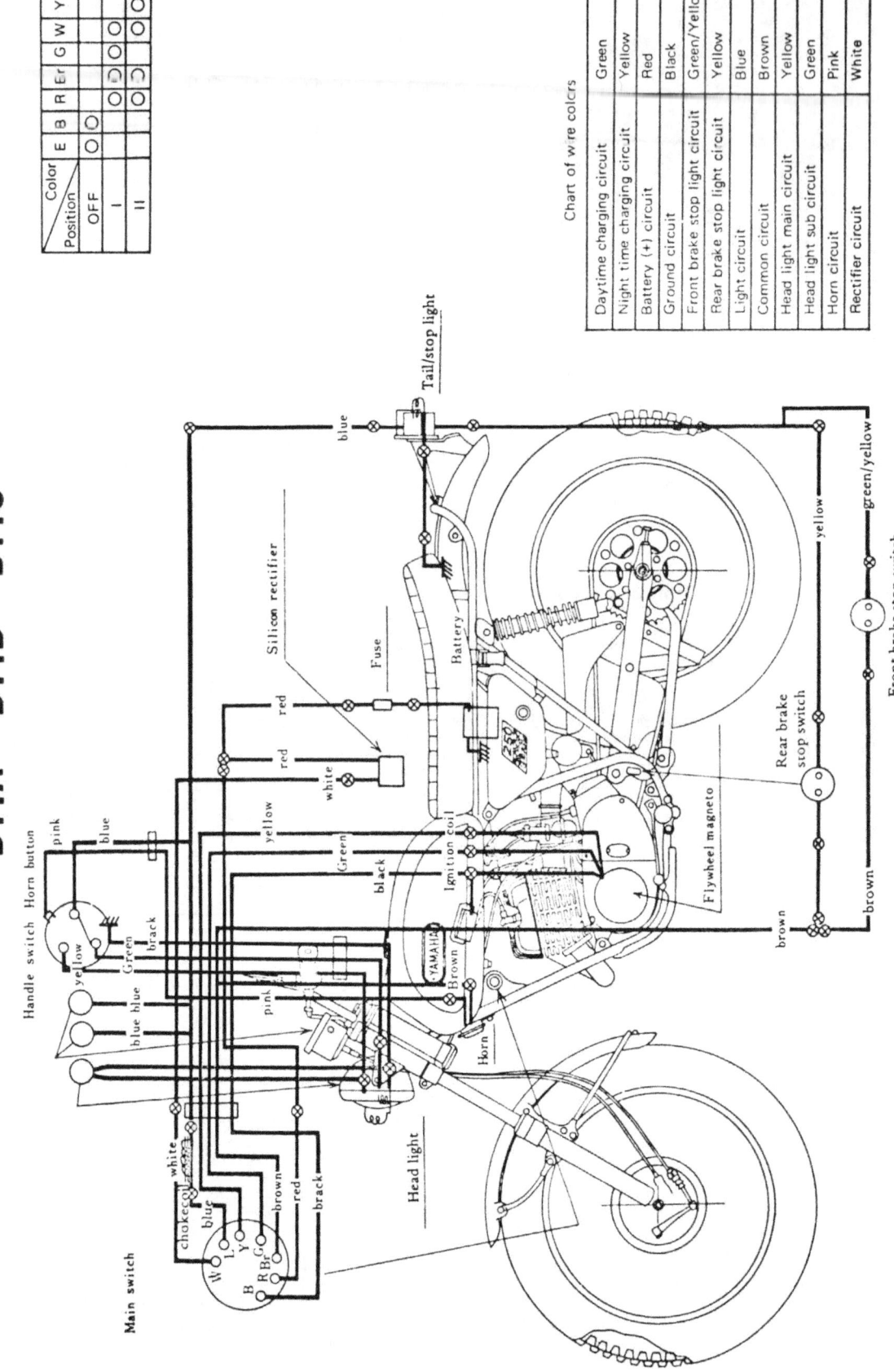

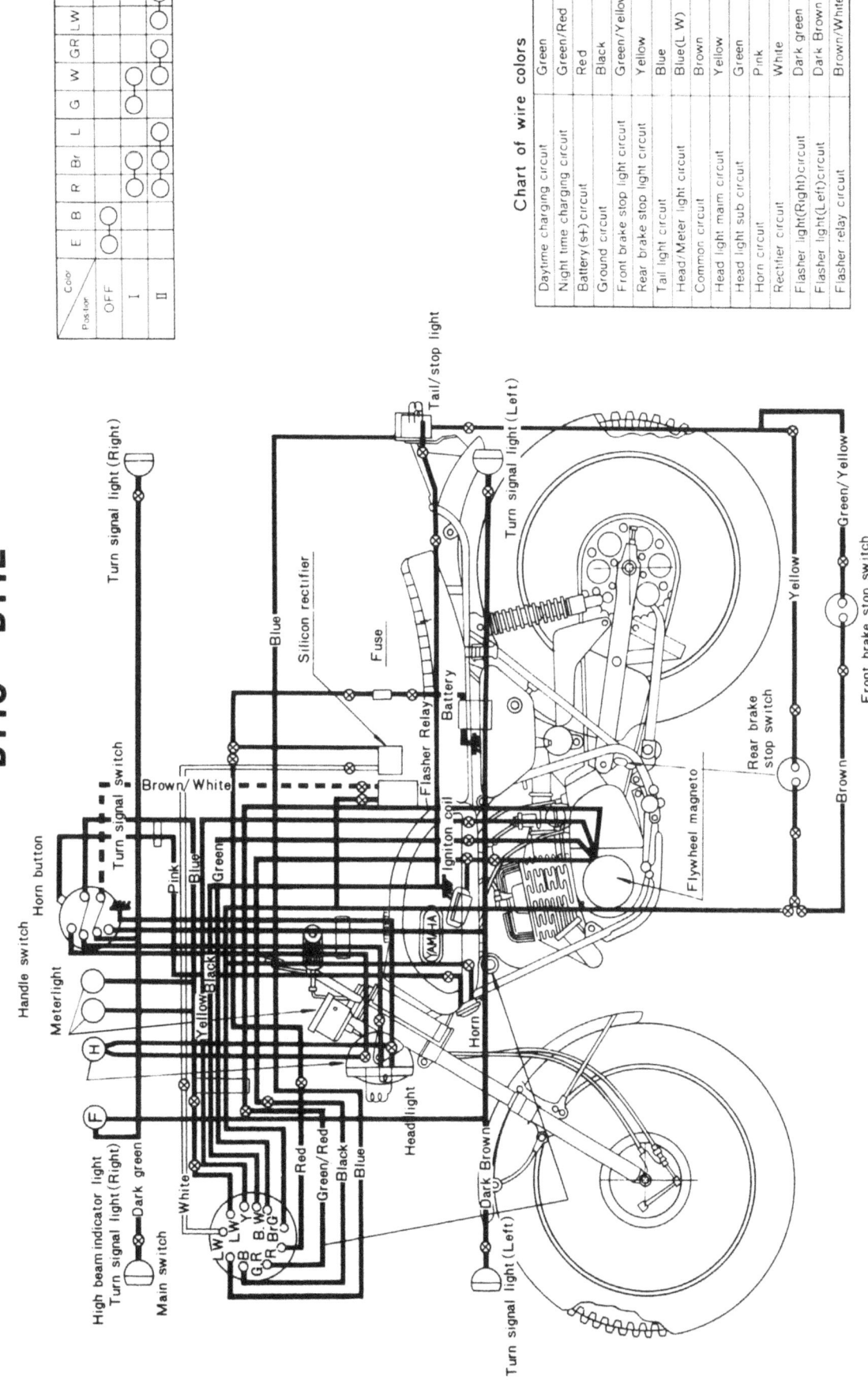

NOTES

DT1A

(1968)

MODEL CHANGES

Note

THE FOLLOWING INFORMATION MUST BE USED AS A GUIDE ONLY TO INDICATE THE DIRECTION TAKEN BY VARIOUS MODIFICATIONS. IT IS INCLUDED ONLY AS AN AID TO SERVICING THE DT1 SERIES AND, SHOULD A QUESTION ARISE REGARDING A CERTAIN PART, THE MECHANIC SHOULD REFER TO AN UP-TO-DATE MODEL PARTS BOOK, SERVICE OR PARTS NEWS BULLETIN, OR THE MANUFACTURER.

Fig. 1 CRANK CASE

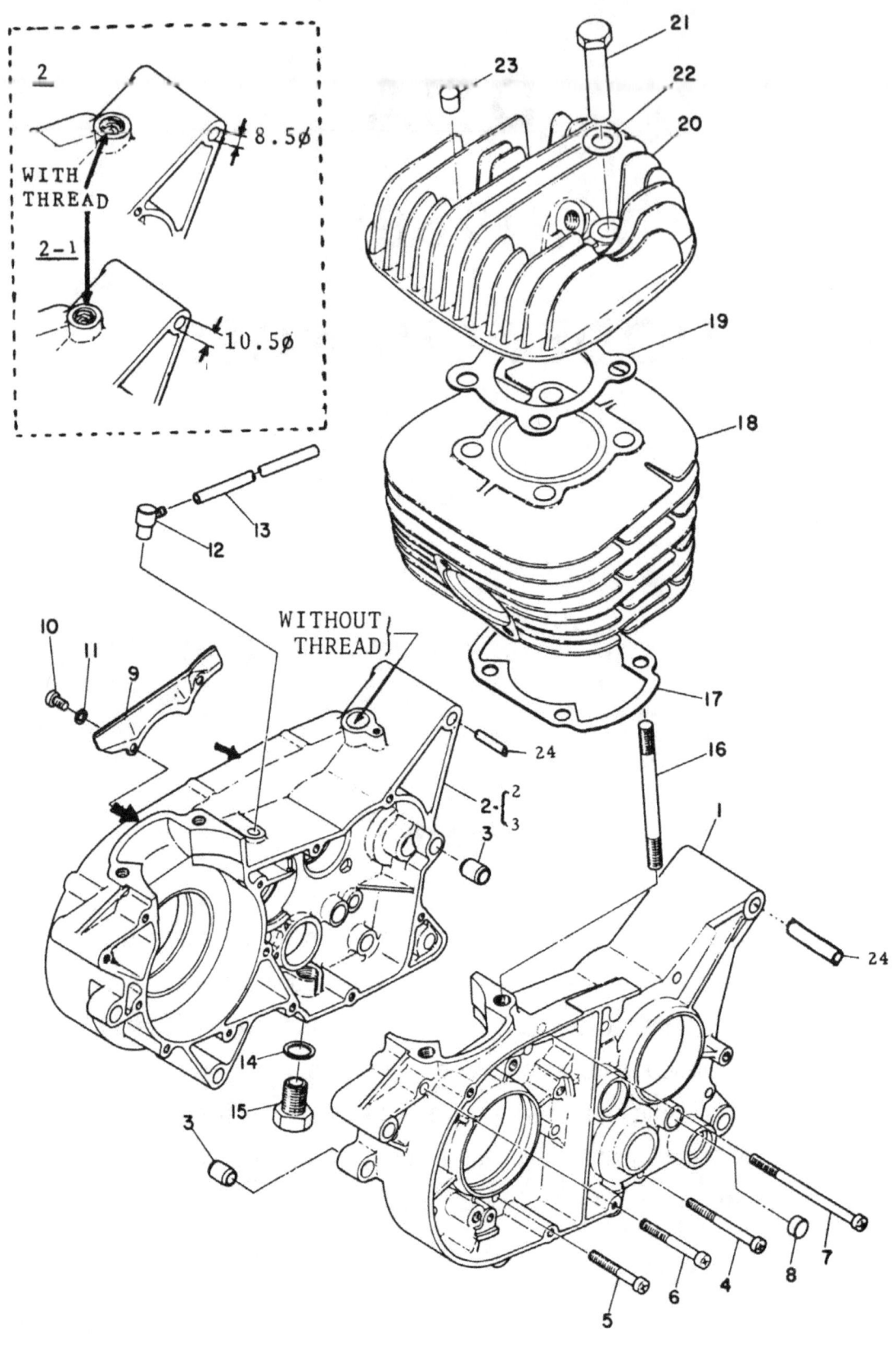

CRANK CASE

Ref No.	Parts No.	Part Name	Description	Q'ty	S·R	Remarks
1- 1	214-15111-00	CASE, crank (L.H). (DISCONT)		1		
1- 1 -1	214-15111-01	CASE, crank (L.H)		1		
1- 2	214-15121-01	CASE, crank (R.H) (DISCONT)		1		
1- 2 -1	214-15121-02	CASE, crank (R.H) (DISCONT)		1		E/#2759~
1- 2 -2	214-15121-03	CASE, crank (R.H) (DISCONT)		1		E/#3383~
1- 2 -3	214-15121-04	CASE, crank (R.H)		1		ISO

NOTE: All pre-ISO crank cases have been discontinued. All new DT1 crank cases ordered will be the ISO (DT1B) edition. (Eng. #15001 and up).

THESE CRANK CASES ARE INTERCHANGEABLE IF the following procedure is adhered to when ordering:
LEFT CRANK CASE HALF:
(00) Eng. #0001-2758. Order one 214-15117-09 spacer metal for upper rear motor mount.
(01) Eng. #2759-(Present). Interchahgeability okay with ISO type. (DT1B)
RIGHT CRANK CASE HALF:
(01) Eng. #0001-2758. Order one 214-15117-09 spacer metal, four 98501-05010 (ISO) pan head screws, one each -01 tach drive housing and associated -01 tach. drive components.
(02) Eng. #2759-3382. Order all of above except spacer metal.
(03) Eng. #3383-15000. Order four 98501-05010 (ISO) pan head screws only.
(04) Eng. #15001-(Present) Interchangeability okay with ISO type. (DT1B)

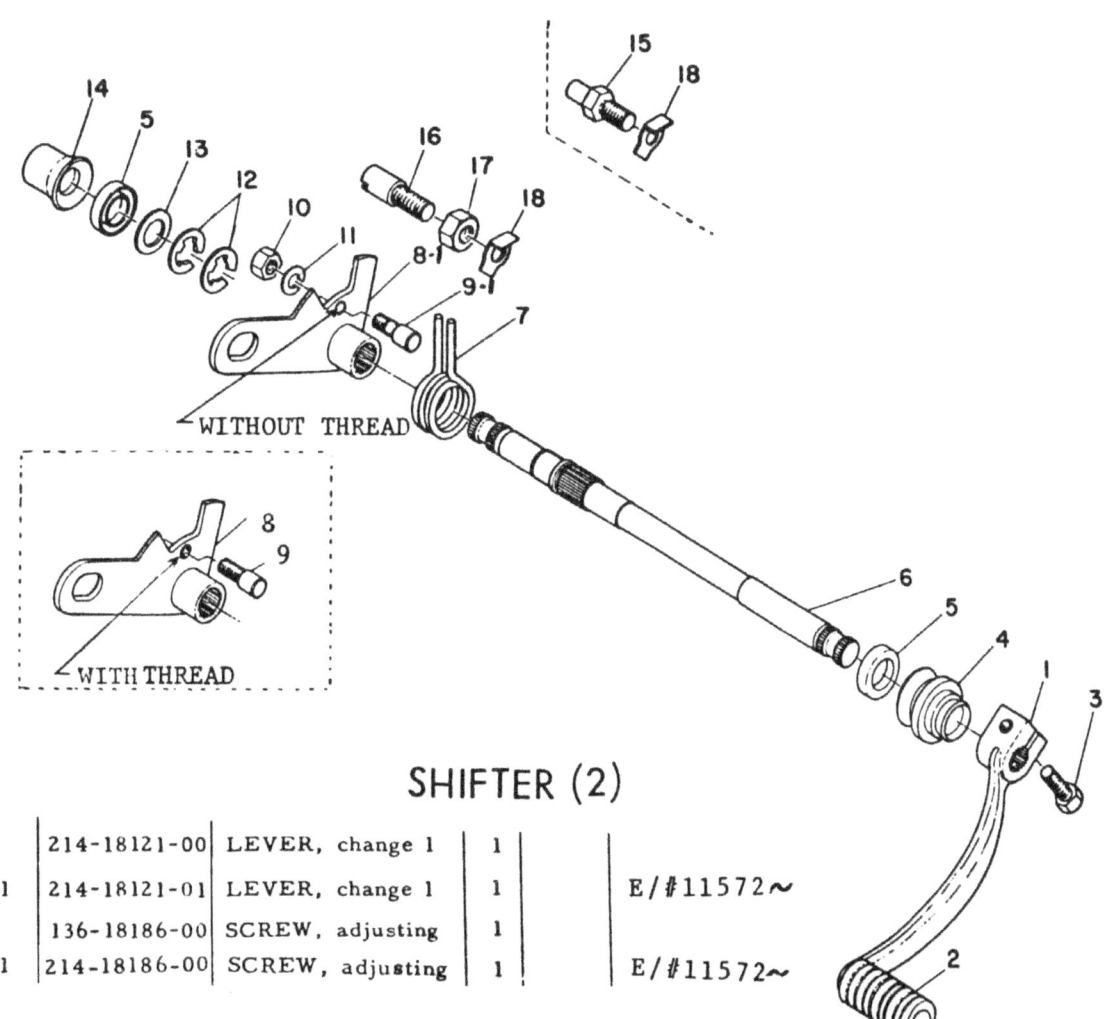

SHIFTER (2)

7- 8	214-18121-00	LEVER, change 1		1		
7- 8 -1	214-18121-01	LEVER, change 1		1		E/#11572~
7- 9	136-18186-00	SCREW, adjusting		1		
7- 9 -1	214-18186-00	SCREW, adjusting		1		E/#11572~

Fig. 9 TACHOMETER GEAR

6	214-17811-01	HOUSING		1	
7	214-17841-01	GEAR, driven		1	
8	93210-13016	O-RING		1	
9	93210-07100	O-RING		1	
10	214-17847-00	SHIM		1	E/#3383~
11	214-17815-00	BUSH		1	
12	214-17812-00	STOPPER		1	
13	92501-06010	SCREW, pan head		1	
14	92901-06100	WASHER, spring		1	
15	214-15353-00	GASKET, drain plug	16.2-24-1	1	
16	214-178 0 00	HOUSING ASS'Y		1	

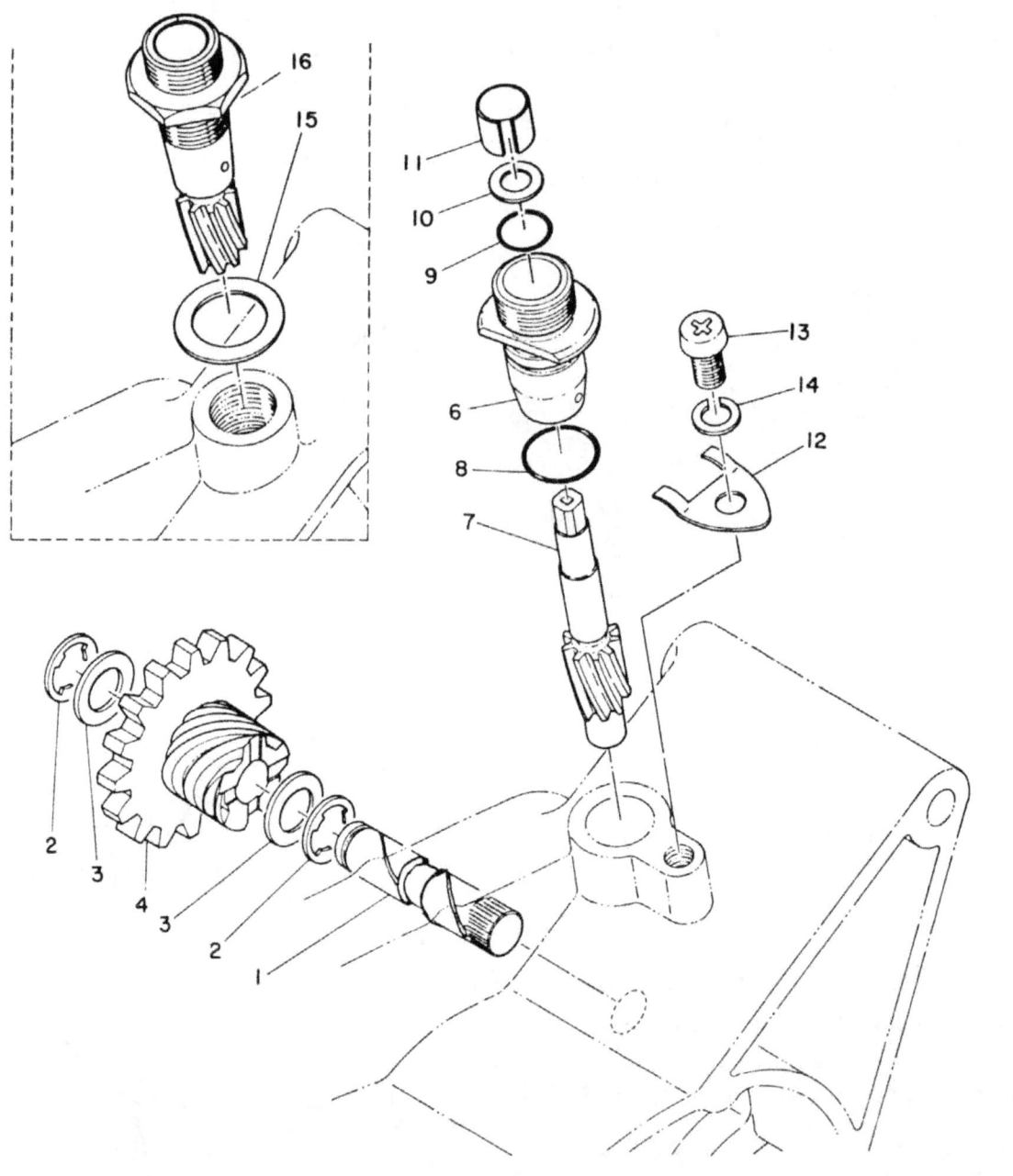

Fig. 13 OIL PUMP

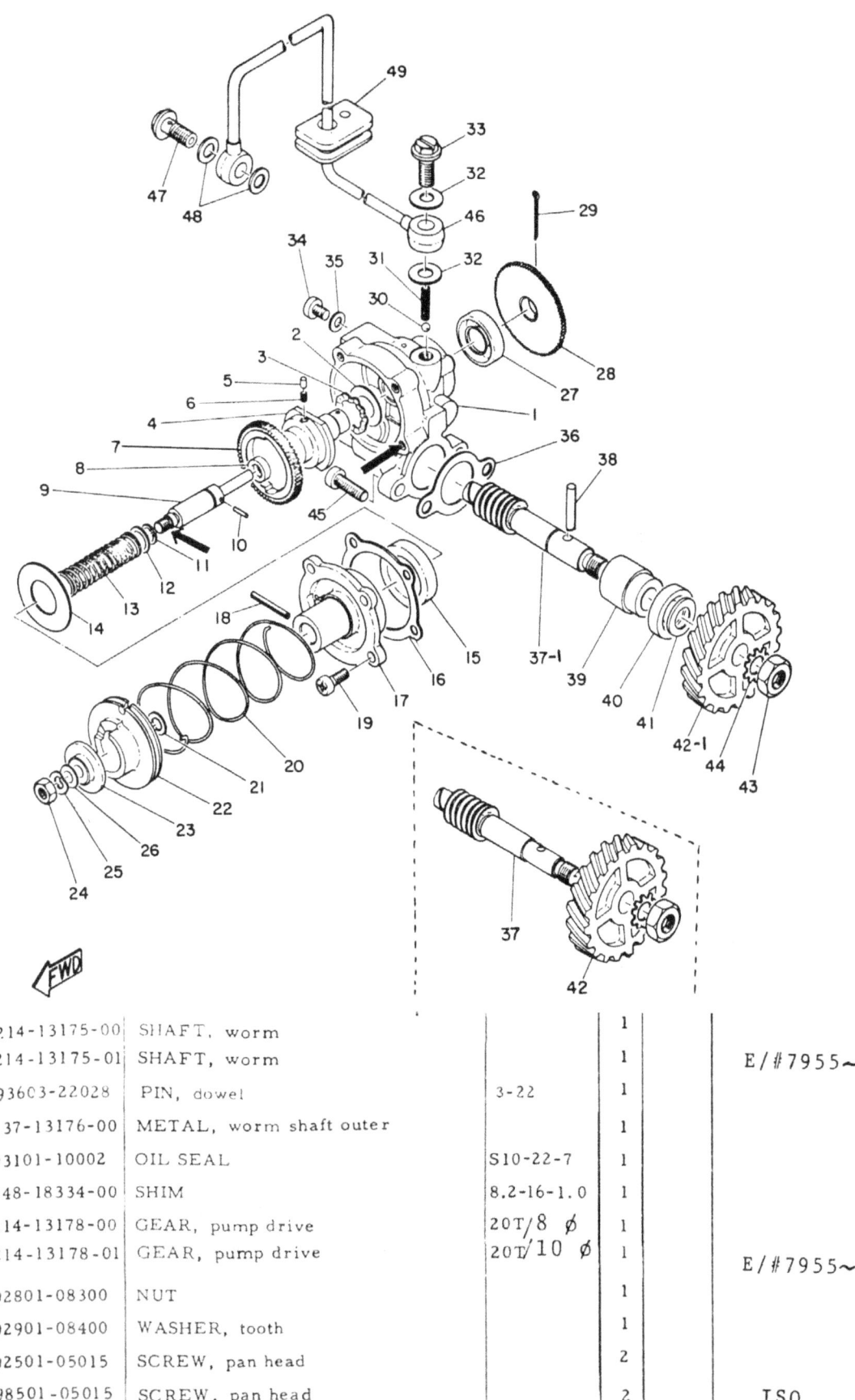

37	214-13175-00	SHAFT, worm		1	
37-1	214-13175-01	SHAFT, worm		1	E/#7955~
38	93603-22028	PIN, dowel	3-22	1	
39	137-13176-00	METAL, worm shaft outer		1	
40	93101-10002	OIL SEAL	S10-22-7	1	
41	148-18334-00	SHIM	8.2-16-1.0	1	
42	214-13178-00	GEAR, pump drive	20T/8 ø	1	
42-1	214-13178-01	GEAR, pump drive	20T/10 ø	1	E/#7955~
43	92801-08300	NUT		1	
44	92901-08400	WASHER, tooth		1	
45	92501-05015	SCREW, pan head		2	
45-1	98501-05015	SCREW, pan head		2	ISO

Fig. 15 FRAME

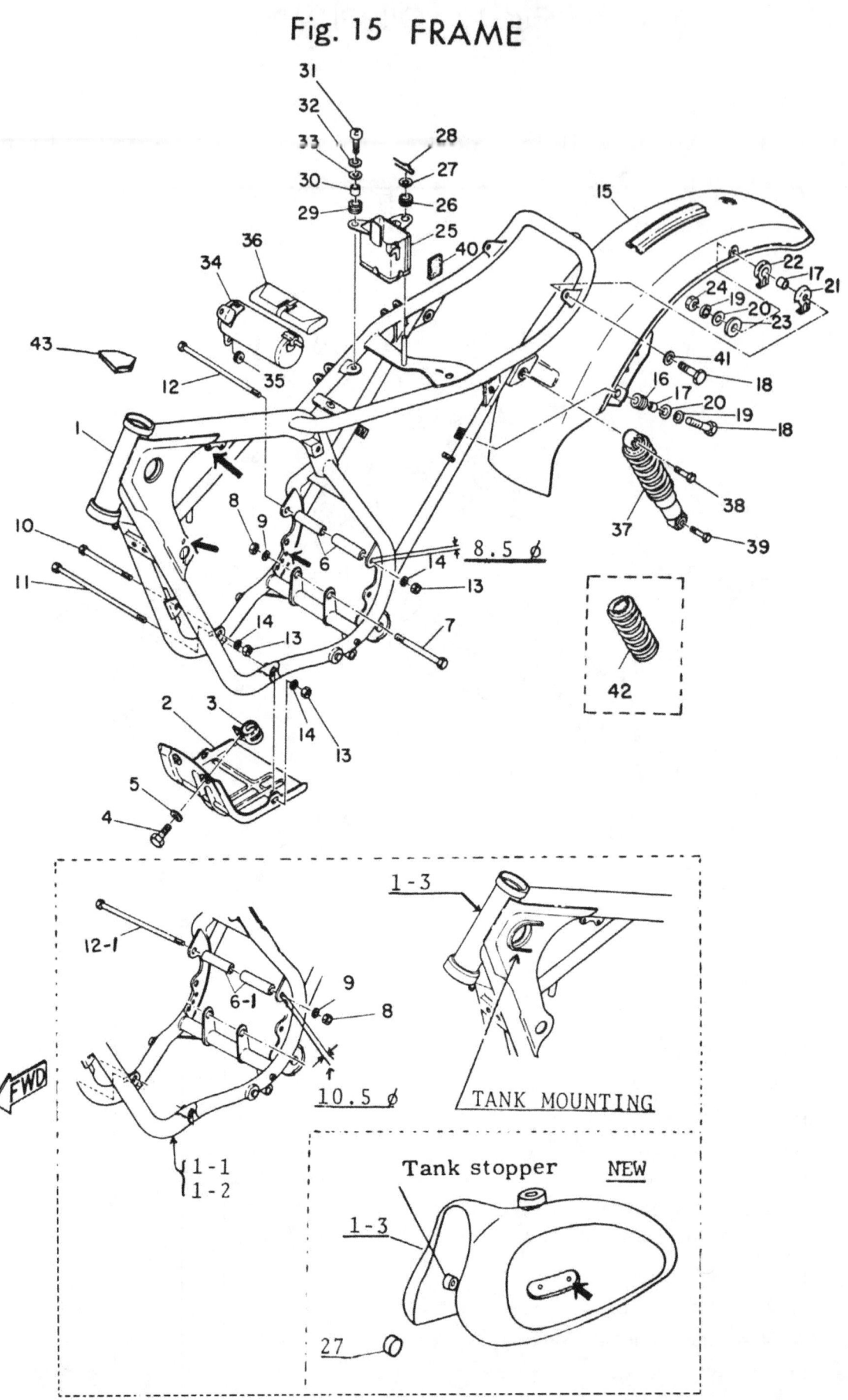

FRAME

No.	Parts No.	Part Name	Description	Q'ty	S·R	Remarks
14	214-21746-00	DAMPER, tool box		1		
15	214-28100-00	TOOL ASS'Y		1		☆
15-1	214-28100-01	TOOL ASS'Y		1		☆ ISO
17	214-22210-20	REAR CUSHION ASS'Y		2		
18	214-22241-00	BOLT, rear cushion upper		2		
19	214-22242-00	BOLT, rear cushion upper		2		
40	214-21268-00	SEAL, battery box		1		
41	92902-06200	WASHER, plain		2		
42	214-22212-10	SPRING ONLY		2		K=1.56Kg/M
43	214-21269-00	SEAL (TANK DAMPER)		1		

NOTE: Make a thorough identification on each DT1 before ordering parts:

(00) Eng #0001-2758. Utilized 8 mm upper rear motor mount bolt. Tap out motor mount bolt hole to 10.5mm to interchange with (01) frame.

(01) Eng #2759-(UNKN) First change was to 10.5mm upper rear motor mount bolt hole. Interchangeability okay with (00) frame.
Second change (engine number unknown) was to add rear turn signal mounts. Interchangeability still okay.

(02) Eng # (UNKN)-13000. Went to ISO standard (Eng # Unknown). Changes in this frame are the 5mm threads for the fittings for the rectifier, ignition switch, brake light switch and ignition coil mounting. To replace a (00 or 01) frame with (02), in addition to above will require purchasing the associated ISO screws for the aforementioned components.
<u>TO IDENTIFY a (02) frame</u>, look for the ISO dot on the heads of the mounting screws on the above components.

(03) Eng #13001-present. Still ISO. Only change here is in gas tank mount. NOT interchangeable with (00-01-02) frames.

NOTE: Changes in the gas tank on the DT1 have made it necessary to pay particular attention to Engine Numbers before ordering replacement parts.

(00) Eng. #0001-4585. Utilized 6mm fuel tank stay mounting bolt. To interchange to (01) tank order two 91202-08015 bolts. To interchange with (02) order (in addition to bolts) four 98501-04008 Emblem mounting screws (ISO). No interchangeability with (03) tank. Frame has to be changed.

(01) Eng. #4586-(UNKN) Utilized 8mm fuel tank stay mounting bolt. During this period the factory changed to ISO system on four Emblem screws. No engine number for change. Check head of screw for ISO stamp (one dot).

(02) Eng. #(UNKN)-13000. Same as (01) tank except for ISO change on four Emblem screws. Interchange to (01) tank will require identification of Emblem screws and their ordering if necessary. Interchange to (00) tank order two each 91202-08015 mounting bolts and 92902-08200 plain washers, also four ISO Emblem screws.

(03) Eng. #13001-(Present). ISO tank utilizing new style tank mount. No interchangeability with earlier tanks. Requires different frame.

NOTE: Figure 20-13 lever fitting screw is used on ALL DT1's. Do not attempt interchange with other pre-ISO models such as YDS3, etc.

NOTES

DT1A TO DT1B
(1968) (1969)
MODEL CHANGES

Note

THE FOLLOWING INFORMATION MUST BE USED AS A GUIDE ONLY TO INDICATE THE DIRECTION TAKEN BY VARIOUS MODIFICATIONS. IT IS INCLUDED ONLY AS AN AID TO SERVICING THE DT1 SERIES AND, SHOULD A QUESTION ARISE REGARDING A CERTAIN PART, THE MECHANIC SHOULD REFER TO AN UP-TO-DATE PARTS BOOK, SERVICE OR PARTS NEWS BULLETIN, OR THE MANUFACTURER.

III. PERFORMANCE CURVES
DT1A - DT1B

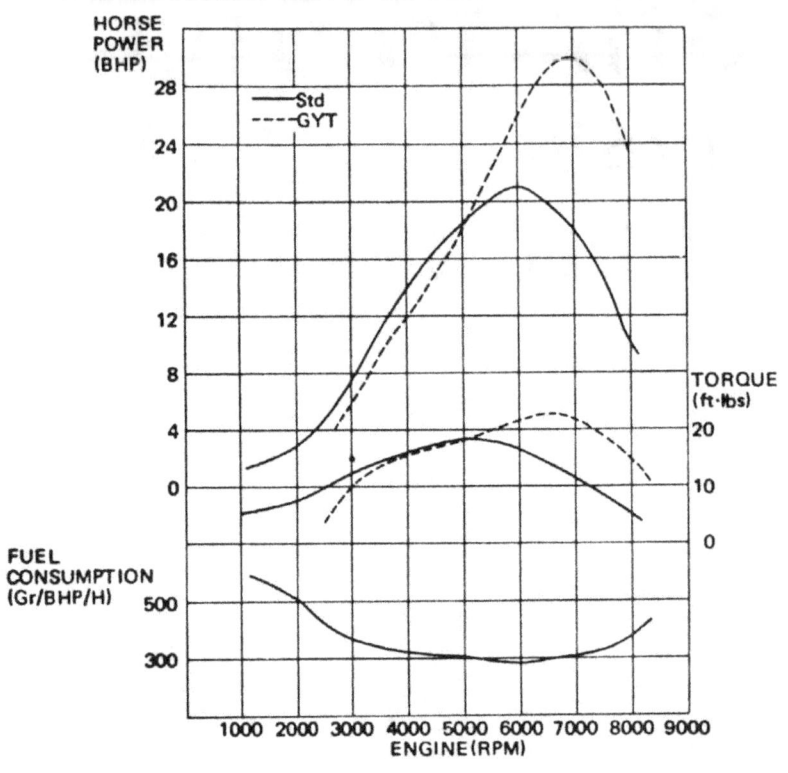

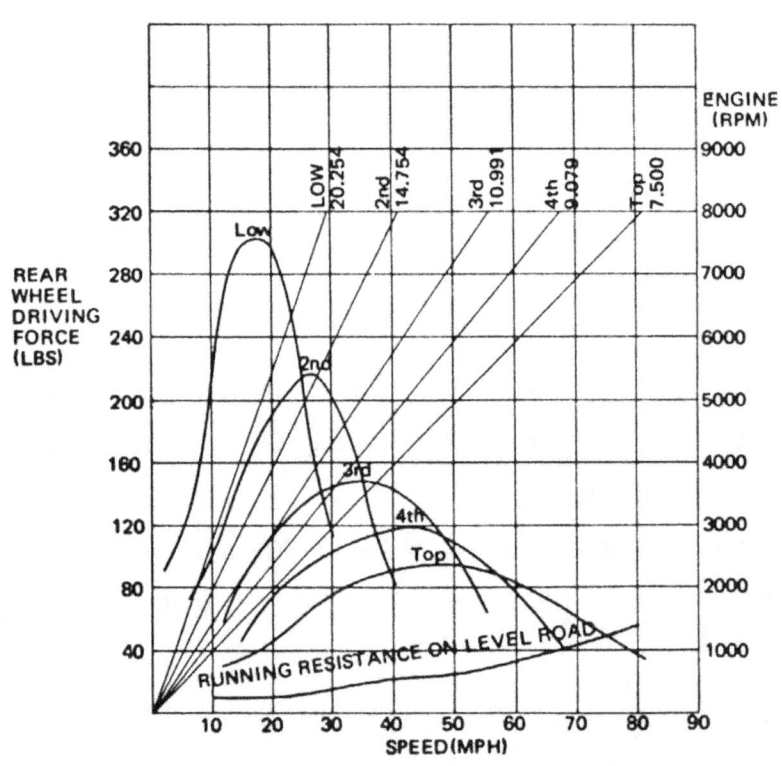

III. PERFORMANCE CURVES
DT1C MX - DT1E MX

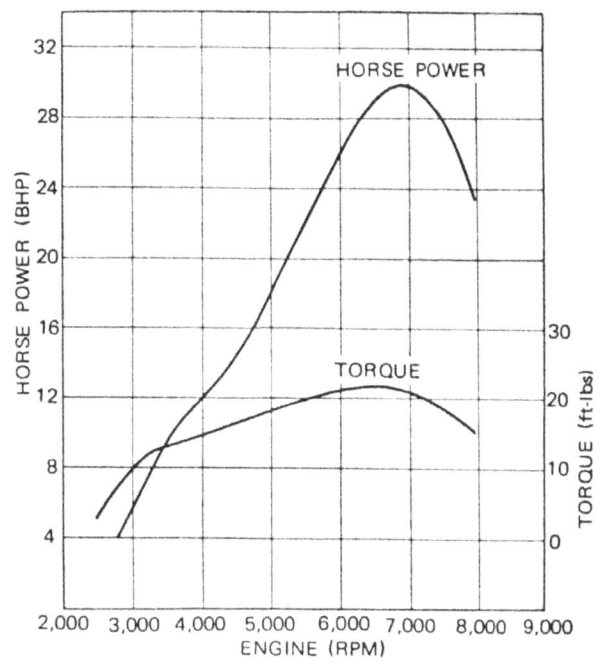

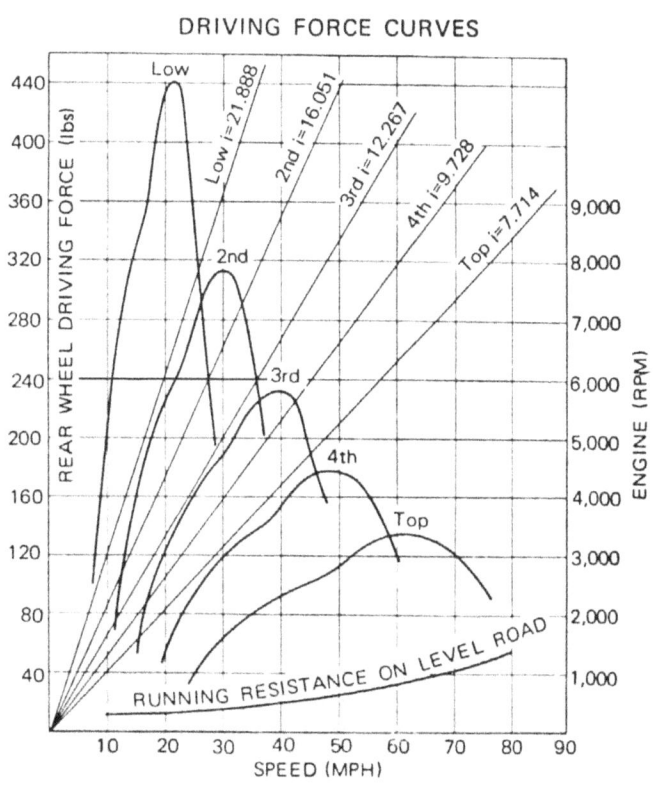

IV. DESCRIPTION
DTIA to DT1B CHANGES

1. **Engine**

   Description will be given as to the differences in the engines between the former and new models.

   1) Cylinder Head

      A hole is added for fitting a compression release or another spark plug. On marketed models, the hole is filled with a blind plug and gasket.

      (The compression release used should be 19 mm reach in length. Do not use any other size.)

      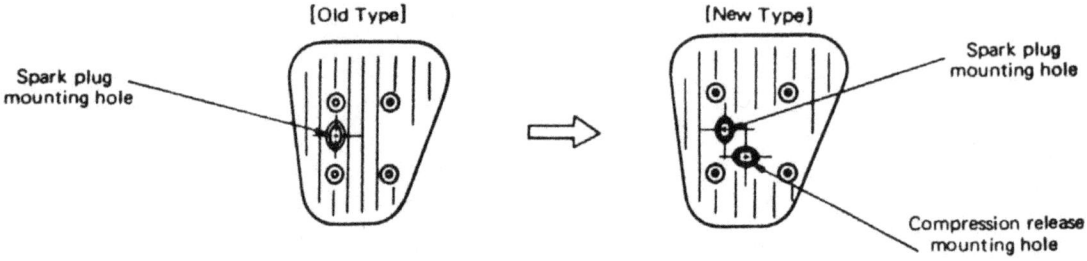

   2) Air Cleaner

      In order to improve both sealing and dust proofing effects, the element and joint rubber are made into one unit. The joint rubber is designed to be connected in a manner such that the raised portion of the upper joint rubber is fitted into the recessed portion of the lower joint.

      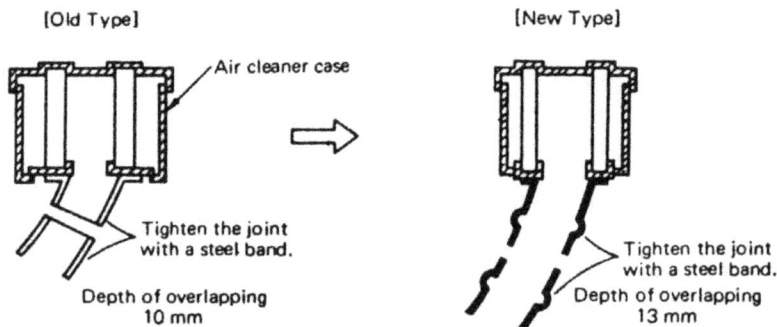

   3) Kick Crank and Kick Lever

      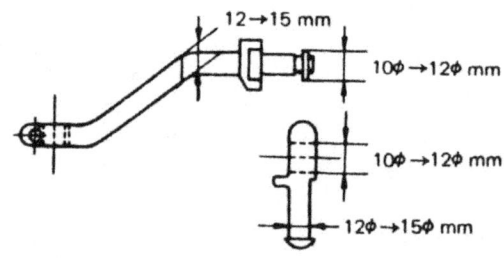

IV. DESCRIPTION
DTIA to DT1B CHANGES

5) Flywheel Magneto Assembly

To prevent the oil seal from coming off the crankshaft, three ribs are provided for the flywheel magneto base.

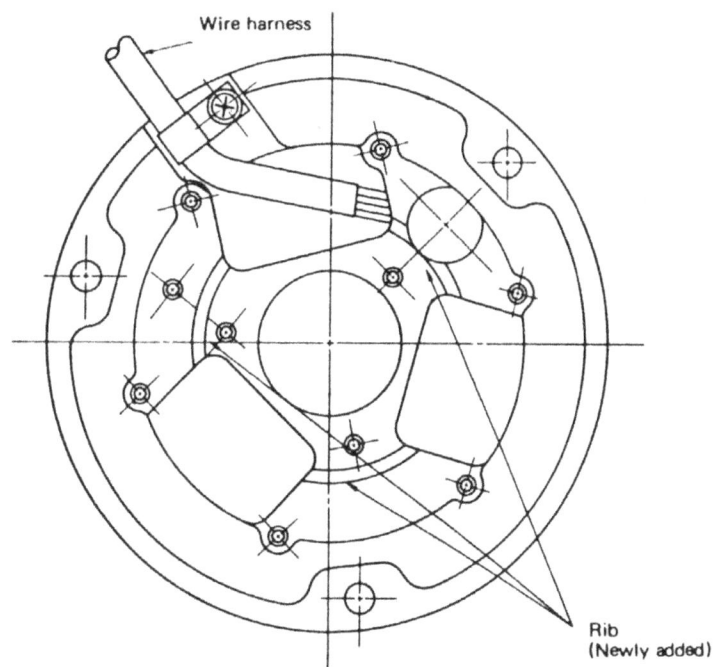

6) Choke Coil

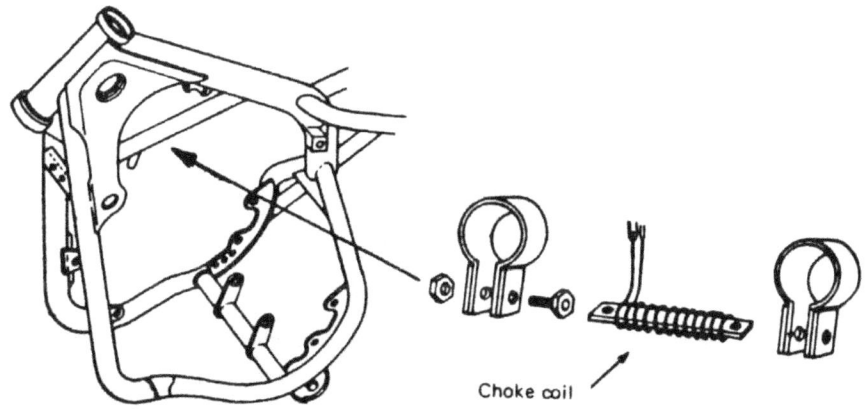

IV. DESCRIPTION
DTIA to DT1B CHANGES

9) **Flywheel Magneto Mounting on Crankshaft**

   To keep the flywheel magneto secured to the crankshaft, improvements have been introduced to these components, and at the same time, the threaded portion has been treated with hardening.

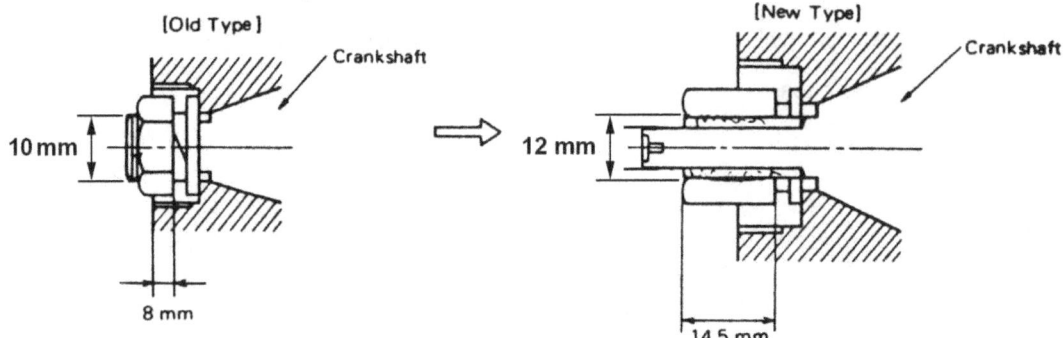

10) **Change Lever 1 and Adjusting Screw**

    The adjusting screw hole tapped in the change lever 1 is no longer in use. No machined portions will be provided for both the 6-mm hole and the screw in order to increase tightness of the screw.

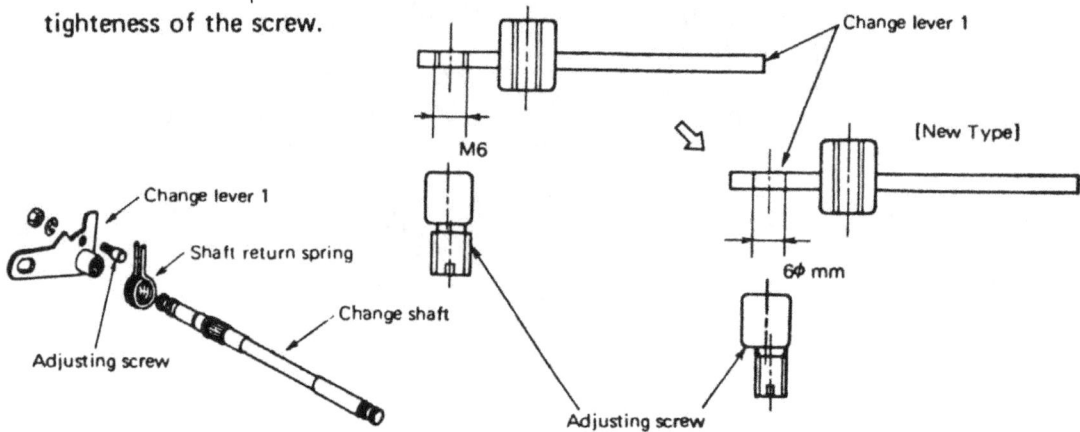

8) **Tachometer Drive Gear Axle**

   To prevent the tachometer drive gear axle from becoming loose, a boss is provided for the crank case cover (right half).

   DT1A (00)   49.6mm L.O.A. (Discontinued)
   DT1A (01)   68.6mm L.O.A.
   DT1B   63.0mm L.O.A. (New cover)

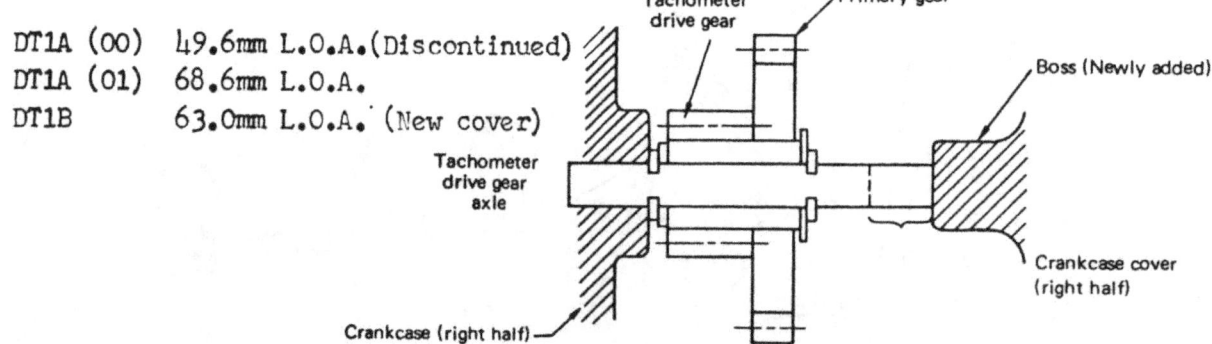

IV. DESCRIPTION
DTIA to DT1B CHANGES

6) Carburetor

1. The idle speed adjustment screw (throttle stop screw) is installed in a horizontal position, instead of the vertical position.
2. Following the change in 1 above, both mixing chamber top and mixing chamber cap are made into one unit.
3. To prevent the mixing chamber cap from becoming loose, a rubber patch is bonded to the cap surface which is in contact with the throttle valve.
4. To tightly secure the throttle wire to the throttle valve, a plate is added.

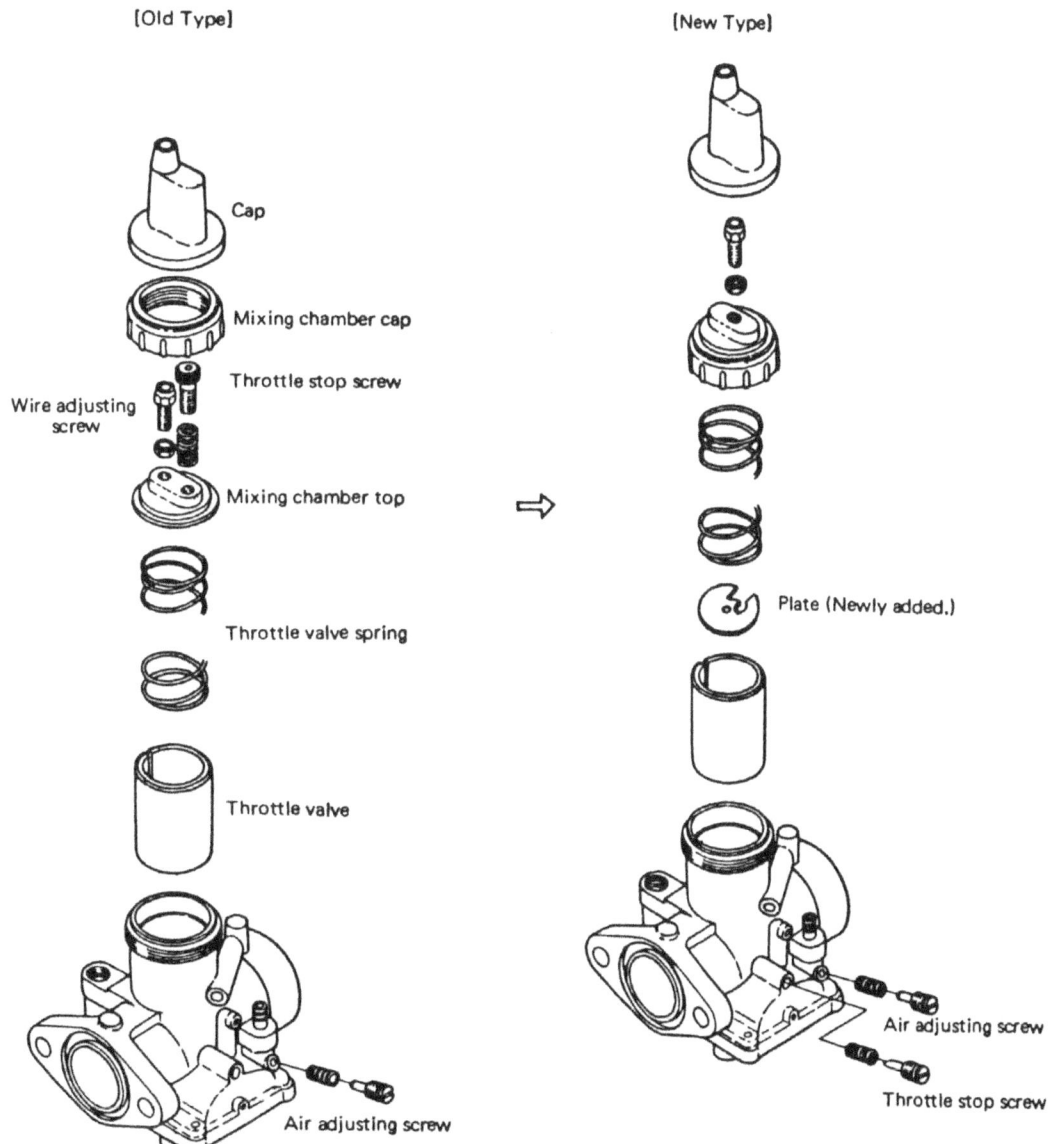

NOTES

DT1 SERIES

PERTINENT PARTS and SERVICE BULLETINS

Note

THE FOLLOWING INFORMATION MUST BE USED AS A GUIDE ONLY TO INDICATE THE DIRECTION TAKEN BY VARIOUS MODIFICATIONS. IT IS INCLUDED ONLY AS AN AID TO SERVICING THE DT1 SERIES AND, SHOULD A QUESTION ARISE REGARDING A CERTAIN PART, THE MECHANIC SHOULD REFER TO AN UP-TO-DATE MODEL PARTS BOOK, SERVICE OR PARTS NEWS BULLETIN, OR THE MANUFACTURER.

MOTORCYCLE SERVICE NEWS

NUMBER 219

YAMAHA INTERNATIONAL CORPORATION
MONTEBELLO, CALIFORNIA
DATE 5/6/69

ENDUROS   INTERCHANGE LIST FOR MODIFICATION AND PERSONALIZATION

The following list has been compiled as an aid to the progressive dealership that wishes to personalize and/or modify any of the Enduro line. The dealer must remember, however, that engine modifications, such as the installation of a GYT Kit head to a stock engine, will void the Warranty on a machine. Customers who desire any engine modifications including those in this list must be advised that the factory and dealer responsibility towards Warranty has been negated and, for all practical purposes, the customer is on his own.

The list below is intended to be used as a guide only and ordering should be done through the parts books for the models involved. This is due to the changing nature of parts and parts numbers.

PART DESCRIPTION	PART NUMBER	ADAPTS TO: AT1	CT1	DT1	REMARKS
AT1 TOP END		X	X		Must be used as a set to convert the CT1 to 123cc.
Cylinder Head	248-11111-00				
Cylinder	248-11311-00				
Piston	248-11631-00				
Piston Rings	248-11601-00				
Piston Pin	137-11633-00				
Head Gasket	248-11181-00				
CT1 TOP END		X	X		Must be used as a set to convert the AT1 to 171cc.
Cylinder Head	251-11111-00				
Cylinder	251-11311-00				
Piston	251-11631-00				
Piston Rings	251-11601-00				
Piston Pin	251-11633-00				
Head Gasket	251-11181-00				
AT1M TOP END		X	X		Must be used as a set on the CT1. Can be used individually on the AT1.
Cylinder Head	248-11111-70				
Cylinder	248-11311-70				
Piston	248-11631-70				
Piston Ring	248-11611-70				
AT1M EXPANSION CHAMBER	248-14610-70	X	X		
AT1M CARBURETOR	248-14101-70	X	X		Mikuni VM26SH (2mm larger than AT1 or CT1.
DT1 GYT CYLINDER HEAD	214-11111-70			X	Increased compression for DT1.
DT1 GYT CYLINDER	214-11311-70			X	Must be used as a set.
DT1 GYT PISTON	214-11631-70			X	
DT1 GYT PISTON RING	214-11611-70			X	
DT1 GYT EXPANSION CHAMBER	214-14610-70			X	
DT1 GYT CARBURETOR	214-14101-70			X	Mikuni VM30SH (an increase of 4mm over standard).
DT1 TACH DRIVE CAP	214-17819-00	X	X	X	Seals tach drive.
DT1 COMPRESSION RELEASE	650-214-002	X	X	X	

MOTORCYCLE SERVICE NEWS

NUMBER 219

YAMAHA INTERNATIONAL CORPORATION
MONTEBELLO, CALIFORNIA
DATE 5/2/69

ENDUROS   INTERCHANGE LIST FOR MODIFICATION AND PERSONALIZATION--cont.

PART DESCRIPTION	PART NUMBER	ADAPTS TO: AT1	CT1	DT1	REMARKS
DT1 DRIVE SPROCKETS					
	214-17461-30			X	13 teeth
	214-17461-40			X	14 teeth
	214-17461-50			X	15 teeth
	214-17461-60			X	16 teeth
DT1 REAR SPROCKETS					
	214-25440-10			X	40 teeth
	214-25442-10			X	42 teeth
	214-25444-10			X	44 teeth
	214-25446-10			X	46 teeth
	214-25448-10			X	48 teeth
	214-25450-10			X	50 teeth
AT1 DRIVE SPROCKETS					
	174-17461-30	X	X		13 teeth
	174-17461-40	X	X		14 teeth
	174-17461-50	X	X		15 teeth
	174-17461-60	X	X		16 teeth
AT1 REAR SPROCKETS					
	248-25443-10	X	X		43 teeth
	248-25445-10	X	X		45 teeth
	248-25447-10	X	X		47 teeth
DT1 FRONT FORK ASS'Y	214-23100-00	X	X	X	Upper/lower bearings identical.
DT1 21" FRONT RIM	94416-21038	X	X	X	To be used as a set with
21" RIM BAND	94327-21024	X	X	X	the appropriate spokes
21" TUBE	94227-21031	X	X	X	as listed below.
21" TIRE	94127-21071	X	X	X	
DT1 21" FRONT SPOKES	214-25104-10			X	
AT1 FRONT SPOKES	248-25104-10	X	X		
HIGH FRONT FENDER & BRACKET	650-980-002	X	X	X	Front fender only = 650-980-003
DT1B PASSENGER PEGS	120-27430-02	X	X	X	ISO
PASSENGER PEG NUTS	98803-12200	X	X	X	ISO

MOTORCYCLE SERVICE NEWS

NUMBER 226

YAMAHA INTERNATIONAL CORPORATION
MONTEBELLO, CALIFORNIA
DATE 2-2-70

ALL DT1/RT1   TRANSMISSION INTERCHANGE

The information listed in this bulletin concerns transmission gear interchangeability among all DT's and RT's. There are three basic transmission gear types in use among these models. The DT1-A and DT1-B employ <u>large</u> tooth, <u>close</u> ratio gears; the DT1-M and RT1-M, small tooth, <u>close</u> ratio gears; and DT1-S, DT1-C, and RT1, <u>small</u> tooth, <u>wide</u> ratio gears. Large and small tooth gears are not interchangeable, except as matching pairs.

Some small tooth gears used in the DT1-M and RT1-M close ratio gear box (low gear wheel and pinion, 2nd gear wheel and pinion, 3rd gear wheel, and 5th gear pinion) are identified by a cut mark on the gear tooth edge. These gears differ in number of teeth from the remaining DT1-S, DT1-C, and RT1 small tooth gears and are not interchangeable with them except as matching pairs.

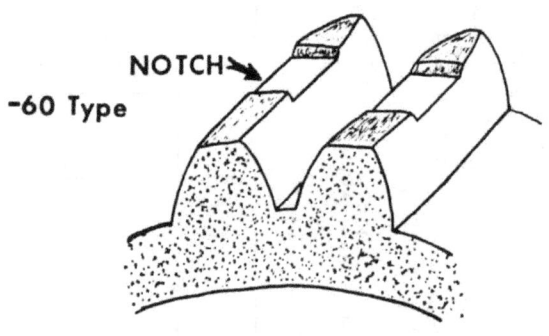

-60 Type   NOTCH→

GEAR	PART NUMBER	DESCRIPTION	CLOSE RATIO				WIDE R.	
			DT1A-DT1B		DT1M-RT1M		DT1S-DT1C-RT1	
			Large Tooth		Small Tooth		Small Tooth	
1	214-17211-	Gear, 1st wheel	00	(29t)	60	*(36t)	10	(38t)
	214-17411-	Axle, main	00	(13t)	60	*(16t)	10	(15t)
2	214-17221-	Gear, 2nd wheel	00	(26t)	60	*(33t)	10	(34t)
	214-17121-	Gear, 2nd pinion	00	(16t)	60	*(20t)	10	(19t)
3	214-17231-	Gear, 3rd wheel	01	(23t)	60	*(29t)	10	(30t)
	214-17131-	Gear, 3rd pinion	01	(19t)	10	(23t)	10	(23t)
4	214-17241-	Gear, 4th wheel	00	(21t)	10	(26t)	10	(26t)
	214-17141-	Gear, 4th pinion	00	(21t)	10	(26t)	10	(26t)
5	214-17131-	Gear, 3rd pinion	01	(19t)	10	(23t)	10	(23t)
	214-17231-	Gear, 3rd wheel	01	(23t)	60	*(29t)	10	(30t)

* Tooth edges are notched. Not interchangeable with -10 type small tooth.

NOTE: For additional information see M/C PNB #260

MOTORCYCLE SERVICE NEWS

YAMAHA INTERNATIONAL CORPORATION
MONTEBELLO, CALIFORNIA
DATE 2-2-70

NUMBER **226**

ALL DT1/RT1   TRANSMISSION INTERCHANGE--continued

MODEL	GEAR	WHEEL	PINION	RATIO	PRIMARY	SECONDARY	*SPEED IN GEAR
DT1A & B	1	29	13	2.231			30.1
	2	26	16	1.624			41.2
	3	23	19	1.211	65/21	44/15	55.3
	4	21	21	1.000	3.095	2.933	67.0
	5	19	23	0.826			81.2
DT1S & C	1	38	15	2.533			26.4
	2	34	19	1.789			37.4
	3	30	23	1.304	65/21	44/15	51.3
	4	26	26	1.000	3.095	2.933	67.0
	5	23	30	0.766			87.5
DT1M	1	36	16	2.250			27.7
	2	33	20	1.650			37.8
	3	29	23	1.261	65/21	44/14	49.4
	4	26	26	1.000	3.095	3.142	62.2
	5	23	29	0.793			79.0
RT1	1	38	15	2.533			26.1
	2	34	19	1.789			36.9
	3	30	23	1.304	65/21	39/15	50.7
	4	26	26	1.000	3.095	2.600	66.0
	5	23	30	0.766			86.2
RT1M	1	36	16	2.250			29.4
	2	33	20	1.650			40.0
	3	29	23	1.261	65/21	39/15	52.3
	4	26	26	1.000	3.095	2.600	66.0
	5	23	29	0.793			83.5

* Stock Rear Tire
   7,000 RPM RT1 Models
   8,000 RPM DT1 Models

DT1A Change Lever and Adjusting Screw (Parts Book Fig. 7-8 & 9)

The adjusting screw diameter between the threads and the eccentric head has been enlarged for increased strength. The change lever hole has also been changed to accommodate the increased screw diameter.

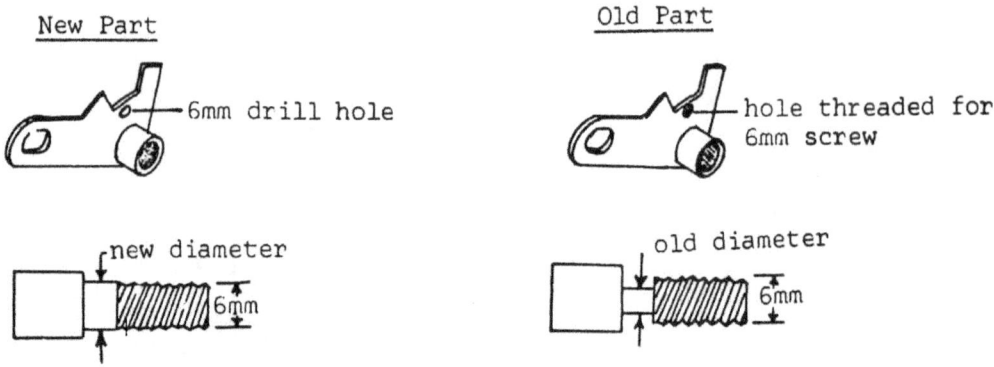

Fig. #	Part Name	Old Part No.	New Part No.	Price
7-8	Change Lever	214-18121-00	214-18121-01	Same
7-9	Adjusting Screw	136-18186-00	214-18186-00	Same

New parts will be fitted on production machines after engine number 11572.

Interchangeability: Before engine number 11572, the parts must be replaced as a set.

DT1A Gear, Pump Drive

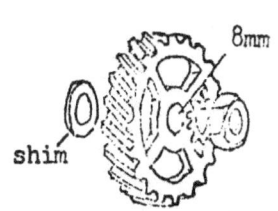 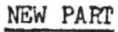 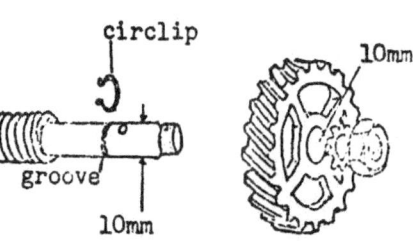

Changes:
1) The new part has a continuous 10mm shaft.
2) The shim that used to hold the gear in place has been replaced by a circlip.
3) Diameter of the gear center hole has been increased to 10mm.

	Old Part No.	New Part No.	Price	Disc.
Worm Shaft	214-13175-00	214-13175-01	No change	
Pump Drive Gear	214-13178-00	214-13178-01	No change	
Circlip	------------	93430-08006		
Shim	148-14334-00	------------		

Interchangeability: The new type parts (worm shaft and gear) must be replaced as a unit until after Engine No. 7955.

MOTORCYCLE SERVICE NEWS

NUMBER 253

YAMAHA INTERNATIONAL CORPORATION
MONTEBELLO, CALIFORNIA
DATE 11/16/70

'70 & '71 MODELS   MECHANICAL DIFFERENCES

The information listed below compares the mechanical differences between the 1970 and the 1971 models. In this way, each mechanic will be made aware of variations in actual service procedures or possible parts interchangeability between '70 & '71 models. If there is no difference listed, then the part (and servicing procedures for that part) remain the same as the preceding year's model.

The following contains a general listing of original machine specifications for last year and this year. Previous SNB's should also be researched to locate any mid-year improvements not listed in this bulletin.

		DT1C	DT1E	Remarks
1.	Muffler	214-14610-01-00 Bullet-shaped diffuser welded in silencer- (silencer/diffuser removeable.)	291-14610-30-00 (Same as RT1B) Bullet-shaped diffuser welded in muffler-silencer dimensions changed (diffuser non-removable). Also larger outlet pipe OD.	Individual old & new muffler components not interchangeable.
2.	Frame	214-21110-03-33	275-21110-01-33	Same as RT1B. Only actual change is main switch location.
3.	Rear swing arm	214-22110-02-33	275-22110-00-33	DT1E same as RT1B. Length from shock pivot to end of arm increased 1". Complete interchangeability between years.
4.	Rear wheel & hub	Standard DT1 parts.	Same as RT1 & RT1B parts.	Interchangeable as a set (including brake rod).
5.	Brake rod	DT1 parts	Same as RT1 & RT1B parts.	Use with RT1(B) rear wheel & hub.
6.	Rear cushion ass'y	214-22210-10-00	291-22210-70-00	New cushion same as on AT1C, CT1C, & RT1B (softer dampening).
7.	Front brake shoe plate	214-25121-00-00	275-25121-00-00 Same as RT1B	Locating notch in plate (& fork leg guide bar) is wider and deeper for more strength.
8.	Front fork ass'y	264-23100-60-52	291-23100-60-71 Same as RT1B	Interchangeable only as a set (extensive change in design & dimensions).
9.	Steering underbracket	214-23340-00-33	275-23340-60-33 Same as RT1(B)	Two pinch bolts instead of one (as on DT1C).
10.	Handle crown	214-23435-02-00	275-23435-01-00 Same as RT1B	Not interchangeable.

MOTORCYCLE SERVICE NEWS

YAMAHA INTERNATIONAL CORPORATION
MONTEBELLO, CALIFORNIA
DATE 11/20/70

NUMBER **255**

DT1/RT1 SERIES   FRONT FORK COMPARISONS

Ever since the first DT1 was sold, Yamaha International engineers have been improving the front fork dampening characteristics. These improvements have required several design changes. To permit a better understanding of parts modifications, and to aid in parts identification, the history and dimensions of the main DT1 front fork parts are listed below. The RT1 series is also listed since DT1 & RT1 front forks each year are identical.

NOTE: Miscellaneous items, such as seals, washers, and clips are not included as these can be easily identified through the parts books.

	DT1-A (1968) DT1-B (1969)	DT1-S (1969½)	RT1 & MX (1970) DT1C & MX	DT1E & MX (1971) RT1B & MX
Oil Capacity	7.1 oz.	7.1 oz.	7.1 oz.	5.9 oz.
Fork Spring	214-23141-00 438mm std. length	214-23141-00 438mm std. length	214-23141-00 438mm std. length	214-23141-00-00 438mm std. length
Inner Tube	214-23124-00	264-23124-60	275-23124-60	291-23124-60-00
Slide metal	168-23125-01 (Steel)	168-23125-01 (Steel)	275-23125-60 (Steel)	None-inside diameter of outer fork leg acts as bushing.
Spacer, lower	NONE	264-23166-60 (Nylon) Plastic	NONE	NONE

MOTORCYCLE SERVICE NEWS

YAMAHA INTERNATIONAL CORPORATION
MONTEBELLO, CALIFORNIA
DATE 11/20/70

NUMBER 255

DT1/RT1 SERIES   FRONT FORK COMPARISONS-continued

	DT1A (1968) / DT1B (1969)	DT1S (1969½)	RT1 & MX (1970) / DT1C & MX	DT1E & MX (1971) / RT1B & MX
Cylinder comp.	214-23170-00	264-23170-60 (Discontinued)	264-23170-61 Interchangeable with DT1S.	291-23170-60-00
Spring (to prevent topping out). Fits over cylinder.	NONE	264-23152-60	264-23152-60	NONE
Piston	214-23171-00	NONE	NONE	278-23171-50-00
Spacer, upper	214-23118-00	264-23118-60	264-23118-60	291-23118-60-00
Outer tube	214-23126-00-35	214-23126-00-35	275-23126-60-35	291-23126-60-00

MOTORCYCLE PARTS NEWS

NUMBER 233

YAMAHA INTERNATIONAL CORPORATION
MONTEBELLO, CALIFORNIA
DATE 11/8/68

DT1(B)   FUEL/FRAME MOUNTING (PARTS BOOK REF. NO. 20)

To provide a stronger method of securing the fuel tank to the frame, the factory has adopted the standard method used on all other Yamaha models. They have done away with the tank stay assembly that was previously used (No. 18 in the fig. below).

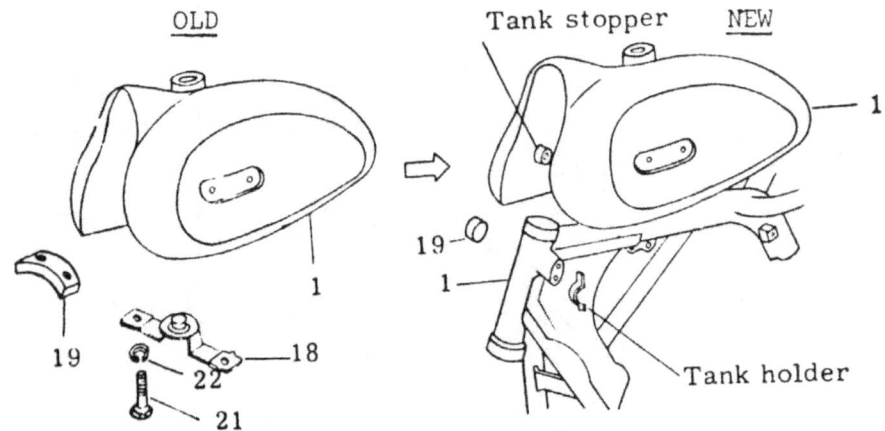

REF. NO.	PART NAME	OLD PART NO.	NEW PART NO.	QUANTITY	PRICE	DISC.
15-1	Frame	214-21110-00	- - - - - -	1		
20-1	Fuel Tank	214-24110-00	- - - - - -	1		
20-18	Stay, Fuel Tank	214-24115-00	- - - - - -	1		
20-19	Damper	214-24183-00	- - - - - -	1		
20-21	Bolt	91202-06015	- - - - - -	2		
20-22	Washer	92902-06200	- - - - - -	2		
15-1-1	Frame	- - - - - -	214-21110-03	1		
20-1-1	Fuel Tank (Pearl White)	- - - - - -	214-24110-03-46	1		
20-19-1	Damper	- - - - - -	156-24181-00	2		

INTERCHANGEABILITY: Must be replaced as a set, including frame and fuel tank, up to and including engine Number 13000.

These parts are stock items on all DT1's after engine Number 13000. The motorcycles after engine Number 15000 are DT1B's, and the color of the tank is changed from Pearl White to Candy Gold.

MOTORCYCLE PARTS NEWS

NUMBER 236

YAMAHA INTERNATIONAL CORPORATION
MONTEBELLO, CALIFORNIA
DATE 11/20/68

CHANGED FROM ENGINE # 16798

DT1B   3rd GEAR WHEEL & 3rd GEAR PINION (PARTS BOOK REF. NO. 5)

Until now it had been possible to install the 3rd gear wheel (same as 5th gear pinion) backwards and remain undetected until the motorcycle was ridden. This happened because the pawls caught in the reversed gear wheel just enough to defy detection when the transmission was checked manually. Both the wheel and pinion have been modified to prevent any further possibility of this happening.

The height of the pawl has been shortened from 14.5mm to 14mm, measuring from the flat side of the gear to the end of the pawl. The 3rd gear wheel web that houses the end of the pawl slots has been increased by ½mm.

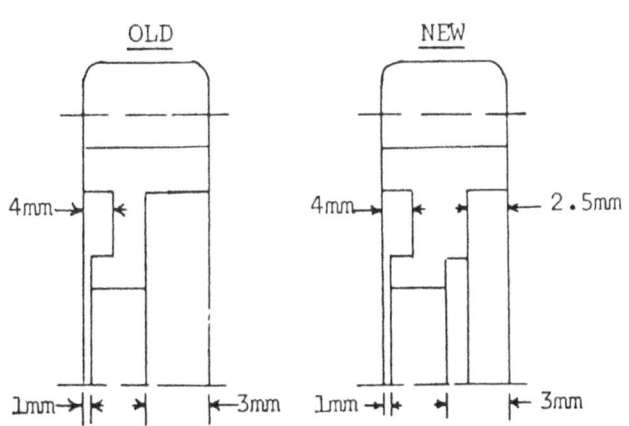
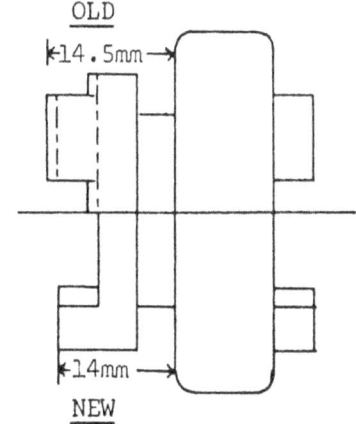

REF. NO	PART NAME	OLD PART NO.	NEW PART NO.	PRICE	DISC.
5-5(21)	Gear, 3rd Pinion (5th Wheel)	214-17131-00	214-17131-01		
5-7(22)	Gear, 3rd Wheel (5th Pinion)	214-17231-00	214-17231-01		

INTERCHANGEABILITY: on all DT1B's, the parts are stock items and can be replaced individually. On all DT1's, the parts must be replaced as a set.

NOTE: the factory has stamped all the new type gears with the letter "N". When installing the gears, always make sure that either both gears have an "N", or neither one is marked. Also be sure that you have <u>not</u> put the gear in backwards to start with.

MOTORCYCLE PARTS NEWS

NUMBER 241

DATE 12/30/68

DT1(A)   OIL SEAL RETAINER (Ignition side) Part No. 214-15317-09

Occasional failures of the crankcase oil seal behind the magneto assembly on DT1A's has prompted the factory to design a seal retainer (see drawing below) for installation behind the magneto backing plate.

This retainer should be installed on any DT1A where the seal has failed. The retainer cannot be installed on the DT1B as this model has an improved magneto backing plate which incorporates its own seal retainer.

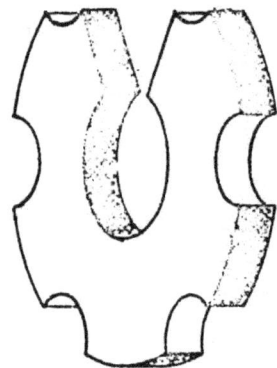

Add to DT1A Parts Book:

Ref. No.	Part Number	Description	Quantity	Price	Disc.
14-18	214-15317-09	Retainer, oil seal	1	.48	50%

(On page 33: sketch in the seal retainer behind the magneto backing plate, mark the sketch with the Ref. No. 14-18.)

Add to DT1A Service Manual:
Add Paragraph "E" (below) to IV-7 on page 31. Include the following text:

    ASSEMBLY INSTRUCTIONS:

1. Remove magneto side cover.
2. Remove magneto rotor assembly.
3. Remove stator backing plate (3 screws).
4. Install oil seal retainer over crankshaft end, slot up, and butt snugly against crankcase surfaces.
5. Reinstall stator backing plate making sure seal retainer is centered correctly.
6. Install magneto rotor assembly.
7. RESET IGNITION TIMING (3.2mm BTDC stock; 2.3mm BTDC GYT kit)

MOTORCYCLE PARTS NEWS

YAMAHA INTERNATIONAL CORPORATION
MONTEBELLO, CALIFORNIA
DATE Feb. 2, 1970

NUMBER **277**
PAGE I

DT1-B   CRANKCASE AND COVER MODIFICATIONS

In order to increase efficiency in the manufacture of DT1-C (and almost identical RT1) crankcases, the factory has designed a new casting mold for the above.

Certain DT1-B's (after E/N 34176) and all DT1-C's utilize this newest improved crankcase. The changes consist of:

(1.) The elimination of a circlip and its retaining groove in the right crankcase half.

(2.) The magneto cover now has four instead of two retaining screws.

(3.) Additional threaded holes added to the left crankcase half to allow for the additional magneto cover screws.

(4.) The length of these two crankcase securing screws has been changed because their threaded anchor points in the R.H. case have been repositioned slightly

The older, two screw magneto cover (No. 214-15411-00) is being discontinued. The new type (-01) will be automatically sent on all orders as soon as the -00 type is out of stock. The new magneto cover can be used on early DT1-B cases. The new crankcases are not interchangeable with early (prior to E/N 34177) DT1-B cases.

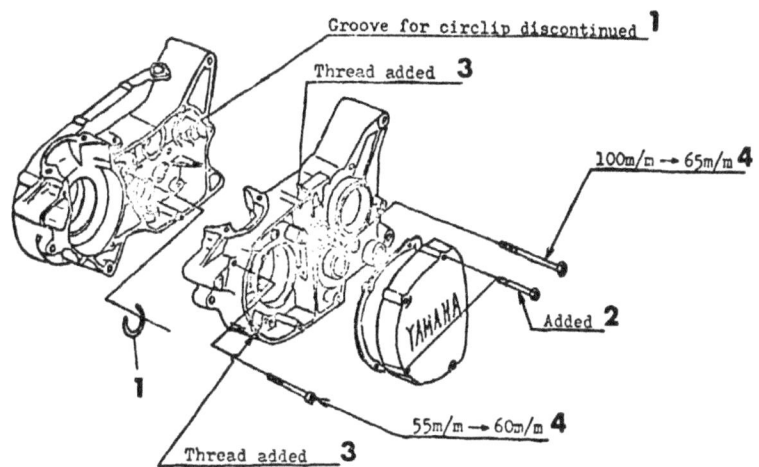

Ref. No.	Old Parts No.	New Parts No.	Description	Q'ty
1-1	214-15111-01	214-15111-02	Case, crank (L.H.)	1
1-2-1	214-15121-04	214-15121-0	Case, crank (R.H.)	1
1-6	92501-06055	96001-06035	Screw, pan head	1
1-7	92501-06100	92501-06060	Screw, pan head	1
2-1	214-15411-00	214-15411-01	Cover, crankcase (L.H.)	1
2-7	214-15451-00	214-15451-01	Gasket, crankcase cover (L.H.)	
2-6	92501-06025	No change	Screw, pan head	
5-15	214-17474-00	Discontinued	Circlip	

PLEASE BRING YOUR PARTS BOOKS UP TO DATE

NOTES

YAMAHA MOTOCROSS DTIB - DTIC DTIS - DTIE

NOTE:

Yamaha Motocross models were released during the DTIC and DTIE model years. However, most parts are interchangeable with the earlier DTIA, DTIB and DTIS models. Most motocross parts differ in design from the DTIA G.Y.T. Kit parts.

Transmission Gear Assembly

4. Transmission Gear Assembly

The constant mesh, close ratio, 5-speed transmission makes it possible to fully utilize the steady performance of the engine throughout the entire speed range from low to high speed. The transmission gear reduction ratio between gears is closer than the DT1-E.
For layout of the transmission and related parts, refer to Fig. 1 and 2.

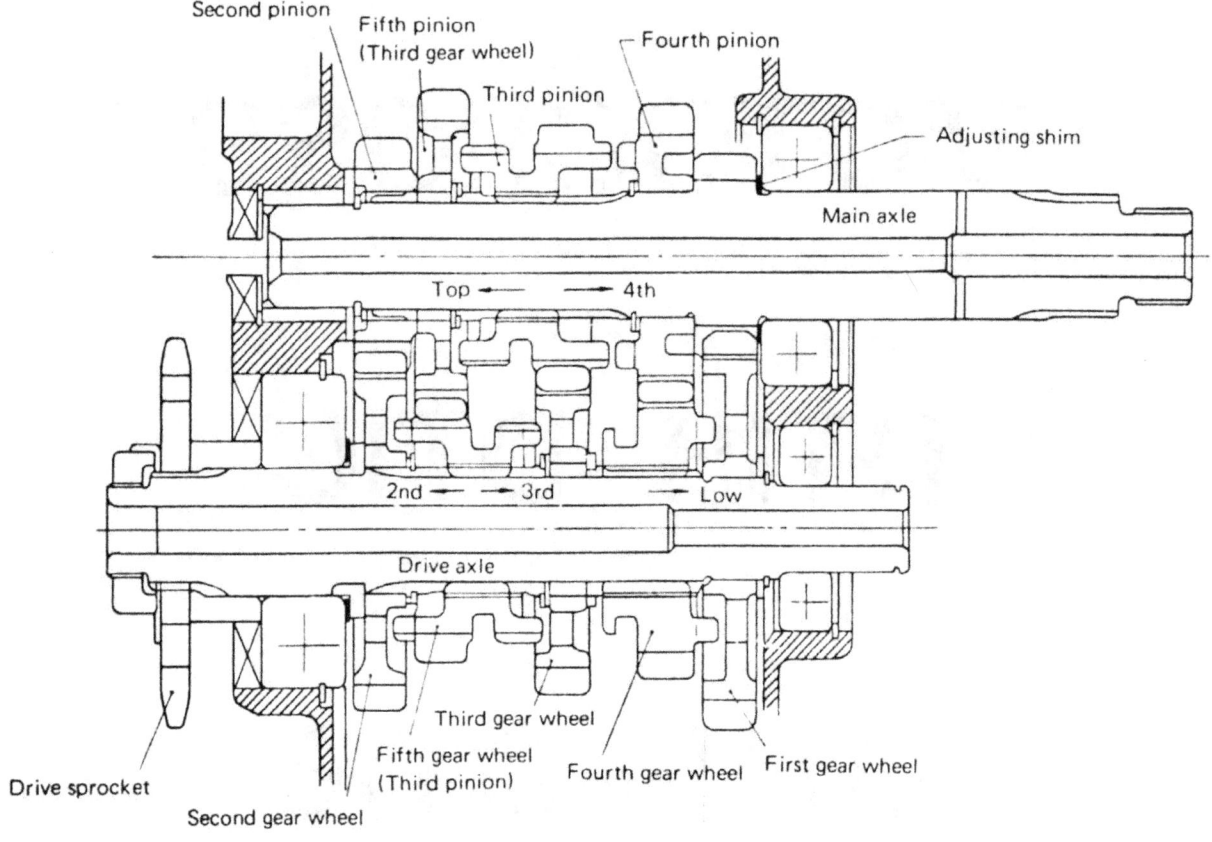

Main shaft overall width (Including shims) = 83.5 mm.
Drive axle overall width (Including shims) = $87.5_{-0.15}^{0}$ mm.

Fig. 1

NOTE:

THIS INFORMATION AND THAT ON THE FOLLOWING PAGES IS FROM THE DT1E-MX SUPPLEMENTARY SERVICE MANUAL. IT IS PERTINENT TO THE DT1C-MX ALSO.

Transmission Gear Assembly

The primary reduction ratio is 65/21 = 3.095
The secondary reduction ratio is 44/14 = 3.142
Therefore the total reduction ratios will be:
Primary reduction ratio x Transmission gear reduction ratio x Secondary reduction ratio = Total reduction ratio.

	Transmission Gear Reduction Ratio	Total Reduction Ratio
1st	36/16 = 2.250	21.887
2nd	33/20 = 1.650	16.051
3rd	29/23 = 1.260	12.265
4th	26/26 = 1.000	9.727
5th	23/29 = 0.793	7.715

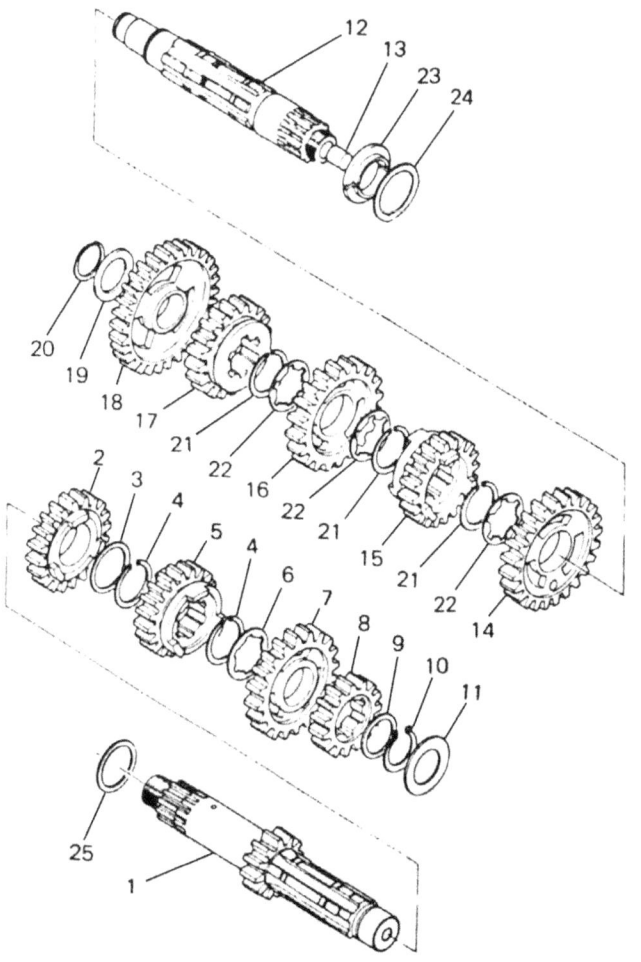

Component parts of transmission
1. Main axle
2. 4th pinion gear
3. Gear holding washer (25-32-1)
4. Circlip
5. 3rd pinion gear
6. Gear holding washer
7. 3rd wheel gear
8. 2nd pinion gear
9. Gear holding washer
10. Circlip
11. Shim (20.2-33-1)
12. Drive axle
13. Blind plug
14. 2nd wheel gear
15. 3rd pinion gear
16. 3rd wheel gear
17. 4th wheel gear
18. 1st wheel gear
19. Gear holding washer (20-30-1.5)
20. Circlip
21. Circlip
22. Gear holding washer
23. Drive axle spacer
24. Drive axle shim
25. Main axle shim (25.1-31)

Fig. 2

Service Data

5. Service Data

- Piston clearance . . . . 0.0018 ~ 0.0020 in. (0.045 ~ 0.050 mm)
- Piston ring end gap . . . . 0.007 ~ 0.015 in. (0.2 ~ 0.4 mm)
  (when ring is fitted in cylinder)
- Spark plug . . . . Standard = B-10EN
- Ignition timing . . . . 2.3 mm B.T.D.C.
- Oil pump
  - Minimum stroke : 0.20 ~ 0.25 mm (0.008 ~ 0.010 in.)
  - Maximum stroke : 1.85 ~ 2.05 mm (0.077 ~ 0.081 in.)
- Fuel mixing ratio

  The DT1-MX, equipped with Yamaha Autolube system, uses mixed gasoline as fuel. The fuel mixing ratio is 30 : 1 for DT1-MX equipped with a Yamaha Autolube pump, and 15 : 1 when not using the Autolube pump.

- Gasoline and Oil
  - Gasoline: Use high-octane gasoline (more than 98 ~ 100 octane)
  - Oil : Use Shell Super 2-stroke oil or oil of similar quality.
- Transmission oil
  - Volume of oil: 1,000 cc. (1.0 U.S. qt)   10W/30
- Carburetor Setting Table

Name of Parts	Abbreviation	Specifications
Main Jet	M. J	#200-220
Air Jet	A. J	0.5
Jet Needle	J. N	5D5-4
Needle Jet	N. J	O-2-O-4
Throttle Valve Cutaway	C. A	#3.5
Bypass Port Diameter	B. P	1.4
Pilot Outlet Diameter	P. O	0.6
Pilot Jet	P. J	#80
Air Screw	A. S	turns out-one turn
Valve Seat Diameter	V. S	2.5
Starter Jet	G. S	#60

Service Data

○ Float Level Adjustment

The carburetor float level is checked by the Yamaha factory during assembly and testing. But rough riding, a worn needle valve, or bent float arm can cause the float level to fluctuate. If the float level raises, this will cause a rich fuel/air mixture that can cause poor performance and spark plug fouling. If the float level decreases, this can cause a lean fuel/air mixture that can result in engine damage. If the machine is subjected to continuous rough riding or many miles of travel, the float level should be checked and set regularly and in the following manner.

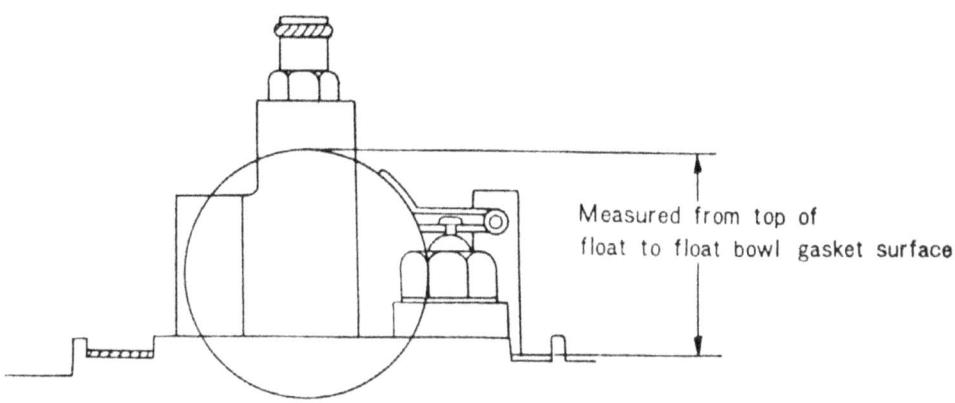

Measured from top of float to float bowl gasket surface

Fig. 3

1) Remove the float chamber body, and turn over the mixing body. Let the float arm rest on the needle valve with the spring fully expanded.
2) Then measure the distance from the float O.D. to the float chamber joint surface.
   Standard measurement : 24 mm. (0.945 in.)
3) When the distance measured is less than recommended bend the tang up. If it is greater, bend the tang down. (with carburetor body upside down.)

○ Cleaning The Air Filter

Wash the foam filter thoroughly in solvent until all dirt has been removed. Squeeze all solvent out. Pour oil onto the filter (any grade of 20 or 30 wt.), work it completely in, and then squeeze out the surplus oil. The filter should be impregnated with oil, but not "dripping" with it.

Change in Specifications

6. Change in Specifications

Participants in racing must change specifications of the machine depending on conditions of the racing course, road surface, coil, length of straightaways, angles of curves, number of curves, slopes, weather, temperature, and skill of the rider.
These factors and conditions must be determined by the rider himself after trial running over the whole race course.

Main Points to be Modified

(1) Carburetor Setting
   In addition to the specified Main Jet, the rider should carry with him spares whose size numbers are larger and smaller than specified by increments of 10 respectively.

(2) Secondary Reduction Ratio
   Consideration should be given to a combination of the drive sprocket and sprocket wheel so that gear shifting to 3rd and 4th is easy and will not cause an undue load on the engine (i.e. lugging).

(3) Spark Plug
   Change the plug by judging discoloration of the plug. Choose the most suitable one from B-9EN, B-10EN or B-11EN after setting carburetion.

(4) Tire Pressure
   Adjust the tire pressure according to road conditions and the rider's choice.

(5) Front Fork
   Adjust the front fork by adjusting the quantity or weight of oil. The oil amount is 5.85 fl. oz. (173 cc). weight is normally SEA #30.

(6) Rear Cushions
   Adjust the spring setting depending on the rider's choice.

(7) Handleber
   Loosen the handle lever holders before racing. This will protect the rider's hands or fingers from getting injured in case of an accidental crash during the race.
   (The lever can easily turn when the machine turns over.)

8. Checks and Service Prior to Racing

The following items should be checked and serviced before racing.
(1) Check the cylinder, piston, and crankshaft ass'y for any defects.
(2) Make sure that the carburetor is clean and correctly set.
(3) Check ignition timing, lead wire connection, and insulation.
(4) Retighten screws, bolts and nuts on all parts.
(5) Check the cables for wear and correct adjustment.
(6) Clean the gas tank and petcock.
(7) Adjust and oil the chain.
Adjust the drive chain so that it has free play of approximately 1 in. (25 mm.) up and down at the center of the lower section with the rear wheel on the ground.
The racer should devote the maximum possible time to inspection and service of the machine prior to racing. "Thorough inspection and service are the first step to victory."

Adjusting Ignition Timing

7. Adjusting Ignition Timing

(1) Tools and instruments for adjusting
Dial gauge (accuracy — 1/100 mm)
Dial gauge stand 2
Continuity testing lamp, YAMAHA electro tester or YAMAHA point checker.
Thickness gauge
Slot-head and Phillips-head screw driver

(2) Adjust ignition timing
a) Set the point gap at 0.30 ~ 0.35 mm (0.012 ~ 0.014 in.). Inspect the breaker points for any pittings. Excessive pitting should be smoothed off with sandpaper (#400 ~ 600), and wiped off with hard, clean, white paper.

b) Remove the spark plug and screw the dial gauge stand 2 into the plug hole. (On the DT1-MX head the spark plug hole is centered and parallel to the cylinder bore).
Next, insert the dial indicator into the gauge stand 2. Bring the piston up to T.D.C. and set the zero on the dial face to line up exactly with the dial indicator needle.
Connect the positive (+) tester lead to the primary ignition terminal. Connect the negative (−) lead to the engine case (ground).

c) Turn the crankshaft back well past 2.3 mm, to eliminate play in the gears, and then bring the piston up to exactly 2.3 mm B.T.D.C.

d) Loosen the breaker plate holding screws and turn the breaker plate. When the points just start to open (the testing lamp lights up) tighten the holding screws. (Do not fully loosen the breaker plate holding screw as the breaker plate tends to shift its position).
Turning the breaker plate in the engine rotation direction causes ignition timing to retard, and turning it in the opposite direction advances ignition timing.

e) After tightening the set screw, recheck timing.

9. WIRING DIAGRAM

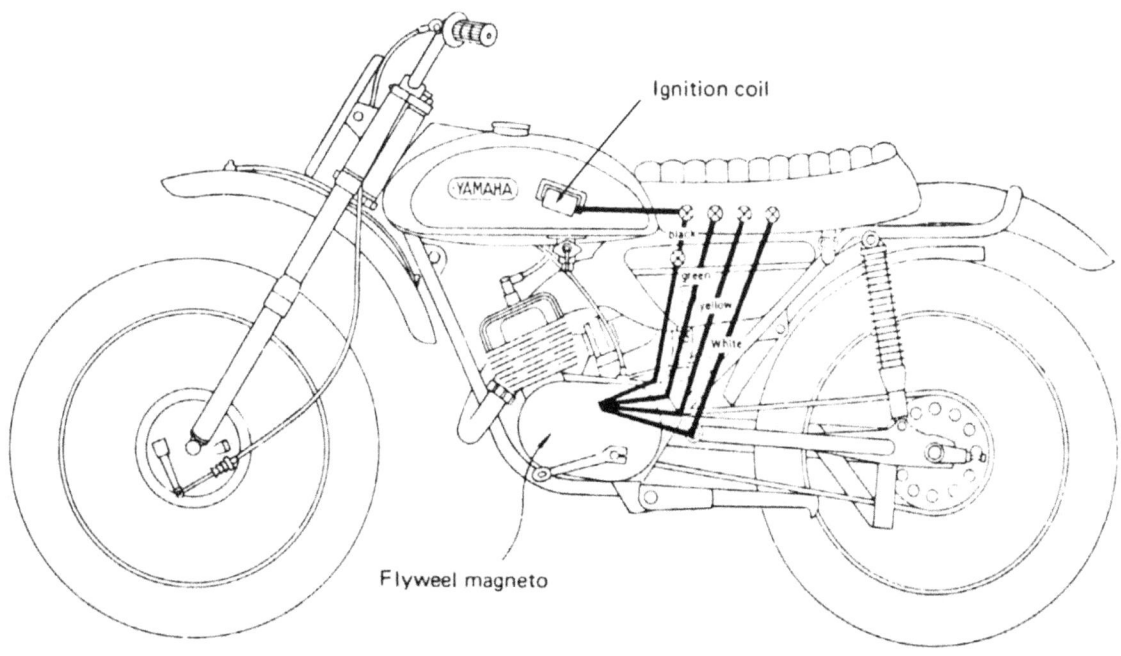

Fig. 32 ENGINE (CYLINDER & TRANSMISSION)

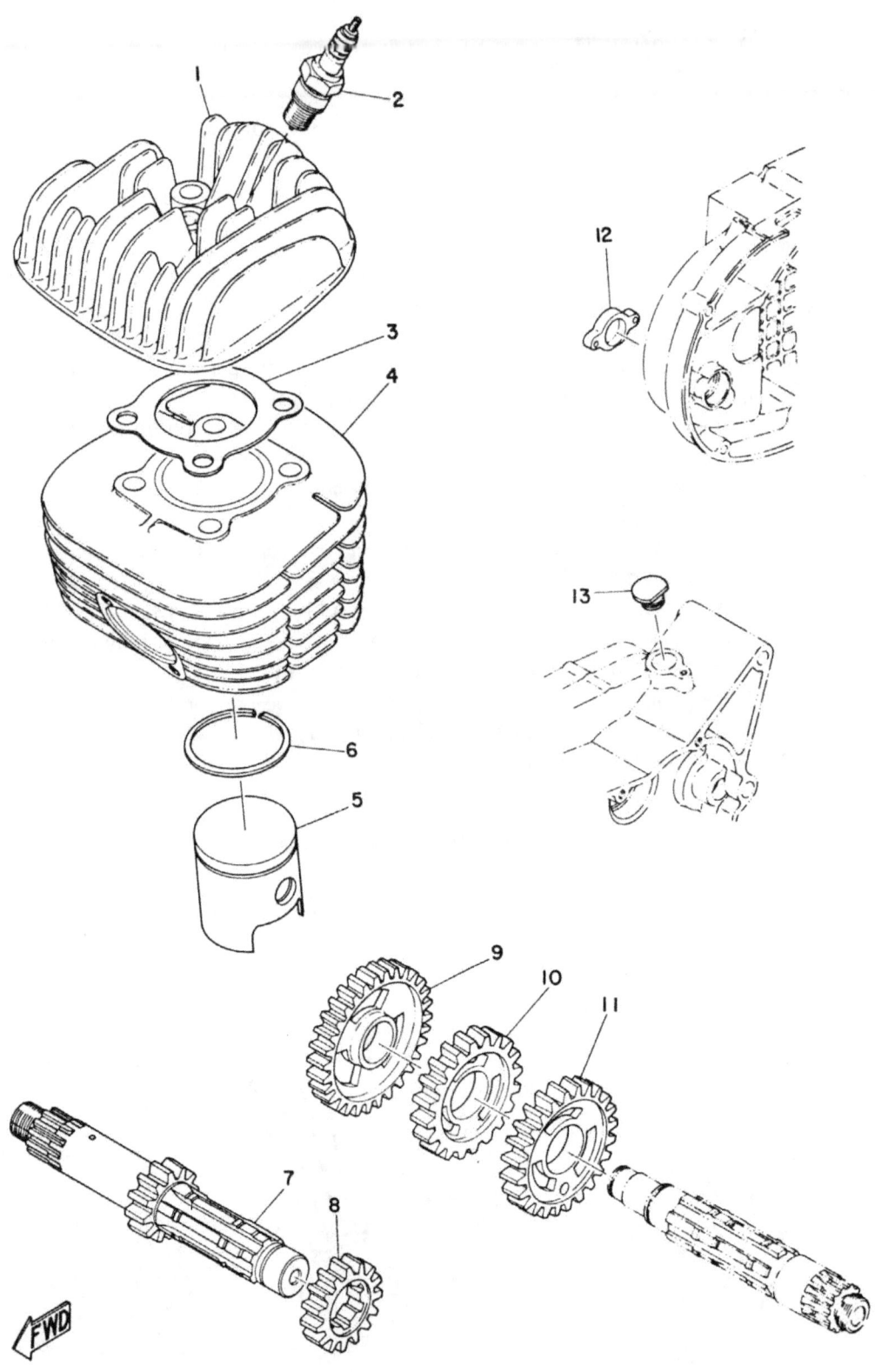

ENGINE (CYLINDER & TRANSMISSION)

Ref No.	Part No.	Description	Q'ty	Applicable Machine No.	Remarks
32-1	285-11111-00	HEAD, cylinder	1		
32-2	94700-00017	PLUG, spark (B-10E)	1		
32-3	285-11181-00	GASKET, cylinder head	1		
32-4	285-11311-00	CYLINDER	1		
32-5	285-11631-00-96	PISTON (S.T.D) 69.96 mm	1		
	285-11635-00	PISTON (1st o.s) 70.25 mm	1		
	285-11636-00	PISTON (2nd o.s) 70.50 mm	1		
32-6	285-11611-00	RING, piston (S.T.D)	1		
	285-11611-10	RING, piston (1st o.s)	1		
	285-11611-20	RING, piston (2nd o.s)	1		
32-7	214-17411-60	AXLE, main (16T)	1		
32-8	214-17121-60	GEAR, 2nd pinion (20T)	1		
32-9	214-17211-60	GEAR, 1st wheel (36T)	1		
32-10	214-17221-60	GEAR, 2nd wheel (33T)	1		
32-11	214-17231-60	GEAR, 3rd wheel (29T)	2		
32-12	241-17819-00	CAP, housing	1		
		ALTERNATE PART (without oil pump)			
32-13	161-15426-00	COVER, oil pump	1		

Fig. 33 ENGINE (AIR CLEANER & EXHAUST)

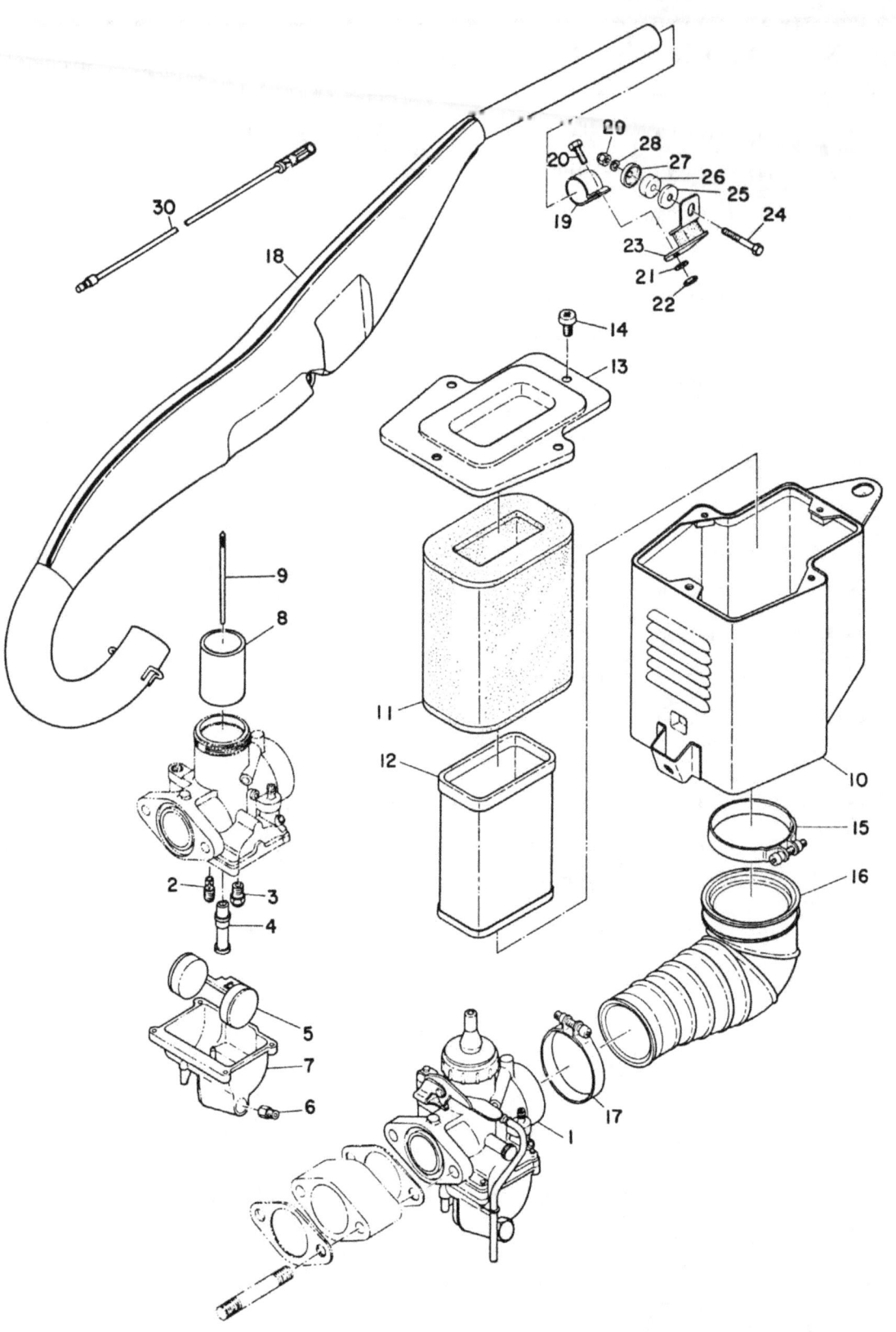

ENGINE (AIR CLEANER & EXHAUST)

Ref No.	Part No.	Description	Q'ty
33- 1	285-14101-60	CARBURETOR ASS'Y	1
33- 2	193-14142-80	. JET, pilot (#80)	1
33- 3	285-14190-25	. VALVE SEAT ASS'Y (#2.5)	1
33- 4	145-14141-32	. NOZZLE, main (0-2)	1
33- 5	285-14185-00	. FLOAT	1
33- 6	137-14143-38	. JET, main (#190)	U.R 1
	137-14143-40	. JET, main (#200)	
	137-14143-42	. JET, main (#210)	
33- 7	285-14181-00	. BODY, float chamber	1
33- 8	211-14112-35	. VALVE, throttle (C.A 3.5)	1
33- 9	168-14116-07	. NEEDLE (5DP7-3)	1
33-10	285-14411-00	CASE, air cleaner	1
33-11	285-14451-00	ELEMENT	1
33-12	285-14458-00	GUIDE, element	1
33-13	285-14412-00	CAP, case	1
33-14	92501-06010	SCREW, pan head	1
33-15	285-14455-00	BAND	1
33-16	285-14453-00	JOINT	1
33-17	170-14455-00	BAND	1
33-18	285-14610-10	EXHAUST PIPE ASS'Y	1
33-19	285-14791-10	STAY, muffler 3	1
33-20	91201-06020	BOLT	1
33-21	92901-06100	WASHER, spring	1
33-22	92801-06100	NUT	1
33-23	285-14781-11	STAY, muffler 2	1
33-24	91201-06045	BOLT	1
33-25	214-14794-00	PLATE, muffler 2	1
33-26	214-14763-02	SPACER	1
33-27	214-14793-01	PLATE, muffler 1	1
33-28	92901-06100	WASHER, spring	1
33-29	214-21635-00	NUT, crown	1
33-30	284-82319-00	WIRE, sub lead	1

Fig. 1 TRANSMISSION GEAR

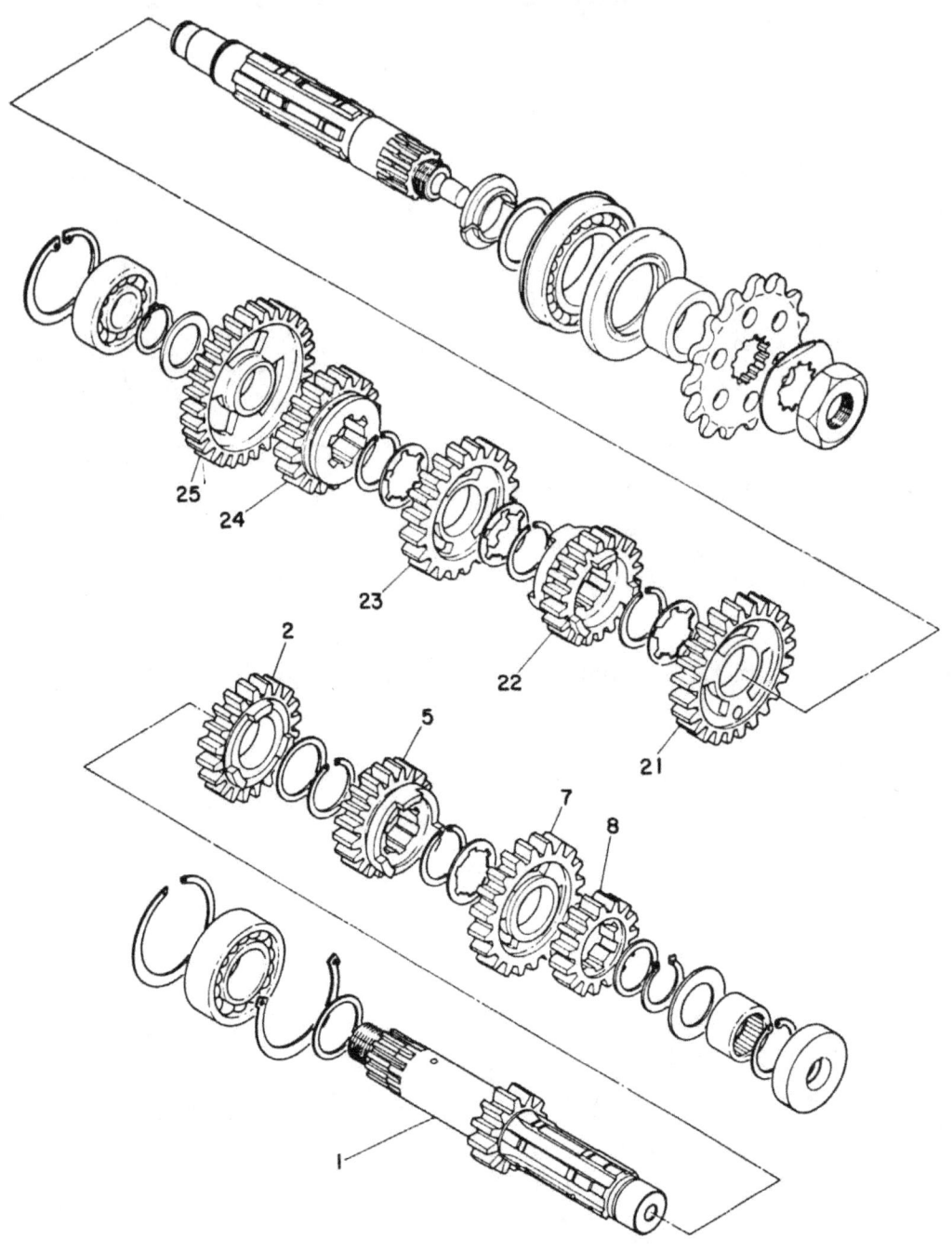

TRANSMISSION GEAR

Ref No.	Parts No.	Parts Name	Description	Q'ty	S·R	Remarks
1- 0-1	214-17401-10-00	MAIN AXLE ASS'Y		1		
1- 1	214-17411-10-00	. AXLE, main	15T	1		Std 13
1- 2	214-17141-10-00	. GEAR, 4th pinion	26T	1		Std 21
1- 3	152-17226-00-00	. WASHER, gear hold		1		
1- 4	93440-25008-00	. CIRCLIP	25ø	2		
1- 5	214-17131-10-00	. GEAR, 3rd pinion	23T	1		Std 19
1- 6	214-17216-00-00	. WASHER, gear hold		1		
1- 7	214-17231-10-00	. GEAR, 5th pinion	30T	1		
1- 8	214-17121-10-00	. GEAR, 2nd pinion	19T	1		
1- 9	132-17216-00-00	. WASHER, gear hold	20-25-1	1		
1-10	93410-19015-00	. CIRCLIP	S-19	1		
1-11	137-17427-00-00	SHIM	20.2-33-1	1		
1-12	93315-22004-00	BEARING	20-26-16	1		
1-13	93420-26024-00	CIRCLIP		1		
1-14	93104-07022-00	OIL SEAL	SO-68-26.1	1		
1-15	156-17417-00-00	SHIM, main axle	25.1-31-$\begin{smallmatrix}0.1\\0.2\\0.3\end{smallmatrix}$	UR		
1-16	214-17474-00-00	CIRCLIP		1		
1-17	93306-20508-00	BEARING	6205Z	1		
1-18	93450-52005-00	CIRCLIP	52ø	1		
1- 0-2	214-17402-10-00	DRIVE AXLE ASS'Y		1		
1-19	214-17421-00-00	. AXLE, drive		1		
1-20	214-17481-00-00	. PLUG, blind		1		
1-21	214-17221-10-00	. GEAR, 2nd wheel	34T	1		
1-22	214-17131-10-00	. GEAR, 5th wheel	23T	1		
1-23	214-17231-10-00	. GEAR, 3rd wheel	30T	1		
1-24	214-17241-10-00	. GEAR, 4th wheel	26T	1		
1-25	214-17211-10-00	. GEAR, 1st wheel	38T	1		
1-26	168-17116-00-00	. WASHER, gear hold	20-30-1.5	1		
1-27	93410-19015-00	. CIRCLIP	S19	1		
1-28	93440-25008-00	. CIRCLIP	25ø	3		
1-29	214-17216-00-00	. WASHER, gear hold		3		
1-30	156-17429-00-00	SPACER, drive axle		2		
1-31	168-17428-01-00	SHIM, drive axle	25-34-$\begin{smallmatrix}0.3\\0.5\end{smallmatrix}$	UR		
1-32	93306-30506-00	BEARING	6305NR	1		☆
1-33	93102-35054-00	OIL SEAL	SD-35-62-6	1		
1-34	214-17462-00-00	COLLAR, distance	25-35-15.5	1		
1-35	214-17461-30-00	SPROCKET, drive	13T	1		

Fig. 2 FRONT FORK

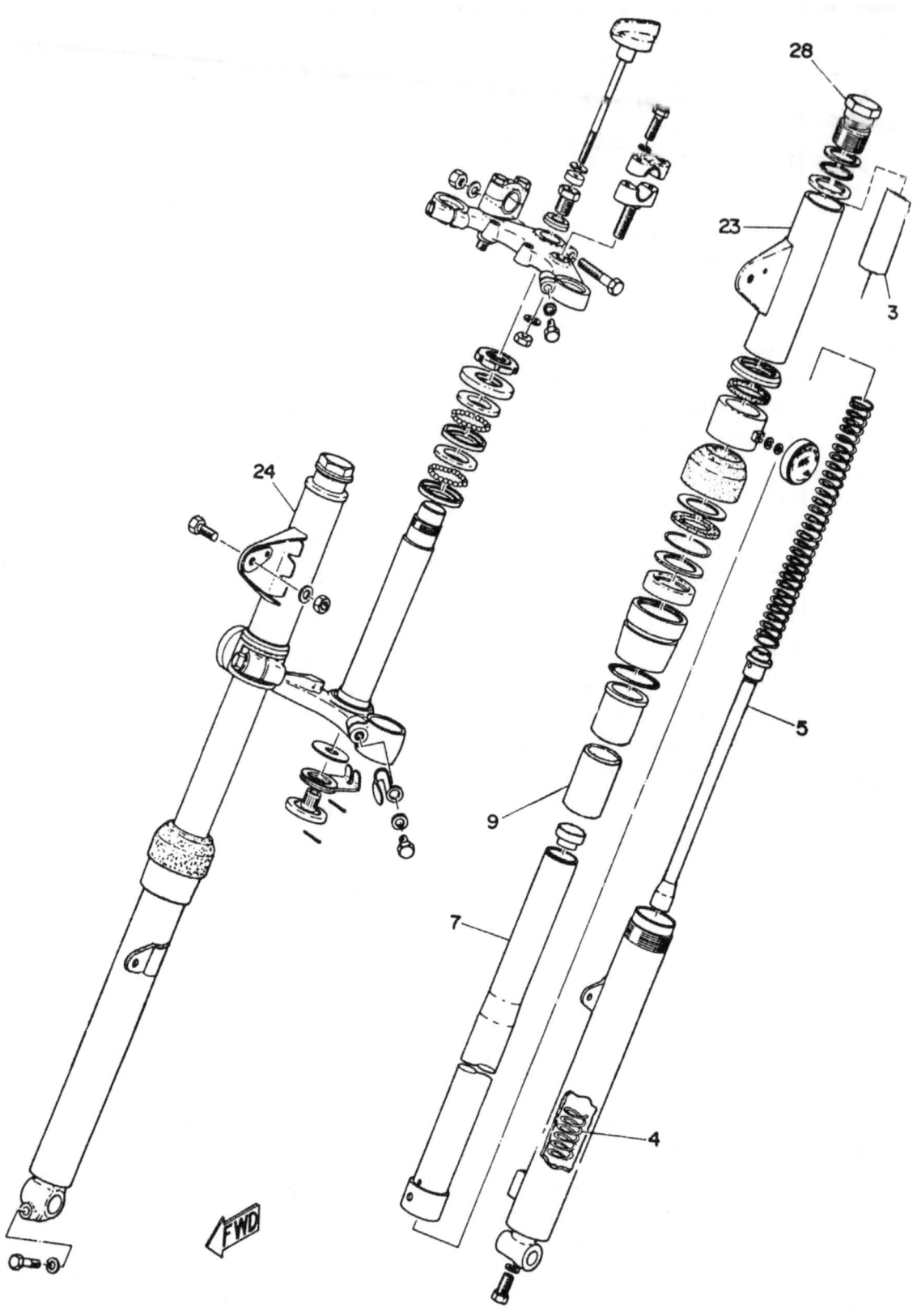

FRONT FORK

Ref No.	Parts No.	Parts Name	Description	Q ty	S·R	Remarks
2 0-1	264-23100-60-52	FRONT FORK ASS'Y	ISO	1		CANDY ORANGE
2 1	214-23126-00-35	. TUBE, outer (L.H)	ISO	1		
2 2	214-23136-00-35	. TUBE, outer (R.H)	ISO	1		
2-3	264-23118-60-00	. SPACER		2		
2-4	264-23152-60-00	. SPRING		2		
2-5	264-23170-60-00	. CYLINDER COMP.		2		
2-6	214-23141-00-00	. SPRING, fork		2		
2-7	264-23124-60-00	. TUBE, inner		2		
2-8	214-23142-00-00	. SEAT, spring upper		2		
2-9	264-23166-60-00	. SPACER		2		
2-10	168-23125-01-00	. METAL, slide		2		
2-11	168-23147-00-00	. O-RING		2		
2-12	214-23127-00-00	. NUT, outer		2		
2-13	168-23145-00-00	. . OIL SEAL		2		
2-14	214-23146-00-00	. WASHER, oil seal		2		
2-15	214-23156-00-00	. CLIP, oil seal		2		
2-16	214-23155-00-00	. RING, felt		2		
2-17	214-23165-00-00	. WASHER, felt ring		2		
2-18	214-23144-01-00	. SEAL, dust		2		
2-19	233-23122-00-00	. COVER, outer (L.H)	ISO	1		
2-20	233-23122-00-00	. COVER, outer (R.H)	ISO	1		
2-21	214-23163-00-00	. PACKING (lamp stay)		2		
2-22	214-23116-00-00	. GUIDE, cover under		2		
2-23	214-23121-01-52	. COVER, upper (L.H)		1		CANDY ORANGE
2-24	214-23131-01-52	. COVER, upper (R.H)		1		CANDY ORANGE
2-25	214-23115-00-00	. GUIDE, cover upper		2		
2-26	214-23114-00-00	. PACKING, (O-RING)		2		
2-27	214-23112-00-00	. WASHER, cap		2		
2-28	264-23111-60-00	. BOLT, cap		2		
2-29	214-23340-00-33	. UNDER BRACKET COMP.		1		
2-30	122-23346-00-00	. BOLT, under bracket		2		
2-31	92901-10100-00	. WASHER, spring		2		
2-32	214-23318-00-00	. HOLDER, wire		1		
2-33	91311-08020-00	. BOLT		2		
2-34	214-23158-00-00	. PACKING		2		
2-35	97201-08030-00	. BOLT	ISO	1		
2-36	92901-08100-00	. WASHER, spring		1		
2-37	164-23462-00-00	SEAL, dust		1		

VELOCEPRESS MANUALS – MOTORCYCLE BY MAKE

AJS 1932-1948 SINGLES & TWINS 250cc THRU 1000cc (BOOK OF)
AJS 1945-1960 SINGLES 350cc & 500cc MODELS 16 & 18 (BOOK OF)
AJS 1955-1965 SINGLES 350cc & 500cc (BOOK OF)
AJS 1957-1966 FACTORY WSM - ALL SINGLES & TWINS
AJS 1959-1969 FACTORY WSM G80CS G85CS & P11 OFF ROAD
ARIEL UP TO 1932 (BOOK OF)
ARIEL 1932-1939 PREWAR MODELS (BOOK OF)
ARIEL 1933-1951 (WORKSHOP MANUAL)
ARIEL 1939-1960 4 STROKE SINGLES (BOOK OF)
ARIEL 1958-1964 LEADER & ARROW FACTORY WSM & PARTS LIST
ARIEL 1958-1964 LEADER & ARROW (BOOK OF)
BMW R26 R27 (1956-1967) FACTORY WORKSHOP MANUAL
BMW R50 R50S R60 R69S (1955-1969) FACTORY WORKSHOP MANUAL
BMW R50/5 R60/5 R75/5 (1969-1973) FACTORY WORKSHOP MANUAL
BRIDGESTONE 90 SERIES FACTORY WSM & PARTS CATALOGUE
BRIDGESTONE 175 SERIES FACTORY WSM & PARTS CATALOGUE
BRIDGESTONE 350 SERIES FACTORY WSM & PARTS CATALOGUES
BSA SERVICE SHEETS MASTER CATALOGUE ALL MODELS 1945-1967
BSA BANTAM D1 TO D7 1948-1966 FACTORY SERVICE SHEETS MANUAL
BSA BANTAM ALL MODELS FROM 1948 ONWARDS (BOOK OF)
BSA BANTAM D14 FACTORY SERVICE MANUAL
BSA DANDY FACTORY WORKSHOP MANUAL (COMPILATION)
BSA SINGLES & V-TWINS UP TO 1926 inc. 1927 SUPPLEMENT (BOOK OF)
BSA SINGLES & V-TWINS UP TO 1930 (BOOK OF)
BSA SINGLES & V-TWINS UP TO 1935 (BOOK OF)
BSA SINGLES & V-TWINS 1936-1939 (BOOK OF)
BSA C10, C11 & C12 1945-1958 FACTORY SERVICE SHEETS MANUAL
BSA OHV & SV SINGLES 250-600cc 1945-1959 (BOOK OF)
BSA C15 & B40 1958-1967 FACTORY SERVICE SHEETS MANUAL
BSA OHV & SV SINGLES 250cc (ONLY) 1954-1970 (BOOK OF)
BSA B31, B32, B33 & B34 1945-60 FACTORY SERVICE SHEETS MANUAL
BSA OHV SINGLES 350 & 500cc 1955-1967 (BOOK OF)
BSA M20, M21 & M33 1945-1963 FACTORY SERVICE SHEETS MANUAL
BSA TWINS A7 & A10 1948-1962 FACTORY SERVICE SHEETS MANUAL
BSA TWINS A7 & A10 1948-1962 (BOOK OF)
BSA TWINS A50 & A65 1962-1965 FACTORY WORKSHOP MANUAL
BSA TWINS A50 & A65 1962-1969 (SECOND BOOK OF)
DOUGLAS 1929-1939 PREWAR ALL MODELS (BOOK OF)
DOUGLAS 1948-1957 POSTWAR ALL MODELS FACTORY SHOP MANUAL
DUCATI 160cc, 250cc & 350cc OHC MODELS FACTORY SHOP MANUAL
HONDA 50cc ALL MODELS UP TO 1970 INC MONKEY & TRAIL (BOOK OF)
HONDA 90cc ALL MODELS UP TO 1966 (BOOK OF)
HONDA TWINS & SINGLES 50cc THRU 305cc 1960-1966 (BOOK OF)
HONDA TWINS ALL MODELS 125cc THRU 450cc UP TO 1968 (BOOK OF)
HONDA C100 50cc SUPER CUB O.H.C. 1959-1962 FACTORY WSM
HONDA C110 50cc SPORT CUB O.H.C. 1960-1962 FACTORY WSM
HONDA 50-65-70-90cc O.H.C. SINGLES 1959-1983 WSM
HONDA 100-125cc SINGLES CB/CD/CL/SL/TL 1970-1984 FACTORY WSM
HONDA 125-150cc TWINS C/CS/CB/CA 1959-1966 FACTORY WSM
HONDA 125-160-175-200cc TWINS 1965-1978 WORKSHOP MANUAL
HONDA 250-305cc TWINS C/CS/CB 1961-1968 FACTORY WSM
HOHDA 250-350cc TWINS CB/CL/SL 1968-1973 FACTORY WSM
HONDA 250-360cc TWINS CB/CL/CJ 1974-1977 FACTORY WSM
HONDA 350F & 400F 4-CYLINDER 1972-1977 FACTORY WSM
HONDA 450cc TWINS CB/CL 1965-1974 K0 TO K7 WORKSHOP MANUAL
HONDA 500cc & 550cc 4-CYL 1971-1978 FACTORY WORKSHOP MANUAL
HONDA 750cc SHOC 4-CYL 1969-1978 K0~K8 WORKSHOP MANUAL
INDIAN PONYBIKE, BOY RACER & PAPOOSE ILL PARTS LIST & SALES LIT

VELOCEPRESS MANUALS – SCOOTERS BY MAKE

BSA SUNBEAM SCOOTER WORKSHOP MANUAL 1959-1965
BSA SUNBEAM SCOOTER 1959-1965 (BOOK OF)
LAMBRETTA 1947-1957 ALL 125 & 150cc MODELS (BOOK OF)
LAMBRETTA 1957-1970 LI & TV MODELS (SECOND BOOK OF)
NSU PRIMA 1956-1964 ALL MODELS (BOOK OF)
TRIUMPH TIGRESS SCOOTER WORKSHOP MANUAL 1959-1965
TRIUMPH TIGRESS SCOOTER (BOOK OF)
VESPA 1951-1961 (BOOK OF)
VESPA 1955-1963 125 & 150cc & GS MODELS (SECOND BOOK OF)
VESPA 1955-1968 GS & SS (BOOK OF)
VESPA 1963-1972 90, 125 & 150cc (THIRD BOOK OF)

VELOCEPRESS MANUALS – MOPEDS & MOTORIZED BICYCLES

CYCLEMOTOR (BOOK OF)
NSU QUICKLY 1953-1963 ALL MODELS (BOOK OF)
PUCH MAXI N & S MAINTENANCE & REPAIR (3 MANUAL COMPILATION)
RALEIGH MOPEDS 1960-1969 (BOOK OF)

J.A.P. ENGINES 1927-1952 & MOTORCYCLES 1934-1952 (BOOK OF)
MATCHLESS 1931-1939 ALL MODELS 250cc THRU 990cc (BOOK OF)
MATCHLESS 1945-1956 350 & 500cc SINGLES (BOOK OF)
MATCHLESS 1955-1966 350 & 500cc SINGLES (BOOK OF)
MATCHLESS 1957-1966 FACTORY WSM - ALL SINGLES & TWINS
NEW IMPERIAL ALL SV & OHV FROM 1935 ONWARDS (BOOK OF)
NORTON 1932-1939 PREWAR MODELS (BOOK OF)
NORTON 1932-1947 (BOOK OF)
NORTON 1938-1956 (BOOK OF)
NORTON 1945-1963 MODELS 16H, Big4, ES2, 19 & 50 WSM'S & PARTS
NORTON 1955-1963 MODELS 19, 50 & ES2 (BOOK OF)
NORTON 1948-1970 DOMINATOR TWINS FACTORY WSM'S & PARTS
NORTON 1955-1965 DOMINATOR TWINS (BOOK OF)
NORTON 1960-1970 TWIN CYLINDER FACTORY WORKSHOP MANUAL
NORTON 1970-1975 COMMANDO 850 & 750cc FACTORY WSM
NORTON 1975-1978 MK 3 COMMANDO 850 cc FACTORY WSM
PANTHER 1932-1958 LIGHTWEIGHT MODELS 250 & 350cc (BOOK OF)
PANTHER 1938-1966 HEAVYWEIGHT MODELS 600 & 650cc (BOOK OF)
PENTON-KTM-SACHS 1968-1975 100cc & 125cc WORKSHOP MANUAL
RALEIGH MOTORCYCLES 1919-1933 (BOOK OF)
ROYAL ENFIELD 1934-1946 SINGLES & V TWINS (BOOK OF)
ROYAL ENFIELD 1937-1953 SINGLES & V TWINS (BOOK OF)
ROYAL ENFIELD 1946-1962 SINGLES (BOOK OF)
ROYAL ENFIELD 1948-1962 350cc & 500cc PRE-UNIT BULLET WSM
ROYAL ENFIELD 1948-1963 500cc TWINS FACTORY WORKSHOP MANUAL
ROYAL ENFIELD 1952-1963 700cc TWINS FACTORY WORKSHOP MANUAL
ROYAL ENFIELD 1956-1966 250cc CRUSADER & 350cc NEW BULLET WSM
ROYAL ENFIELD 1958-1966 250cc & 350cc SINGLES (SECOND BOOK OF)
ROYAL ENFIELD 1962-1970 INTERCEPTOR WSM'S & PARTS (Compilation)
RUDGE 1933-1939 (BOOK OF)
SACHS 1968-1975 100cc & 125cc ENGINES WSM & M/CYCLE PARTS LIST
SUNBEAM 1928-1939 (BOOK OF)
SUNBEAM 1946-1957 S7 & S8 (BOOK OF)
SUZUKI 50cc & 80cc UP TO 1966 (BOOK OF)
SUZUKI T10 1963-1967 FACTORY WORKSHOP MANUAL
SUZUKI T20 & T200 1965-1969 FACTORY WORKSHOP MANUAL
SUZUKI TWINS 1962 ONWARDS 125-500cc WORKSHOP MANUAL
TRIUMPH 1935-1949 SINGLES & TWINS (BOOK OF)
TRIUMPH 1937-1961 SINGLES SV & OHV 250cc-600cc + TERRIER & CUB
TRIUMPH 1945-1955 PRE-UNIT 350cc, 500cc & 650cc TWINS WSM No.11
TRIUMPH 1945-1959 TWINS (BOOK OF)
TRIUMPH 1956-1969 TWINS (BOOK OF)
TRIUMPH 1956-1962 PRE-UNIT 500cc & 650cc TWINS WSM No.17
TRIUMPH 1957-1963 UNIT CONSTRUCTION 350-500cc WSM No.4
TRIUMPH 1963-1974 UNIT CONSTRUCTION 350-500cc FACTORY WSM
TRIUMPH 1963-1970 UNIT CONSTRUCTION 650cc FACTORY WSM
TRIUMPH 1968-1974 TRIDENT T150 & T150V FACTORY WSM
TRIUMPH 1971-1973 650cc OIL-IN-FRAME FACTORY WSM
TRIUMPH 1973-1978 750cc BONNEVILLE & TIGER FACTORY WSM
TRIUMPH 1979-1983 750cc T140, TR7 & TR65 FACTORY WSM
VELOCETTE 1925-1970 ALL SINGLES & TWINS (BOOK OF)
VELOCETTE 1933-1952 MOV-MAC-MSS RIGID FRAME FACTORY WSM
VELOCETTE 1953-1960 MAC SPRING FRAME WSM & ILL PARTS LIST
VELOCETTE 1954-1971 MSS-VENOM-THRUXTON-VIPER FACTORY WSM
VILLIERS ENGINE UP TO 1959 INC. 3 WHEELERS (BOOK OF)
VILLIERS ENGINE UP TO 1969 (BOOK OF)
VINCENT 1935-1955 (WORKSHOP MANUAL)
YAMAHA 1961-1967 YA5 & YA6 (WORKSHOP MANUAL & ILL PARTS LIST)
YAMAHA 1968-1971 DT1 & MX SERIES Inc. GYT WORKSHOP MANUAL
YAMAHA 1971-1972 JT1 & JT2 (WORKSHOP MANUAL & ILL PARTS LIST)

VELOCEPRESS MANUALS - THREE WHEELER'S

BOND MINICAR THREE WHEELER 1948-1967 (BOOK OF)
BMW ISETTA FACTORY WORKSHOP MANUAL
BSA THREE WHEELER (BOOK OF)
RELIANT REGAL THREE WHEELER 1952-1973 (BOOK OF)
VINTAGE MORGAN THREE WHEELER (BOOK OF)

VELOCEPRESS TECHNICAL BOOKS – MOTORCYCLE

1930'S BRITISH MOTORCYCLE CARBS & ELEC COMPONENTS (BOOK OF)
1930'S BRITISH MOTORCYCLE ENGINES (OVERHAUL & MAINTENANCE)
1930'S BRITISH MOTORCYCLE GEARBOXES & CLUTCHES (BOOK OF)
CATALOG OF BRITISH MOTORCYCLES (1951 MODELS)
LUCAS ELECTRONICS BRITISH M/CYCLES REPAIR & PARTS (1950-1977)
MOTORCYCLE ENGINEERING (P.E. Irving)
MOTORCYCLE ROAD TESTS 1949-1953 (Motor Cycle Magazine UK)
SPEED AND HOW TO OBTAIN IT (Motor Cycle Magazine UK)
TUNING FOR SPEED (P.E. Irving)
WIPAC (COMBO) MANUAL NUMBER 3 + M/CYCLE & SCOOTER MANUAL

www.VelocePress.com